The Blue, the Gray, & the Red

The Blue, the Gray, & the Red

Indian Campaigns
of the Civil War

Thom Hatch

STACKPOLE
BOOKS

Published by
STACKPOLE BOOKS
5067 Ritter Road
Mechanicsburg, PA 17055
www.stackpolebooks.com

Printed in the United States of America

10 9 8 7 6 5 4 3 2 1

FIRST EDITION

Library of Congress Cataloging-in-Publication Data

Hatch, Thom, 1946–
    The blue, the gray, and the red : Indian campaigns of the Civil War / by Thom Hatch.
    p. cm.
    Includes bibliographical references (p.) and index.
    ISBN 0-8117-0016-X
    1. Indians of North America—Wars—1862–1865. 2. Indians of North America—History—Civil War, 1861–1865. 3. United States—History—Civil War, 1861–1865.
I. Title.
E83.863 .H374 2003
973.7'4—dc21

2002008088

*To my wonderful wife, Lynn,
and precious daughter, Cimarron,
who are my daily inspiration*

CONTENTS

MAPS

PHOTOGRAPHS

Following page 118

Patrick E. Connor
Henry Hastings Sibley
Little Crow
James H. Carleton
Mangus Coloradas
Christopher "Kit" Carson
King S. Woolsey
John Milton Chivington
Black Kettle

INTRODUCTION

TUCKED AWAY IN RELATIVELY OBSCURE AND SCATTERED PAGES OF CIVIL War history, overshadowed by the microscopic focus on Eastern battles, can be found some of the most dramatic and tragic, yet least known, events of that conflict—those desperate struggles between the white man and the Indian that occurred throughout the frontier West during the years 1861–65.

This subject, other than books about specific high-profile events, such as the Sand Creek massacre, heretofore has been treated as if the Indians simply hibernated and westward migration halted while the war raged in the East. Nothing could be farther from the truth. In fact, it would be safe to say that more whites and Indians were killed in the West during those four years than in any other comparable period in American history. Some of the most captivating, controversial, and noteworthy engagements ever waged between those two races—featuring a fascinating cast of colorful characters, both famous and lesser known—occurred on the frontier while the eyes of the nation were riveted on events in the East.

The Blue, the Gray, and the Red presents an accurate, balanced portrayal of these hostilities as undermanned and inexperienced Union and Confederate soldiers, state militiamen, common citizens, and bands of adventurers, from Minnesota and Utah Territory to the regions of the Great Plains and the Southwest, were called upon to contend with the native red man—and vice versa, for at times it is difficult to distinguish heroes from villains.

In certain cases, it was as if the Indians were being prodded with a sharp stick until instinct and self-preservation compelled them to strike back. In other instances, the Indians took advantage when forts were abandoned when Regular army troops were sent East, and responded with violence to the presence of the white man in their homeland.

One aspect, however, becomes quite clear as the campaigns unfold: The toll of human loss and suffering on both sides due to these encounters is perhaps unparalleled, often beyond comprehension, and proves that savagery is not reserved for any one particular race of mankind.

The significance of this period of conflict on the frontier cannot be understated. When the guns fell silent in the East, there was no truce to hostilities in the West. The army would experience twenty more years of warfare against the Indians, and every battle and every drop of blood that was shed was a direct result of operations conducted during the Civil War.

CHAPTER ONE

The Flight of Opothleyahola

AT THE OUTBREAK OF THE CIVIL WAR, PLEDGES OF LOYALTY TO EITHER
the North or the South created divisions among people who had previously shared the same history, if not the same blood. This pitting of brother
against brother and neighbor against neighbor tore apart families, destroyed
relationships, and divided communities in many parts of the country.

The discord and schism between resolute people with opposing points
of view, however, were not reserved solely for the white man in the East. It
also occurred within one particular tribe of Indians and would result in a
winter of bitterness and violence, with an abundance of blood being spilled
and much suffering endured by thousands of men, women, and children
before the issue was tragically settled.

Admittedly, the tribe involved already had been engaged for decades in
a simmering internal feud of sorts within its ranks. But the contrary alle-
giances embraced by two factions within this tribe would now serve as a
convenient reason to enable one group to take advantage of the circumstances and exact revenge against the other, with assistance from white and
red allies.

In 1861, when the Southern states seceded and the North stood firm,
Indian Territory—present-day Oklahoma—became what could be called a
buffer zone between the Confederate states of Arkansas and Texas and the
Union state of Kansas and the territories of Colorado and New Mexico.
This area was populated for the most part by Indian people, primarily
members of the Five Nations—Cherokee, Chickasaw, Choctaw, Creek, and
Seminole. These tribes some years earlier had been resettled in Indian Territory from various locations within the South and had adopted a lifestyle
based on Southern traditions, such as the practice of slavery. For that reason,
most of these Indians—many of whom were successful plantation owners—

1

were sympathetic to the Southern cause for fear of losing their valuable property, slaves in particular.[1]

There existed, however, treaties between these tribes and the United States, and many members were dependent on the promised food and supplies granted them by the provisions. And there was some doubt about whether the South could provide for them in the same manner as the North. Another problem was that the recently replaced Federal agent was an ardent secessionist from Alabama, and the newly appointed replacement was unable to make contact with the tribes from his post in Kansas. That lack of communication from a representative of the divided United States would soon become a moot point when the disposition of troops in the area was settled.[2]

The question of garrisoning Union soldiers in Indian Territory was addressed in early 1861. Fort Gibson had been abandoned four years earlier and turned over to the Cherokee Nation, and several remaining garrisons, including Fort Arbuckle, Fort Cobb, and Fort Washington, were relatively small and isolated, and therefore vulnerable to an attack. Union colonel William H. Emory had been dispatched in March with orders to assume command at Fort Cobb and determine the prudence of leaving troops at the various posts. Events that occurred during his march through the territory, however, dictated Emory's decision.

Texas volunteers were sweeping through the area, and when Emory passed through Fort Washita and removed the garrison for fear of an attack, he was joined by all the troops from Fort Arbuckle, who also were worried about the advancing Texans. Within days, a courier reached Emory as he led his fleeing Union soldiers toward Fort Cobb. Emory was informed that Fort Cobb had already been evacuated, and he was instructed to march without delay for Fort Leavenworth, Kansas. The Yankees changed course and, with the Texas Confederates hot on their heels, eventually reached their destination without contact being made.[3]

The Southern soldiers, satisfied that their enemy posed no further threat, assumed occupation of the abandoned forts—as well as complete military control of Indian Territory. The Union had, for all intents and purposes, surrendered this vast area to the Confederacy without a shot being fired.

The South immediately sought to arrange treaties with the various Indian tribes. Albert Pike, who would eventually be appointed a brigadier general and placed in command of Indian Territory, was dispatched in June 1861 as a commissioner to the Cherokee capital at Tahlequah with orders to negotiate alliances of mutual assistance with the Five Nations. Pike, a native of Boston and now a prominent Arkansas lawyer, planter, and journalist, was thought to be an ideal envoy. He had already earned the trust of the Creek Nation by representing it in a lawsuit against the U.S. government before the war and winning an $800,000 judgment.

Brig. Gen. Ben McCulloch, a former neighbor of David Crockett who had fought for Texas independence in the 1836 battle of San Jacinto, had been placed in command of Indian Territory. McCulloch accompanied Albert Pike on the initial contact with the tribes in June 1861, when the envoy made contact with John Ross, principal chief of the Cherokee.

The seventy-one-year-old Ross, a wealthy land and slaveowner who was only one-eighth Cherokee, had maintained leadership of the majority element of his tribe since 1828. Ross informed Pike and McCulloch that his tribe would adhere to the treaties that it had made with the Federal government and would remain neutral with respect to the war.

The primary rival to Ross was fifty-five-year-old Stand Watie, three-quarters Cherokee, a successful planter who had been well educated in Tennessee. Watie had already embraced the Confederate cause and was in the process of raising and training a force of mixed-blood Cherokee cavalry to fight for the South.

Ross understood that the Confederates could conceivably remove him from office and replace him with Watie, but for the time being, perhaps in an effort to delay his decision while watching developments, was adamant that his tribe would remain neutral.

The disappointed Albert Pike moved south across the Arkansas River to negotiate with the Creek, while General McCulloch returned to Fort Smith, warning John Ross that if a Union invasion became imminent, "I will at once advance into your country, if I deem it advisable." Pike and McCulloch were comforted in one sense, however, that they could depend on support from Stand Watie.[4]

The Creek would prove to be another tribe that would pose a problem for Pike's effort to form a united Indian Confederacy. The Creek through the years, even before their removal from Georgia and Alabama to Indian Territory, had split into two distinct factions: the mixed-bloods and the full-bloods. The mixed-bloods had embraced the lifestyle of Southern planters—dressing in the finery of gentlemen and wearing their long hair curled at the ends in cavalier fashion—with the ambition of transforming the Creek Nation into more refined and genteel standards. This faction also had been responsible for arranging the earlier sale of the Eastern tribal land and the removal of the tribe to the West.

The full-bloods, on the other hand, shunned many aspects of the Southern way of life and remained loyal to their traditional beliefs. This faction had been outraged at what they considered a betrayal by the mixed-bloods with the treaty that had cost them their land in Georgia and Alabama. Members of both groups, however, had greatly profited from the practice of slavery, with many owning large plantations.[5]

Albert Pike managed to gain signatures on his Creek treaty on July 10, 1861, at North Fork Town by negotiating with mixed-blood tribal leaders Motey Canard (Kennard), Chilly McIntosh, and Daniel N. McIntosh, an ordained Baptist minister. This treaty proved far more favorable to the tribe than any it had ever signed with the United States. The annuities remained the same as in the Treaty of 1856—$71,960—but along with other important concessions, slavery was legalized and placed under Creek jurisdiction. In return, the Creek agreed to furnish a regiment of mounted soldiers— either alone or in conjunction with the Seminoles—which would serve at the pleasure of the Confederate army but only fight within the borders of the Indian Territory.[6]

The full-blood faction of the Creek was not represented at this meeting with Albert Pike but would make its intentions known in the near future.

Pike then met with the Chickasaw and Choctaw, who resided in the southern part of Indian Territory, near the Red River border with Texas. These two tribes were eager to support the South and agreed to raise a mounted regiment to fight for their new allies. The Seminoles were at first reluctant to sign a treaty, but Pike was assisted by influential leader John Jumper, who promised participation by a force of warriors who would join the Creek regiment.[7]

Meanwhile, Cherokee leader John Ross had a change of heart. Ross was aware that the Confederates had routed the Union army back east at Bull Run, or Manassas, and appeared to have seized the upper hand with regard to winning the war. Besides that, General McCulloch had commissioned Stand Watie a colonel in the Confederate provisional army and assigned his Cherokee regiment duty patrolling the northeastern part of Indian territory. Ross addressed a meeting of his tribe, saying: "The State on our border [Arkansas] and the Indian Nations about us have severed their connection with the United States and joined the Confederate States. Our general interest is inseparable from theirs and it is not desirable that we should stand alone." The tribe reluctantly abided by Ross's words and agreed to supply a regiment of Home Guards, which would be led by Col. John Drew.[8]

By then, Pike had drawn up a constitution creating the "United Nations of the Indian Territory," an Indian confederacy that consisted of a Grand Council, which was composed of delegates from each tribe that would meet annually at North Fork Town. Ambitious Mississippian Col.

Douglas Hancock Cooper—a man with the reputation as a hard drinker—who had been an agent to the Choctaw and Chickasaw before the war and was a friend of Jefferson Davis, was appointed commissioner of Indian Affairs.

Although there was some minor disenchantment and disagreement within the tribes, Pike was confident when he departed Indian Territory in October to present the treaties to the Confederate Senate in Richmond that the Five Nations were solidly on the side of the South. Pike, however, had perhaps underestimated the influence of one prominent Creek leader who had been conspicuously absent from the treaty negotiations with his tribe.[9]

Opothleyahola was an older, perhaps elderly (his age has been noted as being from the early sixties to the eighties), full-blooded Creek subchief and wealthy plantation owner. This prominent man, whose name, meaning "Good Shouting Child" in Creek, has been mentioned in various texts as Opothle Yahola, Opuithli Yahola, Opuithi Yahola, Apothleyahola, Opothleyohola, Hopothleycholo, and Hupueheth Yaholo, was a fierce traditionalist with an anti-Southern attitude who had counseled his people to remain neutral with respect to the white man's war.

Over the years, Opothleyahola had played a major role in the history of the Creek people. He was a veteran of the Creek War of 1813–14, serving under Red Eagle (William Weatherford) and fighting against Andrew Jackson. Later, he displayed great oratory skills and became primary speaker for the Upper Creek towns in opposing negotiations over tribal land—and therein was the main reason for his present conflict with tribal leaders over the Pike treaty.

Half brothers Motey Canard and Chilly and Daniel McIntosh were the sons of former Chief William McIntosh, the leader of the Lower Creek, or White Sticks, who had agreed in 1825 to the removal of the tribe from Georgia and Alabama to their present location in Indian Territory. Opothleyahola, as well as other Upper Creek, had at the time vehemently opposed this land cession. In 1825, Opothleyahola had been a member of a tribal delegation that met in Washington with President John Quincy Adams and reluctantly agreed to ceding tribal lands. Nevertheless, his Upper Creek, who lived in towns on the upper tributaries of the Chattahoochie River, refused to leave even after many of the Lower Creek had relocated. And the target of their wrath became William McIntosh. Along with Menawa, a second chief of the Okfuskee towns, Opothleyahola had been involved in the 1828 murder of William McIntosh in retaliation for his betrayal of the Creek.

Opothleyahola headed another delegation in 1832 that met with President Jackson and once again agreed to the treaty. Rather than move, however, he attempted to buy land in Mexico for his people but was rebuffed by the Mexican government. Finally, in 1836, Opothleyahola led about 2,700 people to settle in Indian Territory, where he assumed a leadership role of the reunited tribal faction and encouraged traditional customs among his tribe. He owned about 2,000 acres of land near North Fork Town, which was worked by slaves.[10]

The influence of Opothleyahola created constant tension, which bordered on violence, between the full-blooded leader and the mixed-blood half brothers Motey Canard and Chilly and Daniel McIntosh, who, in addition to disapproving of their enemy's pagan beliefs, were quite aware of the role that Opothleyahola had played in the murder of their father years earlier.

And now, Opothleyahola was disturbed by the signing of the Pike treaty with the Confederacy that William McIntosh's offspring had initiated, particularly the raising of a pro-Southern Creek regiment, fearing that his people would be subject to reprisals by these Lower Creek. Therefore, he vowed to remain loyal to the Union.

In August, Opothleyahola retired to his plantation near North Fork Town and, along with Oktarharsars Harjo, also known as Sands, who had been elected chief of the loyal Creek, wrote a letter to President Abraham Lincoln requesting protection under the Treaty of 1856:

> Now I write to the President our Great Father who removed us to our present homes, & made a treaty, and you said that in our new homes we should be defended from all interference from any person and that no white people in the whole world should ever molest us . . . and should we be injured by any body you would come with your soldiers & punish them. but now the wolf has come. men who are strangers tread our soil. our children are frightened & the mothers cannot sleep for fear. This is our situation now.
>
> When we made our Treaty at Washington you assured us that our children should laugh around our houses without fear & we believed you. . . . Once we were at peace. Our great father was always near & stood between us and danger.
>
> We his children want it to be so again, and we want you to send us word what to do. We do not hear from you & we send a letter, & we pray you to answer. Your children want to hear your word, & feel that you do not forget them.

I was at Washington when you treated with us, and now white people are trying to take our people away to fight against us and you. I am alive. I well remember the treaty. My ears are open & my memory is good.[11]

This plea by Opothleyahola would not reach Washington for almost a month. In the meantime, Col. Douglas Cooper made an effort to contact the dissident group with intentions of smoothing over the relationship between the McIntoshes and Opothleyahola, but the old chief apparently refused to meet with him. Cooper grew worried that Opothleyahola had been in contact with Federal authorities in Kansas and was preparing to ally his people with the Union. Opothleyahola had indeed been in contact with a U.S. commissioner in Kansas but was less than convinced by the promises that Union soldiers would eventually expel the Rebels from Indian Territory. Cooper became frustrated by Opothleyahola's repeated snubs and was also concerned that the slaves who were with the Upper Creek were by now likely armed and could possibly initiate a slave revolt throughout the South. He declared that he would march against the dissidents "and either compel submission" to the treaty or drive them from the territory.[12]

Cooler heads tried to prevail, including Albert Pike, who offered Opothleyahola the opportunity to form a battalion of soldiers exclusively from his followers to fight for the Confederacy; and respected Chief John Ross, who wrote a plea asking the Creek chief to avoid bloodshed at all costs. Opothleyahola, however, stubbornly refused to parley with anyone who represented the Confederacy.[13]

Opothleyahola had caught wind of Cooper's plans for armed intervention and decided that his only logical course of action was to remove his people from the hostile environment before it was too late. If Northern support in the form of troops for protection would not come to him, he would go to them. Opothleyahola would lead an exodus to Kansas, where he hoped that his followers would find relative safety under the protection of Union forces. James Scott of Greenleaf Town, who was ten years old at the time, remembered: "Opuithi Yahola's heart was sad at all the war talk. He visited the homes of his followers or any of the Indians and gave them encouragement to face all these things, but above all things to stay out of the war. It was no affair of the Indians."[14]

Opothleyahola directed his people to prepare stores of food, collect their property and livestock, and gather in a camp situated near his plantation at the junction of the North Fork and Deep Fork—near present-day Eufala.

The loyal full-blooded Creek heeded his call, as did a number of Seminole, Kickapoo, Shawnee, Delaware, Wichita, Comanche, and perhaps 200 to 400 former slaves. As many as 5,000 Indians—at least 1,500 warriors armed with hunting rifles, shotguns, and bows and arrows, who would form the fighting force, along with old men, women, and children—readied their wagons, oxcarts, and all their possessions for the prospect of a most arduous and likely perilous journey.

On November 5, 1861, Opothleyahola broke camp with his caravan of horses, wagons, and herds and headed north up the Deep Fork River to seek sanctuary in Kansas.[15]

Colonel Cooper quickly learned of Opothleyahola's intentions, as well as the time of his departure, and was determined to put down this uprising for fear that other Indians may question their loyalty to the Confederacy and join in this exodus or in some manner create a rebellion.

By November 15, Cooper had assembled a force of about 1,500 troopers, which included a battalion (500 white men) of the 9th Texas Cavalry, under Lt. Col. William Quayle; six companies of the 1st Choctaw and Chickasaw Mounted Rifles; the 1st Creek Cavalry Regiment, under Col. Daniel McIntosh; and the 1st Seminole Cavalry Battalion, led by Lt. Col. Chilly McIntosh and Maj. John Jumper. The column rode out of old Fort Gibson, forded the Arkansas, and turned westward toward the Deep Fork of the Canadian in pursuit of the dissident Creek.[16]

The stage was now set for a civil war within a civil war.

On November 16, Confederate scouts easily located the trail of Opothleyahola's slow-moving procession, and for the next three days, they doggedly closed the gap. Opothleyahola, however, so craftily maneuvered his people through the frosty, rolling prairie that the scouts from time to time would lose the trail. This would require Cooper to call for a halt while fresh sign was sought. On November 19, several Creek stragglers were captured, and it was learned that some of the loyalist Creek were camped just west of the confluence of the Arkansas and Cimarron Rivers. Cooper eagerly drove his men forward, and at about 4:00 P.M. scouts discerned smoke from a number of campfires.[17]

Quayle and his Texans, who let out a whoop at the prospect of a fight, were ordered to charge the camp. Upon arrival, the horsemen were disappointed to find the encampment abandoned. Quayle then ordered his men forward and raced ahead for four miles, until observing fresh wagon tracks that disappeared into a line of leafless trees near two flat-topped mounds known as Round Mountain, near present-day Yale in Payne County. The Texans charged into the timber, confident that their prey was a bay.

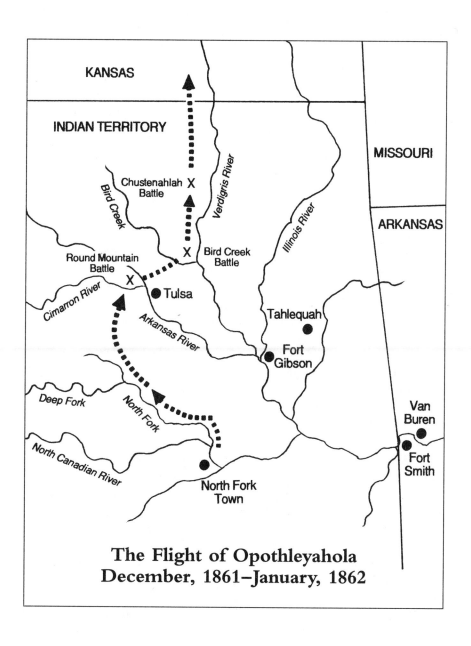

The Flight of Opothleyahola
December, 1861–January, 1862

Opothleyahola, however, had deployed his warriors in the timber and patiently waited for the aggressive horsemen to appear within range of their rifles and bows. The ambush was executed to perfection. When the time was right, the concealed Creek and Seminole marksmen unleashed a furious barrage of rifle and shotgun fire. Lieutenant Colonel Quayle's lead squadron, seventy men led by Capt. M. J. Brinson, was raked by this fusillade—with one man killed instantly—and the Confederates were momentarily stopped in their tracks. Many riders were thrown from their mounts and would have to fight the rest of the way on foot. The Creek also employed an old Indian fighting trick of sending out a pony chased by dogs in an effort to cause a stampede, which added to the confusion. Captain Brinson bravely rallied his men and was joined by two other companies— Captain Berry and Captain McCool, with about eighty men—riding to his right and left in support.

The pro-Union Creek, who outnumbered the Texans, maintained their position while raining constant fire. The bugler finally sounded retreat, and the Confederates pulled back, with Opothleyahola's warriors pressing forward to harass them. By this time, Colonel Cooper had arrived on the field; he decided that it was growing too dark and would be folly to blindly ride directly into the line of fire. He ordered about eighty men from the Choctaw-Chickasaw regiment under Capt. R. A. Young to dismount, form a skirmisher line to reinforce the Texans, and commence shooting at the distant muzzle flashes until the situation was adequately assessed. Any opportunity to flank the Creek was thwarted when Opothleyahola set fire to the prairie. Also, by that time darkness had descended, and it was impossible to distinguish friend from foe.

Opothleyahola, realizing that his men would not be able to hold their positions against Cooper's entire command, used the cover and distraction of the burning prairie to execute a hasty withdrawal. He forded the Arkansas River under the cover of darkness and headed toward a friendly Cherokee village on Bird Creek, which was on his route to Kansas.

Opothleyahola's warriors had left behind at least six dead Texans (one report lists twenty), four others wounded, and one listed as missing. One Texas officer, Capt. Charles S. Stewart of Company I, 9th Regiment, was included in those who were killed.

This engagement at Round Mountain, also known as the battle of Red Forks, had also cost Opothleyahola dearly. He had been forced to discard a large and valuable amount of his own entourage.[18]

Apparently not only material items had been left behind. Creek Indian James Scott gave this account of what he had observed on their flight:

> One time we saw a little baby sitting on its little blanket in the woods. Everyone was running because an attack was expected and no one had the time to stop and pick up the child. As it saw the people running by, the little child began to wave its little hands. The child had no knowledge that he had been deserted.[19]

On November 20, when Cooper was informed by his scouts that the renegade Creek had fled, he advanced his men into the abandoned encampment. He discovered the booty that Opothleyahola had left behind, which included a large number of cattle, oxen, and ponies; twelve wagons; a valuable cache of supplies, including coffee, flour, salt, and sugar; and even a buggy belonging to the old chief. Also found were the mangled bodies of several Confederate prisoners that the Creek women had mutilated with their knives and hominy pestles. There was no mention, however, of whether a little child or its body had been located.

Cooper, in the tradition of Western army officers, embellished his after-action report by claiming that he had killed at least 110 dissident Creek. This number was allegedly provided by Creek prisoners, and Opothleyahola's actual casualties, although unknown, were surely far fewer. The Confederates, confident that they could easily overtake their prey, went into camp at Tulseytown, present-day Tulsa, to rest the horses and bury their dead.[20]

While Cooper contemplated his next course of action, a courier arrived with a dispatch from Brig. Gen. Benjamin McCulloch to inform him that his services were needed elsewhere. To the northeast, in Missouri, Union soldiers under Maj. Gen. John C. Frémont had recovered from their August 10 defeat at Wilson's Creek at the hands of Sterling Price and had occupied Springfield. Reconnaissance reported that these troops had already marched out of that town and down the Telegraph Road toward Arkansas. McCulloch ordered Cooper to abandon his chase of Opothleyahola and move his column to a position near Marysville on the Arkansas line to assist in checking Frémont's advance.

No sooner had Cooper started east toward Concharta when another message from McCulloch reversed the marching orders. Frémont had been relieved of duty in favor of Maj. Gen. David Hunter, who decided that it was too close to winter to risk another campaign. The Union troops were presently falling back to settle into winter camps at Sedalia and Rolla. Cooper was now free to resume his original mission. He moved his command to nearby Spring Hill, where better forage awaited the horses, and ordered his troops to prepare for another march against Opothleyahola.[21]

Cooper took to the field on the morning of November 28 with a column of 780 soldiers—430 from the 1st Choctaw and Chickasaw regiment, 50 members of the Choctaw battalion, 285 from Col. Daniel N. McIntosh's 1st Creek Regiment, and 15 Creek scouts—and rode northwest toward Tulseytown. Upon arrival, a deserter warned Cooper that Opothleyahola was preparing his 2,000 warriors to mount an assault. Cooper sent dispatches to Col. John Drew, the prominent mixed-blood merchant who commanded the 1st Regiment of Cherokee Rifles, as well as requesting the services of Col. William B. Sims of the 9th Cavalry. The two units were ordered to unite and rendezvous with Cooper.[22]

Drew and his 500 Cherokee Mounted Rifles, however, misunderstood the orders and marched directly to Bird Creek, within six miles of Opothleyahola's camp near present-day Turley, and waited for Cooper. By the time Cooper's column approached Drew's position, Opothleyahola began making overtures for peace. A delegation of Drew's Cherokee met with Opothleyahola to assure him that the Confederates wanted peace, not bloodshed. A formal conference was arranged for the following day.

At that time, Cooper dispatched an emissary, Maj. Thomas Pegg, who, accompanied by three other officers, arrived in the dissident camp to observe hundreds of warriors painted and preparing for an attack. These warriors denied the emissaries access to Opothleyahola and shouted threats about an attack planned for that night. Pegg and his companions were fortunate to escape with their lives to report back to Cooper.[23]

Meanwhile, rumors had already reached Drew's Cherokee that an attack was imminent. The unit had little desire to fight an enemy whose offense was simply being loyal to the Union. Therefore, most of the Cherokee slipped away into the darkness, either defecting to the enemy or running away. The surprised Colonel Drew, who was unaware of his men's intentions, was left with a command of only twenty-eight men.[24]

Several of Drew's teamsters reported the desertion to Cooper, who hastily deployed his men into a tight defensive perimeter and dispatched a squadron of Colonel Quayle's Texans to ride to the aid of Drew's remaining troops, who returned during the night. Another patrol, under Capt. Robert C. Parks, was dispatched on a scouting mission.

When no sign of Quayle, Parks, or the enemy was evident by morning, December 9, Cooper sent out a reconnaissance patrol led by his adjutant, Roswell W. Lee. The adjutant returned to report that Quayle had approached Opothleyahola's camp to discover it abandoned, but with tents still standing. Cooper then ordered Drew and his remaining men to sack the enemy camp. This resulted in the confiscation of not only the tents, but additional wagons, horses, and assorted supplies.[25]

Cooper sent out a two-company column under Capt. Adam Foster to sweep Shoal Creek, with orders to keep an eye out for both Opothleyahola's warriors and the Parks patrol, which had yet to return. He then broke camp, forded Bird Creek, and had proceeded along the east bank for about five miles when several of Foster's men galloped up. The detail had located Opothleyahola's Creek up ahead. Within moments, troopers from Captain Parks's patrol arrived to report that they had happened upon the enemy and had been forced to flee.[26]

While Cooper digested this information, he was alerted to the fact that about 200 of Opothleyahola's warriors were attacking the Confederate rear guard. A squadron of Mounted Rifles under Capt. R. A. Young was ordered to reinforce that position. Upon Young's arrival, however, the attackers slowly retreated toward their companions who were hidden in the trees. The wily Opothleyahola had set a trap, but to Young's credit, he recognized the ploy and pulled up in time to avert disaster.

It was evident to Cooper that the only course of action was to engage the enemy with his entire force. He acted swiftly, sending 100 men to guard his wagon train, while separating his command into three columns: The Choctaw and Chickasaw Mounted Rifles under Captains Jones and McCurtin would swing to the right to form a junction with Young; the 9th Texas and the remnants of John Drew's Cherokee regiment would hold the center; and the Creek under Col. Daniel N. McIntosh would ride on the left. Cooper signaled for the bugler to sound the charge, and the white and red Confederates dashed off in a two-mile line through timber and ravines of the prairie along Bird Creek to battle the Union Indians—which now included over 400 well-armed Cherokee who had formerly been members of Drew's regiment.[27]

Opothleyahola had deployed his warriors in the traditional Creek custom of using natural elements for defense: They had assumed a position at a quarter-mile-long horseshoe bend on the east side of Bird Creek, which was known to the Cherokee as Chusto-Talash, or Caving Banks. The terrain in this particular place, which was protected by water on three sides, consisted of fifty-foot sandstone riverbanks with deep water below, tangled thickets, fords known only to the Union Creek, a gouge in the prairie located to the west of the bend in an old stream cut, and a farm—log cabin, corncrib, and fence—at the center of the bend that would provide ample protection. Firing steps for sharpshooters had been cut into the face of the bank to fashion a natural parapet, and trees had been felled in strategic locations.[28]

The Texans, who led the advance, were divided into two columns. Colonel Quayle took about 100 men to the left and reached the horseshoe bend without encountering any opposition. Colonel Sims soon appeared to reunite the regiment as it came under fire from sharpshooters in positions down a ravine. The Texans charged through that swale and onto a second, driving the Union Indians, whom Quayle recognized as the Cherokee who had deserted Drew's regiment, ahead of them, until running into an ambush at the mouth of another ravine. The Cherokee pulled back, and a detachment under Sims pushed toward the east, seeking a place at which to ford the creek—all the while receiving scattered fire from the enemy. Finally, after about a mile-and-a-half march, Sims returned to rendezvous with Quayle, who had become pinned down in a ravine.[29]

On the Confederate right, a detachment of the 1st Choctaw and Chickasaw Mounted Rifles, under Maj. Mitchell LeFlore, rode forward for about a mile and a half before losing sight of their enemy at a cut bank. The regiment dismounted and moved cautiously ahead in a skirmisher line until locating the open end of the horseshoe. From this vantage point, the men observed some warriors around the farmhouse. Captain Young led his squadron in a charge and managed to dislodge the Union Indians from their position. Young's troops aggressively pursued the retreating enemy, but they soon found themselves bogged down within the tangled underbrush and exposed to devastating fire. Young prudently pulled back and re-formed his squadron.

Three companies arrived to reinforce the Mounted Rifles, and Young's men resumed the attack by taking cover behind trees or thick brush and firing, then moving forward to another place of protection and firing again. This tactic proved successful until Opothleyahola's warriors hid and allowed their enemies to pass, then opened fire on their rear and flank. Young was once again forced to retire, and his troops took cover in the house and corncrib.[30]

McIntosh's Creek had swung to the left, where they were met with fierce resistance as they dismounted and advanced into the timber—fighting at times hand-to-hand with their brethren. The regiment was unable to locate an adequate place to cross Bird Creek, however, and before long returned to the main force.

Opothleyahola decided that it was time to take the offensive. To this end, he launched a massive counterattack at the neck of the horseshoe. The battle raged for a half hour, without many casualties, until the Union Indians attempted to capture the Confederates' horses. The troopers of the Mounted Rifles dashed to retrieve their mounts and for the moment abandoned the fighting.[31]

The savage battle—a series of attacks and counterattacks, ambushes and envelopments—lasted for about four hours, until darkness made it impossible to distinguish friend from foe. Colonel Cooper reluctantly recalled his troops, and they retired to camp about five miles from the battlefield.

In the battle of Bird Creek, also known as Caving Banks or Chusto-Talash, the Confederate commander listed his losses at fifteen killed and thirty-seven wounded. There was no official report of Opothleyahola's casualties, but a Union Indian prisoner allegedly told Cooper that 412 had been lost. Cooper wrote in his after-action report that Union losses totaled at least 500. Once again, taking into account that Opothleyahola's warriors had for the most part fought on their own terms, this number was without question highly inflated. In fact, Cooper's men found only 27 enemy bodies on the field.[32]

And much to the disappointment and frustration of Col. Douglas H. Cooper—not to mention the McIntosh brothers—Opothleyahola and his Unionist Creek had for a second time engaged Confederate forces, stopped them in their tracks, and eluded capture. In this case, the Creek chief had withdrawn north up Hominy Creek into the hills and valleys in the Cherokee Cooweescoowee District.

Perhaps Opothleyahola now entertained the thought that his quest to reach Kansas could become a reality after all. His warriors had acquitted themselves with a fierceness that had resulted in success, which would encourage them in future engagements. And the longer they could keep the Confederates at bay, the closer they inched toward their objective and safety.

The following morning, Colonel Cooper sent out a scouting detail in an effort to pick up Opothleyahola's trail, then returned to the battlefield and attended to the grim business of burying the dead. Cooper was ready and willing to give chase, until his chief of ordnance dashed his plans by informing him that they were desperately short of ammunition. The commander grudgingly decided that the column would retire to Fort Gibson and obtain ammo and supplies from Fort Smith before returning to the field.[33]

Cooper was determined to hunt down this dissident force that had caused him such embarrassment. The longer Opothleyahola remained at large, the greater the prospect that other Indians would question their allegiance to the South and defect. Also, there was the distinct possibility that before long, Opothleyahola's Indians might receive aid from the Union, which could conceivably undermine the Confederacy in Indian Territory. Cooper was determined that he would prevent the Creek chief from escaping his grasp at any cost.

Before breaking camp, Cooper sent a message to Col. James McIntosh (no relation to Chilly or Daniel) at Van Buren, Arkansas, near Fort Smith, complaining that Confederate strength in the Indian Territory was inadequate, and requesting that additional troops be dispatched without haste to prevent further Cherokee defections and the threat of a Union takeover. "The true men among the Cherokee must be supported and protected," Cooper wrote, "or we shall lose the Indian Territory." These sentiments were echoed by Southern newspapers in western Arkansas, which warned that if the "rebellion" of the "yankee abolishionist" Opothleyahola and his *four thousand painted warriors* (more likely one-third of that figure) could defeat Cooper, Arkansas and Texas would be in danger of eventual Union control.[34]

Col. James McQueen McIntosh was indeed concerned about the situation among the Cherokee and understood that immediate action must be taken. The West Point graduate, who had finished last in his class but had nonetheless distinguished himself in the August battle at Wilson's Creek, decided to personally accept the assignment. On December 17, McIntosh rode out of Van Buren leading a column of 1,600 Texas and Arkansas cavalrymen "to settle matters in the nation."[35]

McIntosh had failed to inform Colonel Cooper of his intentions, and therefore his arrival at Fort Gibson on December 20 was a pleasant surprise. The two men immediately formulated their plans, a two-pronged approach: Cooper would ride up the north bank of the Arkansas in an effort to get to the rear of Opothleyahola, while McIntosh would head for the Verdigris River to the east of Opothleyahola's assumed position, and then head west to strike the enemy.[36]

Cooper's column was delayed by a series of problems, including the desertion of his Indian teamsters, and McIntosh decided to take to the field alone, with the promise that Cooper would rush to assist if the enemy was encountered.

It was a bitterly cold day, that December 22, when Col. James McIntosh rode out of Fort Gibson at the head of a column of 1,380 troopers.

Cooper finally marched from Choska on December 24, after sending a message for Col. Stand Watie and his 300-man 2nd Regiment of Cherokee Mounted Rifles to join the combined forces as soon as possible on the Verdigris River.[37]

On Christmas evening, McIntosh's command was surprised by the sudden appearance of about 200 mounted Indians, who sat calmly at a distance watching the cavalrymen. McIntosh dispatched one regiment to determine the Indians' intentions, but he soon abandoned that idea when the riders remained just out of the Confederates' reach.[38]

Scouts returned just before dark to report that they had observed smoke rising over the distant hills. This news raised the spirits of the troops, who had for several days heard rumors that Opothleyahola had escaped into Kansas, thereby making their march a waste of time. The men spent the remainder of the evening readying their weapons and equipment for an impending battle.[39]

At the same time, Colonel McIntosh received word that additional difficulties had beset Cooper's column, and any rendezvous would be delayed by at least two or three days. McIntosh, who was convinced from the scouts' reports that he was within striking distance of Opothleyahola's camp, debated his options. If he waited for Cooper, his enemy would likely disappear into the rugged terrain and become closer to sanctuary in Kansas. He decided that his only choice was to press on without Cooper.[40]

At dawn on December 26, McIntosh had his troops in the saddle and thirsting for blood. He dispatched scouts in every direction and proceeded cautiously through freezing rain and sleet westward into the hills, with intentions of forcing a confrontation with the elusive Opothleyahola.

It was just about noon when contact was made with the dissident Indians. McIntosh's vanguard, Capt. D. M. Short's Company E of the 3rd Texas, had just completed fording Shoal Creek, a small tributary of the Verdigris River, when they were fired upon. McIntosh quickly brought up Col. W. C. Young's 11th Texas to reinforce Company E, sent the 3rd Texas Cavalry under Lt. Col. Walter P. Lane to the left, and dismounted his troops.[41]

Opothleyahola had skillfully deployed his men on a rocky hill overlooking Shoal Creek, with about 200 to 300 yards of open prairie between his position and the enemy. A detachment of Seminole under Chief Halek Tustenugge had assumed positions on the slope, concealed by heavy brush, rocks, and trees. The main force remained mounted at the summit of the hill, prepared to attack if the Confederates managed to traverse the open ground and ascend the steep incline.

It was clear to McIntosh and his commanders—all Wilson's Creek veterans—that effectively dislodging the Union Indians from such a defensive position would be a formidable task for the Confederates.[42]

One Texan described the scene that lay before them:

> The warriors, painted in the most hideous manner, and clad in the most outlandish garbs, were perpetrating fantastic antics before high heaven, and the cat-like enemy ready for the fatal spring below. Some gobbled, in imitation of the turkey-gobbler; others, fired by a spirit of emulation, apparently, rivaled the coyote in howling; the game viking of the barn-yard would have recognized his "cock-a-doodle-doo," in the wild pandemonium of sounds, as would the panther, the catamount, and even the domestic dog.[43]

McIntosh wasted little time in planning his attack, which would feature a frontal assault—strength against strength. Colonel Lane's 3rd Texas was ordered to assume a position at the center of the line and would lead the charge. Colonel Young and his 11th Texas Cavalry were sent across the stream to form on Lane's left flank. Lt. Col. John S. Griffith and his 6th Texas Cavalry were dispatched upstream to the right of Lane's troops, with orders to execute a flanking movement to the Union left when the 3rd Texas commenced the frontal assault.

As soon as Griffith's troops had reached their position, Colonel McIntosh gave the order to charge.[44]

The Confederates, yelling wildly, thundered across Shoal Creek and onto the open prairie toward their objective. The Seminole responded with an explosion of rifle fire, which enveloped the entire hillside with plumes of thick smoke. But when the smoke had dissipated enough to restore a view of the surroundings, the Union Indians were dismayed to discover that their volleys had had little, if any, effect on the charging horsemen. The alarmed Seminole quickly scrambled back up the hill.

Lane's men dismounted at the base of the hill and, disregarding the hindrance of their wet and freezing clothing, dashed up the steep slope to engage their enemy in desperate hand-to-hand combat. McIntosh later wrote of this action that the 3rd Texas, "led by those gallant officers Colonel Lane and Major Chilton breasted itself for the highest point of the hill, and rushed over its rugged side with the irresistible force of a tornado, and swept everything before it."[45]

This determined assault by the Confederates proved too much for Opothleyahola's warriors to withstand. The Union Indians retreated in great confusion, while the Arkansas and Texas troopers raced for their horses to give chase.[46]

This part of the battle was later described by one of Colonel Lane's Texans:

A vigorous pursuit was immediately commenced, and many hand-to-hand fights to the death occurred; for, however impotent the Indian may be fettered by disciplined organization, individually, he knows no personal danger, and taking his life in his hands, will accept the challenge to mortal combat with the odds against him ten to one. The Indians scattered in all directions—having Kansas, however, for the objective point—and built fires, or rather "smoke," in order to divert the pursuers, and cause them to relax the pursuit. One instance of their stoical indifference to death will suffice: An old warrior fired upon a party of eight or ten from behind a tree. The men did not wish to kill him, and used entreaties to induce him to surrender; but, with death imminent, he continued to load his old rifle with a sublime indifference never attained by the Cynic philosophers of Greece, and having loaded coolly proceeded with the priming, when his admiring foes were compelled to dash out his brave old life.[47]

The gray-clad horsemen chased the Union Indians for more than two miles before recall was sounded at 4:00 P.M. McIntosh estimated that "upward of 250" of the enemy had been killed, and about 160 women and children and 20 blacks taken prisoner. The deserted camp yielded 30 wagons, 70 yoke of oxen, several hundred head of cattle, 500 horses, 100 sheep, thousands of dogs, and other valuable supplies. McIntosh listed his casualties in this battle, known as Chustenahlah, or Patriot Hills, as 3 killed and 32 wounded. He wrote that "the stronghold" of Opothleyahola "was completely broken up, and his force scattered in every direction, destitute of the simplest elements of subsistence."[48]

Their primary target, Chief Opothleyahola, with about 200 warriors and an unknown number of women and children, however, had managed to vanish into the growing darkness.

While McIntosh tended to his killed and wounded, the regiment of 300 Cherokees under Col. Stand Watie arrived in the Confederate camp. The combined force rode out on the morning of December 27 to finish its mission of destroying whatever remained of the dissidents.

The column had covered almost twenty-five miles before scouts detected a large force of the enemy in the nearby hills. Watie, whose unit was in the advance, dispatched a courier to inform McIntosh of the situation. Although Watie estimated that Opothleyahola had a force of perhaps 500 to 600 warriors spread over a wide area in rugged terrain, much of it inaccessible by horses, he decided to assault the position without waiting for McIntosh. Watie divided his command, sending Maj. Elias C. Boudinot to the left with half the command, while the colonel himself headed to the right with the other half.[49]

While the bitter wind howled, the Cherokee engaged the dissident Creek and their allies in a spirited, running battle that lasted nearly two hours before Opothleyahola was able to break contact and escape. "Every man seemed anxious to be foremost," Major Boudinot later reported, "and the charges made upon the enemy over rocks, mountains, and valley's [sic]—the roughest country I ever saw—were made with the utmost enthusiasm, and with irresistible impetuosity."

Colonel Watie reported back to McIntosh that the bodies of eleven Creek and Seminole had been found on the field, and he turned over seventy-five women and children taken prisoner. Amazingly, Watie's regiment had not suffered even one casualty in this engagement.[50]

Colonel McIntosh was satisfied that this final blow administered by Col. Stand Watie's Cherokee had accomplished his mission. He broke camp on the morning of December 28 and led his troops toward Fort Gibson to prepare for his return to Arkansas. Later that day, his column encountered the late-arriving troops commanded by Col. Douglas H. Cooper.

Although apparently nothing was said at that time, Cooper was later highly critical of McIntosh's recent actions. He believed that had McIntosh waited for Cooper to arrive at Chustenahlah, Opothleyahola's entire force could have been destroyed. Cooper also maintained the same opinion of Stand Watie's impulsive attack. He watched the two offenders head for Fort Gibson, and then led his column north with the intention of sweeping alone up to the Kansas border and overtaking the remainder of the Union Indians.[51]

Meanwhile, Opothleyahola and his band of perhaps several thousand, now scattered into small groups, struggled northward through nearly unbearable cold, without adequate shelter or food. Many people had frozen to death, their bodies left behind to be devoured by scavengers. Children had been born along the way, but most had soon died of exposure to the harsh elements. But there could be no turning back or settling into winter camp until they were safely in Kansas. There would be only misery and more suffering ahead as Cooper's column nipped at their heels.[52]

On December 31, Cooper's vanguard encountered a group of Creek, Osage, and Cherokee. The Texans killed several of the men and captured a number of women and children.

On New Year's Day 1862, Cooper divided his command, sending John Drew's Mounted Rifles to scout a wagon trail, while the main column headed for the Arkansas River. Both columns happened upon the enemy that day. Drew routed a small Cherokee camp, where one man was wounded and several prisoners were taken. Cooper fell upon a Creek camp situated at the foot of a bluff over the Arkansas River. His troops killed one warrior and captured twenty-one women and children. Cooper had now penetrated almost to the Kansas border and decided, given the miserable weather—one of his men had frozen to death—that it was time to retire to Fort Gibson.[53]

The survivors of Opothleyahola's flight—starving, ill, their clothing in tatters, their possessions abandoned—finally straggled across the Kansas border to join other refugees on the upper Verdigris River about fifteen miles south of the Belmont on land reserved for Indians, where white settlers were banned. Conditions in the camp throughout the winter were barren and primitive—people lay on the frozen ground beneath inadequate shelters constructed from tree branches or scraps of cloth. Fuel, food, and medicine were scarce, and scores died from hunger, disease, or effects of the blizzards that roared through the camp. At one point, a visiting surgeon amputated hundreds of limbs. Opothleyahola lay ill with a fever even as he tried to negotiate supplies for his devastated people.

The makeshift camp was soon home to 3,168 Creek, 53 Creek slaves, 38 free Creek blacks, 777 Seminole, 136 Quapaw, 50 Cherokee, 31 Chickasaw, and members of various other tribes. By April, the number of refugees had swelled to 7,600.[54]

The Union Creek who had not departed with Opothleyahola were also terrorized during that winter. Malucy Bear of Greenleaf Town recalled that her once-tranquil community was now a place of desolation. "We would see some lone cow that had been left. The roosters would continually crow at some deserted home. The dogs would bark or howl. Those days were lonesome to me, young as I was, for I knew that most of our old acquaintances were gone." The community was the target of frequent raiding parties that stole everything in sight and even burned down the remaining houses, while the women and children cowered in the thickets during the day and returned to what was left of their homes at night.[55]

By contrast, the Southern Creek benefited from the appropriations they received under the provisions of their treaties with the Confederacy. Albert Pike had been named commanding general of Indian Territory and established a headquarters at Cantonment Davis, across the Arkansas River. He viewed the Indians under his command as a homeland guard, and indeed, these forces were not particularly interested in mobilizing to fight the white man's war in some distant place.

In early March 1862, Union major general Samuel R. Curtis marched against Brig. Gen. Sterling Price in what culminated in the battle of Pea Ridge, Arkansas. General Pike was ordered to advance with his command, which consisted primarily of three Cherokee regiments, and accompanied white Confederate soldiers into the battle. Many of the Creek, Chickasaw, and Chocktaw under Colonels Douglas Cooper and Daniel McIntosh were in no hurry to take the field and arrived a day late.

During the fray, Pike's warriors, shrieking blood-curdling war cries, rashly attacked a Union artillery battery and routed the frightened gunners. The Indians, however, paused to celebrate their great victory and were struck by a Federal counterattack that sent them running away. Pike was unable to reassemble his Indian troops, which contributed to the Confederate defeat, enabling the Union to hold Missouri for more than two years.

Col. Stand Watie's regiment of mixed-blood Cherokees, along with John Drew's full-bloods, had distinguished themselves during the engagement before being driven back and ably covering the Confederate retreat.[56]

The Confederate Indians, however, along with their leader, Albert Pike, were condemned for scalping and mutilating their enemies, which was repulsive to whites on both sides. Also, Drew was accused of purposely turning his guns on Confederate whites during the engagement. For these reasons—as well as white prejudice—Pea Ridge was last time during the war that Indians were integrated with white soldiers on the field.[57]

Pike also came under fire from Maj. Gen. Thomas C. Hindman, the commander of the Trans-Mississippi District, over the handling of money and materials. In fact, Hindman ordered that Pike be arrested and face a court-martial. This conflict perhaps arose from Pike's indignation over the fact that the promise made that the Indians would fight only in their homeland had been broken by having them participate at Pea Ridge. The charges were serious enough that Pike left his command and hightailed it into the Arkansas hills. He submitted his resignation in July 1862, and it was accepted in November. Pike resumed his work as a teacher, lawyer, and journalist, eventually moving to Memphis and then Washington, D.C. He was indicted after the war, but the case never came to trial. In his later years, Pike became a national spokesman for Freemasonry. He died in the nation's capital on April 2, 1891.

James McQueen McIntosh, who had been promoted to brigadier general in January 1862, led a daring yet somewhat foolhardy charge against a Union position during the Pea Ridge battle and was shot through the heart.

Douglas Hancock Cooper was promoted to brigadier general in May 1863. He lobbied for the position of superintendent of Indian Affairs within the district but was passed over due to his constant state of drunkenness. Cooper then influenced the Indians to undermine Confederate authority, until he received the superintendency in February 1865. After the war, he remained in Indian Territory and worked for the betterment of the Choctaw and Chickasaw. He died in poverty at Old Fort Washita on April 29, 1879.

Stand Watie became known as a brilliant commander of guerrilla tactics with effective hit-and-run raids and was promoted to brigadier general in May 1864. That same year, he was made principal chief of the southern band of Cherokee. He finally handed over his sword to the Union on June 23, 1865, thus becoming the last Confederate general to surrender his command. Watie became a farmer and raised a family following the war. He died on September 9, 1871.

Upon arrival in Kansas, Opothleyahola had pleaded with the Union for weapons that would assist his warriors in regaining their homeland. Little at that time was provided, however, and Opothleyahola died in the spring of 1862. His Upper Creek later bravely fought against their rivals—including the McIntosh brothers—and eventually returned to rebuild their homeland.

Remarkably, the Lower and Upper Creek managed to set aside their differences after the war, signed a treaty in 1866, and were reunited as a nation.

CHAPTER TWO

Bear River Massacre

"The mail must go through" remains an adage of the Postal Service to this day—through rain, and sleet, and hail, and snow, and dead of night, the mail must go through. With the advent of the Civil War, however, natural elements and darkness were the least of the worries for those people responsible for transporting mail and maintaining telegraph service through the territories of Nevada, Wyoming, and Utah. Mail stations and carriers would be obliged to contend with a much more dangerous foe—namely, hostile Indians.

Beginning in the 1840s, wagon trains had steadily brought white settlers and miners into those areas along the western trails that had been for centuries inhabited by Indians of various tribes—the Paiute, the Ute, the Bannock, and the tribe that would emerge as the biggest threat to the Overland Mail route, the Shoshone.

The Shoshone had always vigorously opposed the invasion by whites into their homeland, but no group of emigrants would have quite as much of an impact on the tribe as the Church of Jesus Christ of Latter-Day Saints, better known as Mormons. In 1847, the Mormons, persecuted and abhorred for their practice of polygamy, had been driven from their homes in Nauvoo, Illinois, and sought a refuge to escape the mob violence that besieged them. They traveled west and arrived in the Salt Lake Valley in July of that year with intentions of establishing a colony in Mexican territory. The subsequent Mexican cession of that land that followed the Mexican War, however, placed the Mormons under the American flag as a territory, with Brigham Young as governor, but still far from Federal intervention.

Young, who was said to have had twenty-seven wives, administered Utah Territory as if he were the king of a Mormon kingdom. In 1857, President James Buchanan decided to replace Young as governor with

Alfred Cumming, a non-Mormon and former Indian agent. The Mormons made it clear that Cumming would not be allowed to assume office. The president responded by ordering 2,500 troops from Fort Leavenworth, under Brig. Gen. Albert Sidney Johnston, to march into the Salt Lake Valley and seat Cumming by force, if necessary.

The march of the soldiers covered 1,200 miles in almost four months, but the harsh winter weather became a major obstacle and cost the column great numbers of horses and mules—not to mention hardships for the troops. In addition, Brigham Young had directed his militia to employ guerrilla tactics and harass the advancing column by blockading roads, destroying army supply wagons, and committing other acts of terror that would delay or annoy the advancing troops. His tactics were successful. By the time the soldiers had reached the vicinity of Salt Lake, they were in no condition to fight. General Johnston was obliged to wait until spring to complete his mission.

In the meantime, the Mormons offered a compromise to avoid armed conflict. Alfred Cumming would be accepted as governor, but the army must not set foot in Salt Lake City. President Buchanan thought this proposal was best for all concerned and went as far as to pardon those Mormons who had participated in the rebellion. The army was even permitted to save face by marching into Salt Lake City, but continued right on through town and did not halt.

For all intents and purposes, the Mormons had won what became known as the Utah War of 1857–58 without a shot being fired.

Over the next two years, scores of wagon trains filled with Mormons from the East joined their brethren to build farms and settlements that spread out from Salt Lake City into the most fertile valleys of Utah. The Mormon squatters never gave a thought to compensating the local Shoshone Indians for taking possession of their traditional land. To his credit, Brigham Young did announce a policy toward the Indians based on the concept that it was "manifestly more economical, and less expensive to feed and clothe, than to fight them."[1]

In the spring of 1860, hundreds of Mormon wagons rolled into the verdant Cache Valley in response to an announcement by leader Peter Maughan in the church newspaper calling it the "best watered valley I have ever seen in these mountains." In 1855, Brigham Young had successfully petitioned the Utah Territorial Legislature Assembly for exclusive privileges in Cache Valley, and a small settlement called Elkhorn Ranch, near present-day Millville, had been established. Other Mormon settlements in the region also were rapidly growing in population as more and more settlers heeded the church's call to come west.

The Shoshone became quite concerned about the arrival of the migrants into Cache Valley, as well as Bear River Valley and other fruitful food-gathering areas that they regarded to be part of their homeland. Ancestors of the tribe were said to have populated much of present-day Utah since perhaps as early as 400 A.D., although recent archaeological studies have questioned the precise date. Regardless, it would be safe to assume that these Indians had populated the area for hundreds of years before the arrival of white men.

The Shoshone were a nomadic tribe that followed an annual cycle that brought them to prime places for gathering food at the most opportune times. And Cache Valley, with its rich grasses and soil and thick timber stands, provided quite a bountiful menu for the Indians. They could harvest many types of edible greens, roots, bulbs, nuts, seeds to be ground into meal, and wild berries. The mountain streams that flowed into the valley were teeming with trout, whitefish, sucker fish, and salmon. And there was plentiful game to hunt, such as elk, deer, antelope, rabbits, ground squirrels, woodchucks, and various species of birds and waterfowl.[2]

Therefore, it was only natural that the Shoshone would resent the intrusion by whites into Cache Valley and other places within their homeland that were vital to their age-old nomadic lifestyle. The Indians found themselves quickly becoming deprived of their long-standing hunting and gathering grounds, pushed aside by whites and relegated to accept life in desolate deserts and barren mountain ranges that could not provide even their basic subsistence. By 1861, many Shoshone bands that once had thrived were now poverty-stricken, with hundreds of people on the verge of starvation. These proud Indians had been forced by the white man's progress to compromise their dignity and beg for food.

The Mormons, who adhered to Brigham Young's belief that it would be more to their advantage to feed the Indians rather than to fight them, made an effort to provide food for the needy tribe. That gesture, however, was far from adequate. Predictably, given the growing tension between prosperous white settlers and down-and-out Indians, incidences of conflict became more frequent. If the Indians were denied the right to hunt for food, they would attempt to steal it from those with plenty, and the theft of beef and other provisions had become commonplace.[3]

Meanwhile, along the mail route, the famed Pony Express had been inaugurated on April 3, 1860. Twice a day, daring riders would carry mail on horseback halfway across the continent—1,966 miles—supported by stations that had been established every ten to fifteen miles. Mail could travel from Missouri to California in a remarkable, for its time, ten and a half days.

During the summer and fall of 1860, when travel was at its height, these mail stations were repeatedly struck by Ute, Shoshone, and Bannock Indians who were looking for food and horses to steal. The Pony Express and Overland Mail stage service were occasionally interrupted when stations were abandoned for fear of an attack.[4]

At the outbreak of the Civil War, many Western posts were dismantled, and the Regular army troops were sent east to participate in the fighting. Federal soldiers had been garrisoned at Camp Floyd near Salt Lake City; Fort Bridger, then in Utah; and Fort Churchill in Nevada. The presence of these troops may have deterred some problems, but for the most part, they had been ineffectual in preventing many bands of the starving Indians from stealing cattle and looting wagon trains.

Utah and the entire region at that time were left virtually unprotected, a fact that did not go unnoticed by the Indians. Attempts at appeasing the tribal bands with food failed to quell the violence, and brazen raids on mail stations and settlers had become more frequent.

On July 24, 1861, Secretary of War Edwin Stanton informed California governor John G. Downey that the government "accepts for three years one regiment of infantry and five companies of cavalry to guard the overland mail route from Carson Valley to Salt Lake and Fort Laramie." The man who was appointed to raise and command this unit and take it to Utah was Patrick Edward Connor, who began his task of forming the regiment during September. This volunteer unit, however, would be held in California until the following summer, due to the difficulty of traversing the deep snow in the Sierra Nevada, and therefore could not provide any immediate help protecting the besieged mail route and Mormon settlements.[5]

In March 1861, a law had been enacted that rerouted the daily Overland Mail stages and semiweekly Pony Express from the southwestern route to a central route, a move designed to distance it from possible Confederate attacks. These newly constructed stage stations and Pony Express relay stations became the primary target for Shoshone Indians. Although food was their main interest, they also raided to gain tribal prestige by stealing livestock, killing whites—station personnel as well as stage drivers and passengers—and burning coaches, mailbags, and buildings.

In addition to the mail route, Mormon settlers had not been spared in this renewed reign of terror by the Shoshone. Communal cattle herds were constantly being run off and a large number of animals shot dead, which heightened tension between the two races.[6]

Therefore, the presence of as many as 1,500 Shoshone that had gathered at Blacksmith Fork in Cache Valley in mid-July 1861 was viewed with great concern by the Mormons living nearby. The whites were afraid to leave their homes for fear that an attack was imminent, and raids on livestock herds were always a possibility. This threat would require delicate handling by the Mormons, or violence would certainly erupt.

Mormon leaders, including Ezra T. Benson and Peter Maughan, arranged a parley with the Indians, who were represented by chiefs Pe-Ads Wicks, Sagwitch, and Bear Hunter. The Indians mentioned that relations would be greatly improved if the Mormons would present the Shoshone with a peace gift of a wagonload of blankets, shirts, and other goods. Benson explained that they could not provide that much clothing but were willing to donate a gift of 2,400 pounds of flour, several beef cattle, and new shirts for the chiefs. The Indians were quite pleased with the offer and promised to leave the area after they had eaten up the food.

By the end of July, however, many Indians remained in Cache Valley. One chief notified Ezra Benson that he and his band might winter in the valley, and that "the land, water, grass &c are his and [he] wants to sell it to us [the Mormons]." Benson advised the Cache Valley settlement to prepare for an emergency and ordered fifty armed men to assemble to defend Mormon interests in the valley.[7]

Nevertheless, the summer passed without any major incidents, as many of the Shoshone had drifted away to hunt, raid mail stations, or seek a better location to spend the upcoming winter. In September, Chief Bear Hunter offered a gesture of friendship to the Mormons by returning twenty-one horses that had been stolen from a settlement at Logan. Other horses were also returned to owners at Franklin and Richmond. The fall season passed with only a few altercations between the Indians and the Mormon settlers.

But the new year began with a flurry of Shoshone raids on Mormon cattle herds in Cache Valley. Word reached the ears of the settlers that an additional force of Indians was on the way to assist their local brethren in driving away as many head of livestock as they could handle. Peter Maughan dispatched 20 armed men to reinforce the 17 who were already guarding the herd and vowed to assemble another 150, if necessary.

Maughan then advised Dudley J. Merrill, the head herdsmen, to seek a council with friendly Indians, particularly those under Chief Sagwitch, to ascertain that they would take no part in the thievery. The additional guards and assurances from Sagwitch that his band remained at peace with the Mormons apparently defused the situation for the time being. In fact, several Indian bands visited Cache Valley in the next few months to pledge peace with the white man.[8]

In March 1862, another visitor to Cache Valley was James D. Doty, superintendent of Indian Affairs. Doty found the Shoshone in a "starving and destitute condition." Concerned, he wrote, "No provision having been made for them, either as to clothing or provisions, by my predecessors . . . they were enduring great suffering." The superintendent exceeded his budget to provide the Indians with flour, wheat, and clothing. Food was also being handed out to the Indians by the mail company and valley residents. One settler wrote, "[The Shoshone are] flocking in on us very fast [and] they are quite annoying and must be fed."[9]

The desperation and frustration of watching a wife and children slowly starving to death will drive any man to the breaking point and to consider taking matters into his own hands, and the Shoshone men were no exception. That same month, Shoshone warriors went on the warpath en masse and simultaneously attacked every stage station on the Overland Trail between the Platte River bridge in present-day Wyoming and Bear River, Utah. Communication was paralyzed, stages and passengers were stranded, hundreds of animals were stolen, and drivers were killed.

These acts compelled Postmaster General Montgomery Blair to order that all mail to California be delivered by sea until the Indian problem was solved. Along the mail route, the agent at the Pacific Springs Station near South Pass refused to send out any mail coaches until troops were dispatched to protect them.[10]

Violence was also the byword for events taking place in the East. Union and Confederate troops were dying by the thousands at Shiloh, Tennessee, and the nation watched with hope of a swift resolution to the conflict as McClellan commenced his Peninsula campaign. Other troops marched in Virginia's Shenandoah Valley and into New Orleans on the lower Mississippi River. In the Southwest, Brig. Gen. Edward R. S. Canby was in the process of driving Confederate troops led by Brig. Gen. Henry Hopkins Sibley out of New Mexico. In the midst of dealing with these active fronts, however, the problems with the communications and transportation routes through the West were not ignored by Washington.

The incessant attacks on and threats to mail service prompted Frank Fuller, the acting governor of Utah, and officials with the mail and telegraph to petition Secretary of War Edwin M. Stanton, requesting that Superintendent of Indian Affairs Doty be authorized to raise a regiment of mounted rangers that would be activated for a period of three months to protect the state from the Shoshone.

Former governor Brigham Young, the president of the Church of Jesus Christ of Latter-Day Saints, was not about to have his Nauvoo Legion, as this militia unit that was originally organized by Joseph Smith in Illinois was called, be left out of the action. He already harbored distrust and hostility due to the Utah War of 1857–58, when the U.S. government had attempted to assert its authority over the Mormons, and indignantly wired Washington that "the militia of Utah are ready and able, as they ever have been, to take care of all the Indians and are able and willing to protect the mail line if called upon to do so."[11]

On April 24, Young, who evidently had decided not to wait for Washington to respond, instructed Lt. Gen. Daniel H. Wells of the Utah militia to mobilize an escort for the stages. The following day, Acting Governor Fuller made the request formal, ordering Wells to dispatch a force of mounted rangers "for purposes of protection and defense of the United States mails . . . as well as the persons of pasengers [*sic*] and all others connected with the line of the Overland Mail Company, east of Great Salt Lake City." Wells chose Col. Robert F. Burton, the sheriff of Salt Lake County, to command this force of twenty men, which included two sons of Brigham Young.[12]

Colonel Burton and his company marched out of Salt Lake City on April 26, 1862, and arrived nine days later at Fort Bridger. All the stations west of Green River had been abandoned, and Burton discovered twenty-six mail sacks at Ice Spring Station that had been cut open, and their contents "scattered over the prairie." Burton also received reports at other stations about livestock that had been stolen. His company returned to Salt Lake City on May 31 without having encountered any hostile Indians during the march.[13]

In the meantime, on April 28, Brigham Young—surprisingly not Acting Governor Fuller—had received a wire from Army Adj. Gen. Lorenzo Thomas, under orders from President Abraham Lincoln and the secretary of war, authorizing him to organize a company of cavalry for ninety days' service to protect stage and telegraph routes on the Oregon Trail in present-day southwestern Wyoming. Young raised a company of 106 men, who, in the custom of militias, furnished their own horses and equipment. The unit was placed under the command of Capt. Lot Smith, who had commanded Mormon militia troops against the Federal government during the 1857–58 conflict.[14]

Lot Smith's command departed on May 1, marching through rain, snow, and floods, and passed numerous mail stations that lay "in heaps of blackened ashes" as the men patrolled the mail line in the vicinities of Independence Rock and South Pass. At the latter point, they encountered a battalion from the 6th Ohio Volunteer Cavalry, which had been sent west to protect that portion of the Oregon Trail. Inasmuch as his troops were not needed in that area, Smith returned to Fort Bridger, where he established his field headquarters. The men spent May, June, and July guarding stages and wagon trains along the mail routes and rebuilding destroyed stations. In accordance with a reminder from Brigham Young before leaving, the troops refrained from alcohol and profane language, and observed evening prayers.

The only incident that called for Smith's militia to ride after hostile Indians occurred on July 16, when the volunteers responded to a report that Indians had attacked a ranch six miles from the fort and driven off 300 horses and mules. Smith and sixty men followed the trail of the raiders into Indian country, along the headwaters of the Snake River and the Teton Mountains. The detachment became low on food, however, and their horses were exhausted, forcing them to return to the fort without making contact with the Indians. During the march, Smith lost one man, who drowned while swimming his horse across the Lewis Fork of the Snake River.

The term of enlistment of the volunteer cavalry company had expired, and the unit returned to Salt Lake City on August 9, 1862, without having participated in any events of consequence. But at least their presence had discouraged the Shoshone from striking along that stretch of the trail.[15]

By now, the misery and despair of the various bands of Shoshone Indians who resided along the Overland Mail line had reached an unprecedented level. The meager provisions provided by the government, Mormon settlers, and the mail company were insufficient to sustain them. At the end of July, Indian superintendent Doty distributed food to the Shoshone and observed:

> To say they are "destitute" but feeble describes their situation. They took the wheat . . . with the utmost avidity and with hearty thanks; and repeatedly I saw their children, lying on their bellies on the margins of the streams, cropping the young grass. I hope I shall receive the goods from the Dept. in time to clothe their nakedness before the snow falls and winter commences.[16]

To make matters worse, the Shoshone, as well as other tribes, were aware that the whites had a wealth of goods—food, horses, and clothing—that were there for the taking. Raids, thefts, and murders became rampant as the Indians swept through the valleys, unleashing their fury upon the whites in an effort to procure common necessities for survival. The

Shoshone also made entreaties to other tribes to join the fight, boasting to one and all that "when the leaves turn yellow and begin to fall," open warfare would be initiated, with intentions of completely destroying or perhaps driving away the whites.[17]

Under banner headlines, such as "Indian Murders" and "Murders of Emigrants in the Humboldt County," newspapers reported all the gruesome details of massacres, mutilations, and scalpings, often greatly exaggerated, as in the following colorful sentence: "Rivers of blood and mountains of Indians rush into *bona fide* existence and the end of the world is near at hand." Nearly every story ended with a demand for protection of the victimized settlers.[18]

The prayers and pleas of Utah residents were about to be answered. A column commanded by the capable Col. Patrick E. Connor, comprising the 3rd California Infantry and part of the 2nd California Cavalry—more than 1,000 volunteer troops—was on its way and ready and willing to collide with the hostile Indians.

Patrick Edward Connor was born on St. Patrick's Day, March 17, 1820, in Kerry County, Ireland. At an early age, he emigrated with his parents, then named O'Connor, to New York City. In November 1839, O'Connor enlisted in the army as a private. He served on the Iowa frontier for five years. Upon his discharge, he returned to New York and worked in the mercantile business. O'Connor immigrated to Texas in early 1846, just in time for the Mexican War. He joined a regiment of Texas volunteers as a first lieutenant under the command of Col. Albert Sidney Johnston and at that time changed his named to Connor. Connor was promoted to captain in February 1847 and fought in the battle of Buena Vista, where he distinguished himself. Gen. Zachary Taylor wrote in his official report: "Captain Connor's company of Texas Volunteers . . . fought bravely, its captain being wounded and two subalterns killed." Although Connor had received a severe wound to the hand, he refused to leave the field and directed his men throughout the battle. He resigned his commission in May 1847, remaining in Texas.

In January 1850, Connor departed Texas to participate in the California gold rush. He survived a brush with death while aboard the U.S. Navy brig *Arabian,* which he and others had chartered in an attempt to locate a settlement at the mouth of the Trinity River. A whale boat in which he was riding capsized while attempting to land in heavy surf, and of the eleven aboard, only five made it to shore.

After suffering a failed business in San Francisco, Connor joined a band of twenty California Rangers that had been established by the state legislature to hunt down the famous outlaw Joaquin Murietta. The rangers supposedly captured Murietta in July 1853 and received the $1,000 reward for killing him. One account named Connor as the person who killed the outlaw.

Connor then ended his career as an adventurer by marrying Johanna, who hailed from the same county in Ireland where her husband was born, and settled down in Stockton, California. He raised one son (two others died in infancy) while becoming the owner of various businesses—a surveying company, a gravel company, the city waterworks—and was fulfilling a contract to build the foundation of the new state capitol at Sacramento when he was called into military service in July 1861.

During September, Connor recruited his regiment, which would be garrisoned at Camp McDougall, located three miles south of his hometown of Stockton. Prominent members of the Stockton community joined up, including a surgeon and chaplain, as did quite a few men with Irish heritage. The ten companies, only seven of which would travel to Utah, trained at the Agricultural Park in Stockton—renamed Camp Halleck— and wintered in the Benicia Barracks.

The California column finally marched in July 1862, heading east across the mountains to Nevada, with Salt Lake City as the intended destination.[19]

On August 1, 1862, when the column arrived at Fort Churchill near Carson City, the feisty, red-bearded Connor, who was also known for his short temper, assumed command of the Military District of Utah, comprising Utah and Nevada Territories, by order of Brig. Gen. George Wright. Connor assigned one company each of cavalry and infantry at that fort, with orders to watch the Paiute Indians and pro-Southerners, and resumed his march east with the remainder of his command. In early September, Connor and his troops reached the verdant Ruby Valley, near the Nevada-Utah border, where Fort Ruby was presently under construction. While his men pitched in to help build the fort, Connor decided to venture alone into the Mormon capital of Salt Lake City to confer with the governor and other officials, arriving on September 9.[20]

The prevailing mood in the capital was contentious, at best, due to Brigham Young's attitude toward Federal authorities based in Utah. The Mormons had recently written a state constitution, elected two shadow senators and a congressman, and petitioned for admission to the Union as the state of Deseret. That bold request had been rejected by Congress in July, and that body also snubbed its nose at Young and his people by passing an antipolygamy act.

Colonel Connor expressed quite a critical, to say the least, opinion of the Mormons when he wrote to General Wright: "It will be impossible for me to describe what I saw and heard in Salt Lake, so as to make you realize the enormity of Mormonism; suffice it, that I found them a community of traitors, murderers, fanatics, and whores."[21]

The least of Connor's immediate concerns, however, were in Salt Lake City. On his return to Fort Ruby, he was confronted by a scheme concocted by his men that threatened to end the mail route operation. The troops had requested that the paymaster apply $30,000 of the wages due them to pay for transport to the "soil of Virginia," where they could "serve their country in shooting traitors instead of . . . eating rations and freezing to death around sage brush fires."

Oddly enough, this patriotic gesture was embraced by Connor, who wrote to General-in-Chief Henry W. Halleck in Washington, asking for permission to send the infantry—and perhaps himself—at the men's own expense to fight the war in the East. After all, Connor pointed out, there was enough cavalry available to patrol the Overland Mail route, and foot soldiers were basically useless in that endeavor. Permission was denied, which served to fuel the motivation of the troops to hunt down and kill some Indians.[22]

The first opportunity for the soldiers to vent their frustration came when it was reported that twenty-three emigrants had been killed by the Shoshone, perhaps with assistance from pro-Southern guerrillas, eight miles from Gravelly Ford on the Humboldt River.

On September 29, Connor dispatched Maj. Edward McGarry, in command of cavalry Companies H and K, with the following orders: "Destroy every male Indian whom you may encounter in the vicinity of the late massacre" and "immediately hang them, and leave their bodies thus exposed as an example of what evil-doers may expect while I command this district." He added, "In no instance will you molest women and children."[23]

McGarry, the cavalry commander, who was known as a tough-as-old-boots, hard-drinking man, reached the desert country around the Humboldt River on October 5 without encountering any Indians. His men, however, managed to lure three male Indians into camp. Then, because there were no nearby trees large enough to hang them from, the cavalrymen mercilessly shot their captives. A patrol led by Capt. Samuel P. Smith flushed out fourteen Indians, nine of whom were shot while attempting to escape. Two of the remaining Indians were held hostage, while the other two were released with the understanding that they would later return with those who had participated in the massacre. When the two Indians did not return by nightfall, McGarry ordered the hostages executed. The next day, another detachment of troops killed eight more Indians.

McGarry returned from his mission and reported to Connor that he had killed a total of twenty-four Indians, none of whom he could say for certain were involved in the massacre. Connor wrote General Wright that McGarry's action was "the only way to deal with those savages." He continued, "I hope and believe that the lesson taught them will have a salutary effect in checking future massacres on that route."[24]

On October 2, Connor departed Fort Ruby with 750 men—leaving behind two companies to garrison the fort—and arrived in Salt Lake City eighteen days later. He had originally planned to establish his headquarters at Fort Crittenden but now altered his plans. Connor had earlier sized up the local political situation and realized that Brigham Young maintained a despotic control over Federal officials. He also was aware that Young resented the presence of the Federal troops, and he fully anticipated the threat of the Mormon militia attacking the California volunteers at some point. With that in mind, Connor established a new post, Camp Douglas, three miles east of Salt Lake City, on a foothill bench that overlooked the city. As an added deterrent, a cannon was mounted that was aimed directly at the city. This would enable the troops to keep an eye on the Mormons, as well as carry out their mission of policing the Overland Mail route. Young responded to this affront by forbidding his people to have any contact with the soldiers, except for a committee that was formed to conduct trade.[25]

Brigham Young personally might have taken issue with the intrusion by Connor's troops, but the army was a mixed blessing to the Mormon settlers. The starving Shoshone had continued their relentless raids on farms and cattle herds, and the losses mounted daily. The settlers had sought help from Young's militia, but the Mormon leader remained resolute in his belief that violence should be avoided. His order to feed the Indians and negotiate for the return of stolen livestock had become a tiresome routine. Now, with soldiers ready and willing to fight, the settlers could obey Young and remain detached but look forward to perhaps the prospect of an end to the thievery. In November, reports reached Colonel Connor that a white captive boy was being held in Cache Valley by a band of Shoshone headed by Chief Bear Hunter. This chief had vigorously resisted white colonization of the area and was the prime suspect in numerous raids targeting Mormon settlers, mail stations, miners, and passing wagon trains.

The boy, ten-year-old Reuben Van Orman, had been captured by the Indians along with his three sisters in the fall of 1860, after his father, mother, and brother had been killed in the Otter Massacre on the Snake River in Idaho. The three girls had subsequently died of starvation. Connor assigned Maj. Edward McGarry to lead an expedition to Cache Valley to rescue the boy.

Major McGarry arrived in the valley on November 22 and was informed that a band of thirty to forty Indians were presently camped near the town of Providence. At dawn the following morning, McGarry located, surrounded, and attacked the camp. The Indians, however, had evidently received word that the soldiers were on the way and fled to a more defensible position down a canyon. McGarry followed and was confronted by Chief Bear Hunter, who rode out on a rise and "made a warlike display, such as shouting, riding in a circle, and all sorts of antics known only to their race."

The major responded to Bear Hunter's challenge by dividing his men into three groups and, with orders "to kill every Indian they could see," assaulted the Indian position. The two sides battled for about two hours, until finally Bear Hunter appeared, waving a white flag of truce. McGarry ordered a cease-fire and permitted the chief and his warriors to surrender. The troops had killed three Shoshone and wounded one during the skirmish, "without the loss or scratch of man or horse."

Bear Hunter professed his friendship and claimed that the boy had been sent away a few days earlier. McGarry demanded that Bear Hunter hand over the boy and decided to hold the chief and four of his warriors hostage overnight until the boy was delivered. The next day, Reuben Van Orman, whom McGarry described as acting "like a little savage," was turned over to the troops. The chief and his warriors were released, and the triumphant McGarry rode back to Camp Douglas, where he received his commander's praise.

The yellow-haired, blue-eyed boy, who did not speak English, would spend the winter at the army camp. During that time, his identity would come into question when reliable information was presented from a Shoshone that the boy was actually the half-breed son of a Frenchman and the sister of Washakie, chief of the eastern Shoshone.[26]

Chief Bear Hunter was furious about this indignity that he had endured at the hands of the soldiers. On November 25, he assembled his warriors near Providence and "made hostile demonstrations" against the Mormon settlers, whom he accused of feeding the soldiers. One account reported that the chief "abused the people for not helping them to retain the boy . . . declaring that the settlers were cowards and dared not fight." The Logan militia—seventy armed men—was called out and hurried to Providence to mount a defense. Mormon leaders Ezra Benson and Peter Maughan, however, were able to pacify Bear Hunter with two beef cattle and a large supply of flour, which apparently satisfied the chief enough to end the threat.[27]

Within a week of that incident, Colonel Connor learned that Bear Hunter's band had raided settlers near Bear River and stolen a large number of stock. On December 4, Maj. Edward McGarry was once again dispatched, this time with about 100 cavalrymen, and rode to Emprey's Ferry, west of Brigham City, where the Indian encampment was said to be located. McGarry arrived to discover that the Indians were across the Malad River and the ferry rope had been cut. The soldiers left their horses behind and painstakingly crossed the river on a scow. McGarry grabbed four unwary Indians and sent a message warning the Shoshone that the hostages would be killed if the stolen livestock was not delivered by noon the following day. The Indians answered his threat by hastily packing up the camp and moving north. McGarry was incensed by this disrespectful act. He ordered that the hostages be tied by their hands and executed. Their bodies were riddled with a total of fifty-one bullets, then tossed into the river.[28]

These murders, in addition to the confrontation with Chief Bear Hunter in Cache Valley and the liberation of the boy who likely was Wakaskie's nephew, were an outrage that the Shoshone could not ignore. They responded with hostility, intensifying their raids on Mormon farms in Cache Valley and vowing to kill every white in the area. The Indians were described by the *Deseret News* as "mad, and determined to do as much injury as possible to the white race."[29]

Reports of depredations by Bear Hunter's band were constant during the early part of January 1863. On January 5, a party of ten prospectors was killed while coming south from the mines in present-day Idaho to buy supplies in Salt Lake City. The next day, eight men traveling from the Grasshopper mines in Dakota Territory to Salt Lake City through Cache Valley were attacked on the Bear River near Franklin. One man was killed, and their wagons and most of their stock was stolen. One of the survivors filed charges in Salt Lake City, and arrest warrants were issued for chiefs Bear Hunter, Sanpitch, and Sagwitch. Territorial marshal Isaac Gibbs was ordered to seek assistance from Col. Patrick Connor in apprehending the guilty parties. While the countryside cowered in fear, the attacks by the Shoshone were relentless. On January 14, Connor received news that two expressmen had been brutally murdered on the Cache Valley Road.[30]

Naturally, the public and press demanded that measures be taken that would result in safe travel throughout the region. Connor, however, was way ahead of them. In order to maintain the element of surprise, he had been planning a campaign in secret with the mission of eliminating Bear Hunter and his band once and for all. Connor wrote: "Being satisfied that they [the Indians] were part of the same band who had been murdering emigrants on the overland mail route for the past fifteen years and [were] the principal actors and leaders in the horrid massacre of the past summer, I determined, although the weather was unfavorable to an expedition, to chastize them if possible." In fact, he understood that winter by far was the most opportune time of the year to attack the village of a nomadic tribe, given the lack of forage for ponies and the encumbrance of the women and children.[31]

On January 22, 1863, in the midst of a heavy snowstorm, Capt. Samuel N. Hoyt of Company K, 3rd California Infantry Regiment, with sixty-nine volunteers, fifteen baggage wagons carrying a twelve-day supply of rations, and two howitzers under Lt. Francis Honeyman, started north toward the Shoshone winter camp on Bear River. The Indians would certainly notice this slow-moving column, but Connor hoped that the soldiers would be mistaken for merely an escort on a routine detail headed to Cache Valley to obtain grain.[32]

After sundown on January 25, Connor covertly departed the camp with his main force of 225 men from Companies A, H, K, and M of the 2nd California Cavalry, under Maj. Edward McGarry, and rode for sixty-eight miles before halting at dawn at Brigham City. Marshal Isaac Gibbs, arrest warrants in hand, accompanied Connor's column but had been told by the colonel not to expect to be able to serve the warrants to living Indians.

Capt. Charles H. Hempstead described that "fearful night march" thusly:

Clear and brilliant shone the stars upon the dreary earth mantled with deep snow, but bitter and intense was the cold. The shrill north wind swept over the lakes and down the mountain sides freezing with its cold breath every rivulet and stream. The moistened breath freezing as it left the lips, hung in miniature icicles from beards of brave men. . . . All that long night the men rode on, facing the wintery wind, and uncomplainingly endured an intensity of cold rarely if ever before experienced even in these mountain regions . . . the sufferings of that night march can never be told in words. Many were frozen and necessarily left behind.[33]

Captain Hoyt's command moved by day and Connor's by night, stealthily traveling separately through the deep snow and below-zero temperatures, plodding toward their objective, where they intended to combine forces and attack Bear Hunter's camp.

While the army marched, Bear Hunter and some of his braves visited the settlement of Franklin on January 27 and demanded a present of wheat.

When none was given, the Indians held a war dance around the house of Bishop Preston Thomas. They returned the next day and received nine bushels of wheat. At that time, the chief noticed the infantry column approaching and hurried from the town.[34]

That night, Connor passed the infantry, which had been hindered by deep, drifting snow and for that reason was compelled to abandon the howitzers. The colonel's column arrived on the bluffs overlooking Bear River on January 29, just as dawn was breaking. The soldiers could observe smoke rising from the seventy-five lodges that were home to perhaps 450 Indians, including as many as 200 to 250 warriors.

The Shoshone camp was situated about 500 yards to the east, beyond an open, treeless plain on a tributary then called Beaver Creek, now known as Battle Creek. The location of the camp afforded the Indians an excellent defensive position, in the bed of a thirty- to forty-foot-wide ravine with banks that rose up to twelve feet in height. Exits large enough for a horse to pass through had been cut into the banks on the east side of the camp, and the Indians had lined the embankments with concealed firing positions made from thickly woven willow branches and brush.[35]

Chief Sagwitch had risen early and happened to glance through the frosty air in the direction where the troops were poised on the ridge. He alerted the camp, but apparently no one, including War Chief Bear Hunter, was too concerned. The prevailing thought was that the soldiers had come to seek the arrest of those Indians who had killed the miners and those who had been stealing stock in Cache Valley. It was assumed that representatives from the army would, as was the custom, initiate a parley and request that the guilty parties be handed over.[36]

Colonel Connor, however, was in no mood to negotiate. He ordered Major McGarry to cross the river "and surround before attacking," while the main force waited for the infantry to arrive.

McGarry rode off with Companies K and M in the lead, and began to ford the river. The half-frozen water, blocked in spots by huge chunks of floating ice, was deep enough to pour over many saddles, and a few horses lost their footing or balked and carried their helpless riders downstream. But each company of troops, wet uniforms frozen to their skin, managed to cross, and then dismounted to form a line of skirmishers facing the Shoshone camp, which lay about 400 to 500 yards of open ground away.[37]

The Indians, at this point, understood that the army had not ridden that far in such miserable conditions to merely talk, and they emerged from their camp on foot and on horseback to taunt the soldiers. Connor wrote that the Indians "sallied out . . . and with fiendish malignity waived [*sic*] the scalps of white women and challenged the troops to battle."

The only correspondent accompanying the column, a gentleman from the *San Francisco Bulletin,* wrote:

> Here redskins were evidently full of good humor and eager for the day. One of the chiefs was galloping up and down the bench in front of his warriors, haranging them and dangling his spear on which was hung a female scalp in the face of the troops, while many of the warriors sang out: 'Fours right, fours left, Come on, you California sons of b—s.'[38]

The enraged Connor, calculating that it would be impossible to surround the camp with his small body of men, ordered a frontal assault by those troops who had crossed the river. While the horseholders, every fourth man, maintained the mounts, Company K, under Lt. Darwin Chase, and Company M, led by Capt. George F. Price, charged on foot across the open plain to assault the camp.

The Indians rose up from their protected positions on the east bank of Battle Creek to fire a murderous volley, which wounded one trooper and compelled the men to halt and take cover wherever they could find it. The soldiers hugged the ground as the warriors blasted away from the willows along the riverbank.

Company H, commanded by Capt. Daniel McLean, and Lt. John Quinn's Company A were brought up by Major McGarry to reinforce the line. These troops fared no better than their comrades. The Indians held the advantage due to their excellent defensive positions. They were elusive targets, popping up to snap off quick shots at the exposed soldiers, then dipping back down into the safety of their hiding places.

Lieutenant Chase, a flashy dresser mounted on a horse with gaudy trappings, quickly attracted the attention of the Indians' fire. He was first shot in the wrist, then caught a ball through the lung, but remained in the saddle to direct his men. Captain McLean was also struck, first in the hand, then by a severe wound in the thigh. Within a half hour of fighting, at least seven troopers had been killed and perhaps twenty others wounded.

When Colonel Connor arrived on the field, Lieutenant Chase, who believed himself mortally wounded, requested and was granted permission to retire. McLean eventually lost his horse and also removed himself from the fray. The Indians fought "with the ferocity of demons," Connor reported.

"My men fell fast and thick around me." McGarry was forced to order his men to fall back out of range of the furious and effective fire.[39]

Connor realized that an alternate strategy would be necessary to dislodge his stubborn enemy. He ordered Major McGarry to take twenty men along the bluffs and work their way down the ravine toward the camp in an attempt to turn the Shoshone left flank. By this time, Company K of the 3rd Infantry, under Capt. Samuel Hoyt, had arrived on the opposite side of the river and had commenced crossing. The water, however, was too deep and swift, and many men were dunked into the icy river. Connor dispatched the horseholders to ferry the infantry across, then sent Hoyt and his foot soldiers to support McGarry's men. Meanwhile, Lt. Cyrus D. Clark was ordered to take Company K, 2nd Cavalry, and block any escape at the mouth of Battle Creek. Lieutenant Quinn was sent west across the creek with orders to attack the rear of the village and prevent any escape in that direction. The remainder of the troops formed a skirmish line on the plain facing the Indian camp. Connor had successfully surrounded the Shoshone position.[40]

McGarry moved his troops down the ravine and opened fire, which was the signal for the other four units to simultaneously attack the camp. The troopers closed in on the Shoshone, and a fierce battle, often hand-to-hand, moving from lodge to lodge and into the willows, was waged for a period of about two hours. Connor's aide, Maj. Patrick A. Gallagher, sustained a painful wound in his left arm. Captain McLean, after having a pistol shot from his right hand, drew another with his left, only to be shot in the groin. But the Indians were no match for the superior weapons of the soldiers and endless supply of ammunition.

Eventually, as Connor's men steadily overran the camp, the Indians were flushed out and made an effort to escape the deadly trap by dashing away in every direction. In what most historians have called a battle that turned into a massacre, dozens of Indians were ridden down and slaughtered. Riflemen on the riverbanks picked off warriors who attempted to swim across the icy river.

The soldiers, urged on by their officers, had lost control of their senses as they systematically combed every inch of the camp in a killing frenzy. Any Indian found alive by being prodded with a bayonet was brutally executed—shot an excessive number of times, or stabbed, or struck by axes that split their heads open. Soldiers held infants by their heels and "beat their brains out on any hard substance they could find." A dead woman was found by a soldier clutching an infant that was still alive. The soldier "in mercy to the babe, killed it." Other women "were killed because they would not submit

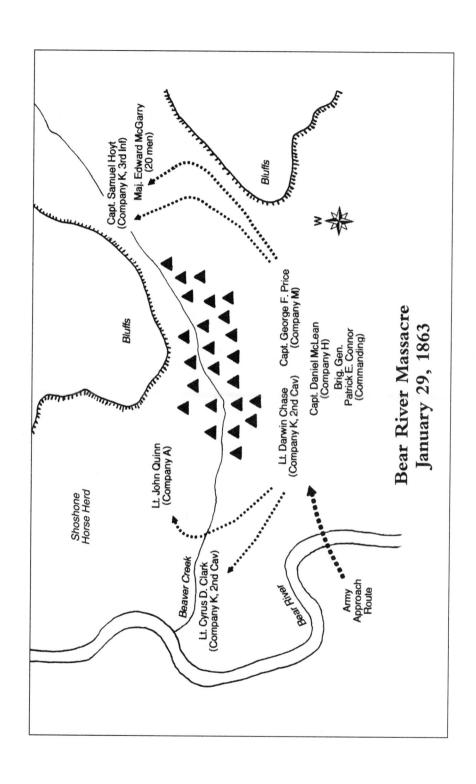

Bear River Massacre
January 29, 1863

Capt. Samuel Hoyt
(Company K, 3rd Inf)

Maj. Edward McGarry
(20 men)

Bluffs

W

Bluffs

Capt. George F. Price
(Company M)

Capt. Daniel McLean
(Company H)

Brig. Gen.
Patrick E. Connor
(Commanding)

Lt. Darwin Chase
(Company K, 2nd Cav)

Lt. John Quinn
(Company A)

Shoshone
Horse Herd

Beaver Creek

Lt. Cyrus D. Clark
(Company K, 2nd Cav)

Bear River

Army
Approach
Route

to lie down and be ravished." A number of women were raped while dying from their wounds.

Among the dead was Chief Bear Hunter, who was said to have been shot and toppled into a campfire. Another version, written by the grand-daughter of Chief Sagwitch, claimed that after the soldiers shot Bear Hunter:

> they whipped him, kicked him and tried several means of torture on him. Through all of this the old chief did not utter a word, as crying and carrying on was the sign of a coward. Because he would not die or cry for mercy, the soldiers became very angry. One of the military men took his rifle, stepped to a burning camp-fire and heated his bayonet until it was glowing red. He then ran the burning hot metal through the chief's ears.

Chief Sagwitch, although wounded, managed to escape with a small group of other survivors.[41]

When the mayhem had finally ended, at least 250 Shoshone men, women, and children lay dead. They would remain where they had fallen, prey to scavengers. Another 120 women and children were initially taken captive, then left in the camp with a small amount of food. Seventy lodges were burned, large quantities of provisions were appropriated or destroyed, and about 175 horses were confiscated. The soldiers sustained 23 killed, 41 wounded, and 75 men with frostbitten feet from a force of about 200 that had engaged the Indians.[42]

The grateful Mormon settlers in Cache Valley offered the hospitality of their homes to the soldiers on their return march, caring for the wounded, serving hot meals, and providing beds. They considered "the movement of Col. Connor as an intervention of the Almighty."

Leader Peter Maughan summed up the feelings of the settlers toward the fate of the Shoshone Indians when he wrote to Brigham Young:

> I feel my skirts clear of their blood. They rejected the way of life and salvation which have been pointed out to them from time to time (especially for the last two years) and thus have perished rely-ing on their own strength and wisdom.[43]

This rather contradictory attitude by a religious group, when taking into respect the words contained in the Good Book, certainly would not have been echoed by citizens across the nation had they not been distracted by events of the war in the East. Later, more highly publicized, engagements between the army and the Indians—George Armstrong Custer and the 1868 battle of the Washita comes to mind—had none of the characteristics of this incident, though they have been classified by revisionists as massacres.

The massacre at Bear River goes down in history as perhaps the least-known act of brutality in warfare between the military and Indians. Some may justify the actions of the soldiers by pointing out that the Indians had been tormenting the settlers, and this was the only manner in which to punish them, in order to discourage further raids. This argument holds little water when taking into consideration the brutal rapes and murders of women and children.

Col. Patrick E. Connor, however, was hailed a hero by such luminaries as Brig. Gen. George Wright, commander of the Department of the Pacific; California governor Leland Stanford; and General-in-Chief Henry W. Halleck, who on March 29, 1863, rewarded Connor with a commission to brigadier general.[44]

There was only one problem: The Indian tribes in Connor's district shared none of that respect for the new general or his alleged accomplishment. Some tribal members and chiefs may have been frightened, but others—Shoshone, Bannock, and Ute—were enraged by the slaughter of their relatives and resumed raiding in Cache Valley and the Overland Mail route.

Ezra T. Benson and Peter Maughan wrote that the Shoshone:

> now threaten to steal some of the Mormon women . . . their intention . . . is to not only steal but kill us . . . the hostile Indians are the remains of the Bands that were in the fight at Bear River last winter and they say they intend having their pay out of the Mormon as they are afraid to tackle the soldiers.[45]

General Connor, however, was not afraid to tackle the Indians. His troopers relentlessly hounded the hostiles and engaged in a series of skirmishes. The Shoshone had gained little by their raiding and remained a destitute and desperate tribe. In addition, the possibility of another massacre like the one at Bear River weighed heavily on their minds.

Finally, in the summer of 1863, James D. Doty, former Indian Affairs superintendent and now governor of Utah, met with chiefs of nine bands of Shoshone at Brigham City and negotiated the Treaty of Box Elder, which would provide subsistence to the Indians and bring an end to their depredations. The Shoshone were eventually settled west of Fort Hall in Idaho Territory, relinquishing their homeland to the Mormons.

By fall, all routes of travel through Utah Territory to Nevada and California were declared safe for travel. The mail could now go through.[46]

In 1865, Patrick Connor briefly left Utah to head a three-pronged operation north of the Platte, which, although the general had several successful fights against the Indians, ended in an embarrassing failure. Connor, breveted major general for his actions during the war, was mustered out of the army on April 30, 1865. He remained in Utah, maintaining his staunchly anti-Mormon sentiment, and started the first daily newspaper in the territory. Connor also owned the first steamboat on Salt Lake and became known as the "father of mining." He died in Salt Lake City on December 17, 1891, and was buried with full military honors.

CHAPTER THREE

Sioux Uprising

By the fall of 1862, the war in the East between the Union and Confederate armies was shifting north, away from Richmond and closer to Washington. Gen. George B. McClellan's ambitious Peninsula campaign had ended in a bitter failure when Union troops were forced to withdraw. With McClellan's threat on Richmond repulsed, Gen. Robert E. Lee seized the initiative and began moving his army north, which would culminate in the defeat of Maj. Gen. John Pope at the second battle of Bull Run and the bloodiest single day of the war on the killing fields of Antietam.

Meanwhile, 1,000 miles to the west of those significant battlefields that captured the attention of the nation, a conflict in the border state of Minnesota was about to provoke one of the most brutal reigns of terror and carnage ever recorded in the annals of warfare between Indians and whites. Perhaps as many as 800 white settlers and soldiers, and countless Indians, would lose their lives before hostilities could be brought under control.

In 1862, Americans regarded Ohio, Michigan, Indiana, and Illinois as the boundaries of the West. Minnesota Territory, a virtual wilderness roamed mainly by Indians and fur traders, was considered to be part of the Far West. This area was first settled by French missionaries and trader-explorers in the seventeenth century and was notable for the next 100 years on account of its abundance of fur-trading wealth. By 1849, the year Minnesota achieved territorial status, the 6,000 whites said to be living in that area were outnumbered two to one by the Indian inhabitants. By 1858, when the territory gained statehood, the lure of inexpensive land with rich soil for farming had dramatically increased the population, primarily German and Scandinavian immigrants, to 200,000—with St. Paul, the capital, boasting 10,000 people.[1]

Naturally, a white invasion of such magnitude was bound to affect relations with those Indians who had inhabited the region for centuries. One such tribe was the Dakota, or Santee, an eastern division of the Sioux.

The Dakota Nation of Sioux, along with their brethren the Lakota and Nakota Sioux, had migrated from the South in the sixteenth century to settle the headwaters of the Mississippi in northern Minnesota. Over time, the three groups had split into distinct nations, each speaking a different dialect and occupying its own territory; collectively they were known as Sioux. That title, however, a French interpretation of the Chippewa word *Nadoue-is-iw,* meaning "enemy," served only as a generic name for the three separate nations. In the late eighteenth century, the Lakota Sioux became the final major group of Indians to arrive on the Great Plains; the Dakota and Nakota Sioux remained in Minnesota. The Dakota tribe consisted of four bands—the Mdewakanton and Wahpekute, known as the Lower Sioux; and the Sisseton and Wahpeton, known as the Upper Sioux.[2]

The initial contact between these Indians and French, British, and American traders could be called peaceful, if not amicable. These trappers and traders introduced the Indians to guns and manufactured goods, which were in great demand. The Dakota assisted the trappers with their work and in return received those valuable items that complemented their basic subsistence. The settlers and trappers, however, eventually pushed farther into Indian land, filling the fertile valleys with farms and towns and taking great amounts of game.[3]

By 1837, the pressure of more and more people arriving in the territory had nearly depleted game and, with it, that golden goose of prized provisions provided by the trappers. Concerned about their economic survival, the Mdewakanton band agreed to sell a portion of their holdings on eastern side of the Mississippi River to the government in order to survive. The tribe was promised $1 million in annual deliveries of food, supplies, and other benefits in return for some 5 million acres of land. The Mdewakanton received enough food to stave off starvation, but other provisions of the treaty—including cash, an educational fund, and a farm program that was designed to help the Indians become successful farmers—for one reason or another failed to materialize.[4]

When Minnesota became a territory in 1849, the appointed governor, Alexander Ramsey, vowed to buy up all available Indian land to make room for additional settlers and the comforts and security of civilization. By that time, the Dakota had been weakened by decades, if not centuries, of warfare with the Chippewa, their more populous and better-armed neighbors to the north—not to mention the loss of resources due to the encroachment of whites and an inability to prosper from farming the land. The summer hunt that year had been less than successful, and floods had devastated the corn crop. Although the obligations of the previous treaty had been for the most part unfulfilled, the desperate tribe listened to proposals to cede more of their country.[5]

On July 23, 1851, the Sisseton and Wahpeton bands of Upper Sioux signed the Mendota Treaty with the United States, which ceded their lands in southern and western Minnesota territory for the price of $1,665,000 in cash and annuities. The Mdewakanton and Wahpekute bands of Upper Sioux followed suit on August 5, signing away their land in the southeast quarter of present-day Minnesota for $1,410,000. In total, almost 24 million acres of prime agricultural land was ceded to the whites for the governmental promise to pay nearly $3 million in annuities over the next fifty years.

The two bands of Sioux—numbering perhaps 6,500 tribal members—were given adjoining reservations, each twenty miles wide and seventy miles long, that bordered the banks of the upper Minnesota River. The Sisseton and Wahpeton bands settled in villages around the Yellow Medicine Agency, and the Mdewakanton and Wahpekute bands around the Redwood Agency. The terrain within this combined reservation was composed of great stands of timber and rich bottomlands—the perfect setting, to the white man's way of thinking, in which to transform wild Indians into civilized farmers. In 1853, Fort Ridgely was established about ten miles below the Redwood Agency to maintain control over the occupants of the reservations.[6]

The ink on these treaties was barely dry when traders, agents, and politicians—particularly Governor Ramsey—concocted reasons to divert most of the nearly half a million dollars promised up front to cover the immediate subsistence needs of the Indians. The biggest chunk went to the American Fur Company, whose representative, Henry Hastings Sibley (no relation to Henry Hopkins Sibley, the Confederate general), claimed that his company was owed $145,000. Governor Ramsey arbitrarily took another 10 to 15 percent of the money off the top to compensate for his troubles in handling the transactions, and other traders, lobbyists, advisers, ex-agents, and countless numbers of opportunistic contractors produced claims.

When the dust had settled, the Sisseton and Wahpeton received about $100,000. The Mdewakanton received nothing, except for prominent chief Little Crow, who was promised a new wagon. Alexander Ramsey, who subsequently was replaced as territorial governor, was later charged with fraud, but the ensuing Federal investigation cleared him of any wrongdoing.[7]

To add insult to injury, the Senate held up the treaty in debate, which delayed implementing the provisions, and then, in their typical infinite

wisdom, that body decided to eliminate the clause that permitted the Indians to occupy a reservation in Minnesota. In the meantime, settlers refused
to wait for ratification of the treaty and commenced occupying the villages
and farms of the soon-to-be-homeless Dakota Indians and tramping across
their hunting grounds. The aggrieved Indians, however, in order to clear
the way for these white intruders, were magnanimously assigned temporary
residence on the reservations that had been set aside for them in the treaty.
It was not until three years later that President Franklin Pierce, at the urging of the secretary of the interior, signed an executive order allowing the
Dakota to remain on the reservations promised them in the treaties until
he, the president, "shall consider it proper to remove them."[8]

The Dakota had agreed to subject themselves to the humiliation and
demoralization of becoming reservation Indians, a decision driven by starvation and not by a desire to become farmers, but their grievances simply
continued to mount. The cash payments were generally late, and the supplies were of poor quality, or less than promised, or stolen by unscrupulous
traders or government officials, which compelled the Indians to buy on
credit from the traders at exorbitant prices. Missionaries encouraged the
tribe to build cabins and houses, wear white's man's clothing, cut their hair,
and ignore the religious teachings of their fathers to accept Christianity, all
of which created further animosity. Those Indians who trekked to old
hunting grounds or young warriors who took part in raids on the
Chippewa were severely punished by government agents.

This attempt at transforming the Indian into following the ways of the
white man was summed up by Jerome Big Eagle, speaker of the Mdewakanton band:

> There was great dissatisfaction among the Indians over many things
> the whites did. The whites would not let them go to war against
> their enemies. This was right, but the Indians did not know it.
> Then the whites were always trying to make the Indians give up
> their way of life and live like white men—go to farming, work
> hard as they always did—and the Indians did not know how to do
> that, and did not want to anyway. It seemed too sudden to make
> such a change. If the Indians had tried to make whites live like
> them, the whites would have resisted, and it was the same way
> with many Indians. The Indians wanted to live as they did before
> the treaty—go where they pleased and when they pleased; hunt
> game wherever they could find it, sell their furs to the traders and
> live as they could.[9]

Perhaps worst of all was the growing number of settlers—mainly German, Scandinavian, and Irish immigrants—who did not respect the boundaries of the Dakota reservation, much less its inhabitants. By the summer of 1855, settlers, in this case German immigrants, had pushed up the Minnesota River and built farms and a town called New Ulm in a location at the juncture of the Big Cottonwood near the lower boundary of the reservation, in an area that had been promised to be added to Dakota land. To protest this intrusion, several Dakota men pulled up surveyor stakes near New Ulm and killed a few oxen.

The growing tension between red and white had become as taut as a bowstring, and it was inevitable that these heated emotions would escalate into violence. In 1854, a whiskey seller named Henry Lott and his son had slaughtered nearly a dozen Wahpekute, mainly women and children, allegedly in retaliation for Indian depredations committed at an earlier date. The Lotts had not been brought to justice for their brutal murders of innocent people.

One of the Indian victims was said to have been the brother of Inkpaduta, a Dakota outcast who had been expelled from the tribe for killing a chief and was the leader of a nomadic band of about a dozen followers. Inkpaduta had not taken part in the 1851 treaty but would occasionally appear at the reservation to obtain supplies. The murders committed by the Lotts festered in his heart and mind, and he vowed to someday seek revenge.

The winter of 1856–57 was unusually severe, and Inkpaduta's outlaws were able to survive only by begging and, when that failed, by raiding white settlements. On one occasion, a settler's dog bit a member of the band. The angry Indians then killed the dog, an act that caused a posse to chase down and forcibly disarm the band. Inkpaduta's men were now unable to hunt, which created a desperate situation and called for a remedy.

To that end, in early March 1857, Inkpaduta and his warriors attacked a settlement on the Okooji Lakes, where they killed thirty-four people and took three women prisoner. Another settlement, at Spirit Lake, was subsequently victimized, and one man was killed and his wife captured. Several more whites were killed a week later in Springfield.

The Spirit Lake Massacre, as these atrocities collectively became known, created near hysteria throughout Minnesota. Militias were hastily formed to protect settlements, as residents feared that their farm or town might be next on the list of this savage named Inkpaduta. Although Dakota leaders were quick to disassociate themselves from Inkpaduta, the acts by their brethren served to further isolate their people from the whites and subject them to a higher level of discrimination.

The people called for a response from the government. A company of Federal troops was dispatched from Fort Ridgely, and even Chief Little Crow, in a gesture of goodwill, joined in the search for the outlaws. Inkpaduta, however, managed to elude capture, and the pursuit was finally called off.[10]

The result of the Inkpaduta affair had a profound effect on both Indians and whites alike. The Indians certainly noticed with great interest that, in spite of threats to the contrary, attacks resulting in the murder of whites could go unpunished. The whites, on the other hand, became more hostile toward the Indians and loudly called for their removal from the territory and the opening of the reservation to settlers. The latter proposal was seriously considered by the government. In March 1858, Mdewakanton chief Little Crow led a delegation of tribal leaders to Washington for the purpose of readjusting the present treaty.

Little Crow, who was born about 1810 at Kaposia on the Mississippi, was the son and grandson of chiefs. In his youth, he was known as arrogant, domineering, and immoral. In fact, he was forced to leave Kaposia due to threats against him by husbands of wives with whom he had dallied. He subsequently lived with the Wahpekute, where he married and discarded two women, then moved to a Wahpeton village, where he married four sisters, who became his permanent wives. This last polygamous matrimonial arrangement apparently changed his life, and he became admired by the tribe for his "smooth speech and agreeable manners."

In 1834, Little Crow returned to Kaposia upon the death of his father to assume his hereditary leadership role of the Mdewakanton band. This claim was disputed by his two half brothers—as well as some of the wronged husbands. In a violent confrontation, Little Crow was shot through the wrists. With treatment from the medicine man, he emerged from the conflict with disfigured arms, but he had gained the support of his sympathetic people.

Little Crow's ascension to chief engendered dramatic changes in him. He vowed to "stop whisky drinking, to encourage members of his band to become industrious and thrifty, and to promote morality among them." When questioned by the wronged husbands about this change of heart, he replied, "I was only a brave then; I am a chief now." Although he did not entirely forsake his own tribal religious beliefs, he allowed a missionary to establish a mission at Kaposia.

Little Crow accepted a policy of accommodation with the whites and had adopted some aspects of their culture while maintaining essential parts of his own Dakota culture. He was instrumental in promoting the 1851 treaty over the objections of others, and now, in 1858, he would represent his people as the primary negotiator in Washington.[11]

Over a four-month period in 1858, the delegation frequently met with Charles E. Mix, the acting commissioner of Indian Affairs, a fellow Minnesotan who had a reputation for cheating the Indians in various devious schemes. Mix, however, was quite persuasive. He pointedly reminded the Dakota that they were being permitted to reside on their reservations only as long as the president desired. At any time, they could be forced to move out, which would leave them homeless and at the mercy of the people of Minnesota. And given the present climate among the populace, that was an unsettling thought to the Indians.

Through chicanery, misinterpretation, misrepresentation, misunderstanding, and the relentless brow-beating of commissioner Mix, two treaties that proved highly favorable to the U.S. government were signed on June 19—one with each band. The Dakota relinquished permanent title to a ten-mile strip of prime farmland on the northeast bank of the Minnesota River, a parcel that constituted basically half of their reservation. In return, the Indians were offered a strip of land of lesser value on the southwest bank; some trinkets and material goods, including ceremonial swords and flags; and the promise that Congress would *consider* future annuities. The Dakota had in effect given the government virtual carte blanche to do as it pleased with the disposition of the tribes and their property—including entitlements from previous treaties.[12]

Delegation member Jerome Big Eagle later spoke about the treaty:

> In 1858 the ten miles of this strip belonging to the Mdawakanton and Wahpekute bands, and lying north of the river were sold, mainly through the influence of Little Crow. That year, with some other chiefs, I went to Washington on business connected to the treaty. The selling of that strip north of the Minnesota caused great dissatisfaction among the Sioux, and Little Crow was always blamed for the part he took in the sale. It caused us all to move to the south side of the river, where there was but very little game, and many of our people, under the treaty, were induced to give up the old life and go to work like white men, which was very distasteful to many.[13]

Some evidence exists, however, that Little Crow at least offered token resistance to the treaty. He had told Mix, "We have been so often cheated that I wished to be cautious, and not sign any more papers without having them explained, so that we may know what we are doing." Mix was said to have ridiculed Little Crow, calling him a child for his wariness. Perhaps Mix took it upon himself to patiently explain the treaty, at least his biased interpretation of it, until the chief was finally satisfied. More than likely the acting commissioner bullied the delegation with repeated reminders that if they refused to sign, they could have all their land turned over to the state of Minnesota at the discretion of the president. Regardless of the tactics employed, the treaty was finally signed, and the delegation headed for home the following morning.[14]

Predictably, when the treaty was ratified by Congress and the Dakota were awarded $266,880 for 889,000 acres—30 cents an acre—once again the creditors descended with palms up. Nearly all the money owed to the lower bands—the Mdewakanton and Wahpekute—went to pay debts to traders (Henry Sibley, now governor of Minnesota, was paid $12,000), and the upper bands—the Sisseton and Wahpeton—escaped with about $85,000.[15]

During the next several years, the troubles continued to mount for the Dakota tribe, and the reservation was a place of many miseries. The people had gradually separated into three distinct factions: the "blanket Indians," those who pursued their age-old hunting and fishing culture; the "cut-hairs," or "breeches Indians," who had chosen to adopt the white man's methods of cultivating the land; and mixed-breed families with bonds to the whites, some becoming churchgoing Christians. Sadly enough, a great number of these mixed-breeds were fatherless children, the result of the seduction by whites of Indian girls and women.

This cultural division was combined with the problems associated with sharing the cramped reservation; the threat of settlers crowding close to reservation boundaries—settlers who flaunted their perceived superiority over the Indian; inferior government rations—wormy, mealy flour and rancid bacon—in less-than-adequate quantities; deductions from annuities to pay alleged depredation claims; and payments to the traders, who kept the members of the tribe debt-ridden with inflated charges or by cheating them by falsifying account books. Additional frustration and resentment came from the knowledge that the troops at Fort Ridgely were always prepared to inhibit any serious display of Indian militancy.[16]

At the outbreak of the Civil War, Minnesota was the first state to respond to President Lincoln's call for troops. More than 5,000 Minnesotans marched off to fight for the Union in the East, including Regular army soldiers from Fort Ridgely. The responsibility of garrisoning the three frontier forts—Ridgely, Abercrombie, and Ripley—was placed in the hands of Minnesota volunteers. This mass disappearance of young white men from the surrounding farms and settlements did not go unnoticed by the Dakota.

Also due to the war, the government was neglecting many of its responsibilities to the Dakota, and only a small amount of provisions were being doled out. To add to the predicament and increased discontent, the tribe's corn crop planted in 1861 had been damaged by cutworms. By early 1862, the Dakota were becoming desperate for food, and their debts to the traders were mounting. Some Indians hatched a scheme that called for buying as much food on credit from the traders as possible, then refusing to pay. Word of that plan reached the ears of the traders, who cut off all credit to the Dakota tribe.[17]

The starving Dakota people were in dire need of provisions by the time cash and food annuities were scheduled to be distributed in June. But these annuities, which were traditionally handed out "as soon as the prairie grass was high enough for pasture," were—much to the chagrin and outrage of the Indians—postponed. Two reasons were given for this delay: Congress had been tardy in appropriating the funds, and the Treasury Department was undecided about whether to pay the Indians with new wartime paper greenbacks instead of gold, which was scarce. June turned into July, and still the money did not arrive. The Indian agent, Maj. Thomas J. Galbraith, had adequate provisions on hand stored in a warehouse, but he refused demands to open the doors, adamantly insisting custom dictated that food and cash be distributed at the same time.

By July 14, about 5,000 angry Indians had assembled at the agency and once again demanded that the warehouse provisions be handed out to the starving people. Galbraith grudgingly issued a small amount of food, barely enough to keep the Indians alive. Only the presence of two companies of the 5th Minnesota Regiment, under Lt. Timothy Sheehan, prevented the Indians from entering the warehouse by force. The sullen Indians had no choice but to return home as ordered with their meager rations.[18]

On August 4, violence broke out at the agency. About 500 Sioux, on foot as well as on horseback, surrounded the warehouse, while others broke down the door with hatchets and began carrying away sacks of flour. Lieutenant Sheehan and his troops quickly arrived and aimed a howitzer at the warehouse door, which caused the Indians to back away. The Indians complained to the army officer that their women and children were starving and the food inside rightfully belonged to them. Sheehan conferred with Galbraith and persuaded the reluctant agent to immediately issue small portions of pork and flour. A meeting was then arranged for the following day between Dakota leaders and Galbraith.

This council was attended by agent Thomas Galbraith, a trader named Andrew J. Myrick, several clerks from agency stores, and a young missionary, John P. Williamson, along with a delegation from the tribe. Chief Little Crow assumed the role as primary spokesman for the Dakota. He summed up the predicament facing his people, noting that the government payment was overdue and a solution must be found. The chief reasonably suggested that agent Galbraith enter into some arrangement with the local traders to supply provisions until the annuities arrived, which had been practiced occasionally in years past. He concluded his plea with what could be construed as a warning, saying, "When men are hungry they help themselves."[19]

The interpreter was alarmed that this last statement would be taken as a direct threat and refused to translate it into English. Galbraith, however, insisted that Williamson, the missionary, who was proficient in the Dakota language, translate. Williamson complied, and Galbraith turned to the traders, saying: "Well, it's up to you now. What will you do?"

Trader Myrick was incensed by Little Crow's menacing remark and replied, "So far as I am concerned, if they are hungry, let them eat grass." The translation into Dakota of that cruel response provoked the Indians to leap to their feet and storm out, chilling the air with loud war whoops and vicious threats.[20]

This unsympathetic retort by Myrick was even more of an affront to the Dakota given the fact that he and many of his fellow traders had married into the tribe, as had their clerks and other reservation shopkeepers. Nevertheless, all had thus far ignored any responsibility to the tribe and refused to provide assistance to their starving relatives. That fact, coupled with Myrick's insult, constituted an unpardonable sin to the Dakota.

Word of this confrontation reached Fort Ridgely and was received with apprehension, and perhaps disgust, by Capt. John S. Marsh, commander of the garrison. Marsh understood the danger of allowing circumstances to fester and called for an immediate council in an attempt to defuse the situation. The captain dominated the meeting, ordering Galbraith and the traders, under the threat of arrest, to open the warehouse and issue the food annuities at once. Galbraith grudgingly complied with this order, and rations—130 barrels of flour and 30 barrels of pork—were distributed to the Dakota over the next two days. The Indians, now pacified to some extent by the prospect of full bellies, took their goods and returned to the reservation or went out hunting, while awaiting word about the cash annuities that were still owed them.[21]

The deep-seated hatred between the Dakota tribe and the white farmers, however, had not abated, and on Sunday, August 17, 1862, this animosity erupted into violence.

On that day, four Dakota Indians—Brown Wing, Killing Ghost, Runs Against When Crawling, and Breaking Up—all under the age of thirty, were returning home to the Rice Creek village after a five-day deer-hunting trip. These young men were Wahpeton who had married Mdewakanton women and were all related by blood, either brothers, half brothers, or cousins.[22]

The supplies that the four Indians had brought along had been depleted, and they were hungry and thirsty. In addition, their hunt had been unproductive, and their foul moods reflected that fact. Beyond the reservation boundary, at the white settlement of Acton in Meeker County, they approached the home of Robinson Jones, which also served as a public house and post office. One of the men casually reached through the split-rail fence and grabbed a few eggs from a hen's nest. One of his companions objected to the theft, warning that they could get into trouble. The Indian who had taken the eggs angrily threw them to the ground and bragged to his companions that he was not afraid of the white man. This instigated a heated argument among the four, with taunts and boasts, and the thief finally bragged that he was not afraid to even kill a white man.[23]

Robinson Jones appeared to greet the Indians, whom he had known from previous visits to his store. The five of them then walked over to the log home of Jones's stepson, where several children were present, including fifteen-year-old Clara Wilson. The Indians became quarrelsome, and Jones, who, like most frontiersmen of the time, was carrying his gun, ushered the rowdy men out of the house. They moved on to the Howard Baker house, where new arrivals Viranus Webster and his wife had temporarily parked their covered wagon.[24]

The Indians by that time had calmed down and, after some friendly conversation, proposed that they all engage in a target-shooting contest. In the subsequent match, Robinson Jones easily outshot his competition, which did not set well with the Dakota men.

Perhaps angry words were exchanged or one of the Indians was goaded by his companions into making good on his earlier boasts. Regardless, without warning, the Indians turned their rifles on the whites and commenced firing. Viranus Webster was the first to fall, then Howard Baker, then Mrs. Jones, who had run to the door to see what was happening, then Robinson Jones was shot dead. The surviving women were screaming hysterically as the Indians turned to dash away. The disturbance drew the young Clara Wilson to the doorway of the Jones house. One of Indians paused to sight in on her and yanked the trigger. The girl toppled backward into the house, dead. The four Dakota murderers then stole some nearby horses and excitedly raced for their village.[25]

The four killers of the Acton settlers galloped into their village that evening and bragged to one and all about what they had done. This disconcerting news quickly passed from village to village and came as quite a shock to the Dakota people. Ordinarily, the four culprits could have been handed over to authorities for punishment, and the matter would have been settled. August 1862, however, was not an ordinary time in the relationship between the two races, which could be called contentious at best and in most cases hostile. Therefore, the consensus opinion of the Indians was that, in the words of Little Crow, "the whites would take a dreadful vengeance because women had been killed."

This statement was spoken at an all-night meeting held at Little Crow's house, where chiefs and warriors from the various villages had gathered, and a debate raged about what course of action to take. Other grievances against the whites were aired, and although many considered it folly to engage in war against such a strong adversary, it was finally decided that they could not simply wait for retaliation. The Dakota must seize the offensive.

Little Crow, whom the others believed had the prestige and ability to lead a fight against the white man, was at first reluctant to participate—until he was called a coward by one of the more hot-blooded warriors. That insult aroused Little Crow, who threw that warrior's headdress to the ground and delivered an impassioned speech in which he announced that he would lead an attack on the white man in the morning. This decision certainly contradicted the chief's past behavior, and even now he held to the opinion that his people were doomed in any fight with the whites. Little Crow, however, had chosen to follow what he believed were his obligations to his tribe as a warrior.[26]

On the warm summer morning of August 18, Dakota Sioux warriors, led by Chief Little Crow, went on a rampage that left a trail of bloodletting perhaps unparalleled in recorded history. Robert Utley, in *Frontiersmen in Blue,* perhaps summed up the carnage best:

> The warriors swept through Redwood Agency, killed the men, took the women and children captive, and put the buildings to the torch. In wide-ranging parties they spread over the countryside, killing, raping, pillaging, and burning. Surprised, unequipped for defense, unversed in frontier life, the farmers fell by the score, dispatched with a savagery rarely equalled in the history of Indian uprisings—families burned alive in their cabins, children nailed to doors, girls raped by dozens of braves and then hacked to pieces, babies dismembered and their limbs flung in the mother's [*sic*] face.[27]

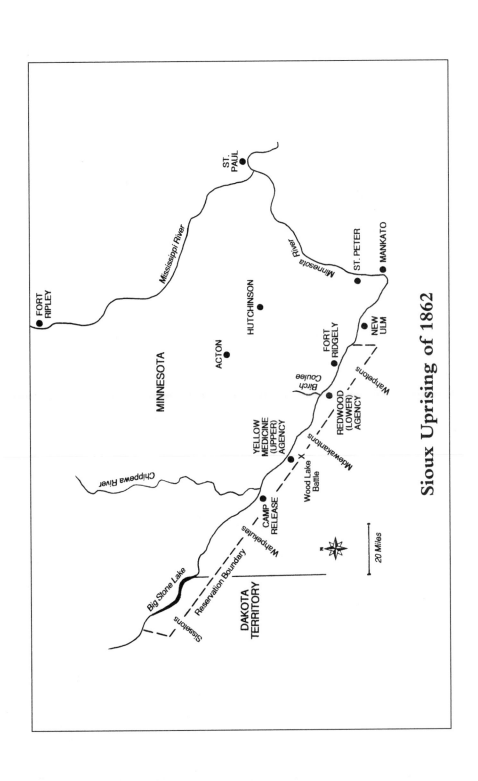

Sioux Uprising of 1862

The violence was initially centered around the two agencies but spread rapidly down the Minnesota River, as bands of vindictive Sioux swooped down on farms and settlements like swarms of locusts ravenously devouring everything in their path. In a furious frenzy of merciless acts, entire families of innocent people were massacred—the men were riddled with bullets or arrows, or stabbed or hacked to death with knives or tomahawks, and those women and young girls who were not killed before, during, or after being raped were taken prisoner, along with scores of children. Houses, barns, and buildings were set afire, possessions ransacked and stolen or destroyed, the Indians lingering in each area only long enough to fulfill their propensity for torture before moving on to the next farm.[28]

One of the early casualties was trader Andrew Myrick, who was singled out for special treatment. He was slain while trying to escape from a second-floor window of his store. His body was mutilated with a scythe and countless arrows, and according to Big Eagle, the Indians "stuffed his mouth full of grass," apparently in retaliation for the cruel comments made by the trader at that earlier meeting.[29]

At about 10:00 that morning, word of the uprising reached Fort Ridgely, which was manned by two officers and seventy-six men from Company B of the 5th Minnesota Infantry. Capt. John Marsh immediately sent a message to Lieutenant Sheehan at Fort Ripley to return at once with his fifty men. Marsh then assembled forty-six men and set out for the Redwood Agency. Along the way, the column encountered fleeing settlers, who warned them that the Sioux were in great numbers and could likely overwhelm such a small detachment. Nevertheless, Marsh marched onward and eventually approached the ferry that crossed the Minnesota River to the agency.

An Indian beckoned from the other side, bidding the soldiers to come across for a council. At that moment, a shot rang out, a signal that brought fire from the rifles of countless Indians concealed in nearby brush. According to Sgt. John Bishop, "About one-half of our men dropped dead where they had been standing." Marsh deployed his remaining men behind the dense foliage, and a battle ensued that lasted most of the afternoon. Finally, the Indians closed in. The soldiers were forced to fight hand-to-hand and were in danger of being of overwhelmed by the sheer number of warriors. Marsh frantically ordered the men to swim across the river in an attempt to escape. The captain led the way but soon suffered a cramp and slipped beneath the water's surface. Despite the efforts of others to save him, Capt. John Marsh, the man who just days before had ordered that rations be issued to the desperate Dakota, drowned. A total of twenty-four soldiers were killed in the day's fighting.

The surviving troopers safely returned to the fort that night, where nineteen-year-old Lt. Thomas P. Gere, who was suffering from the mumps, and twenty-nine other men frantically worked to shore up defenses in case of an attack. The fort boasted several pieces of powerful artillery—two 12-pounder and one 24-pounder mountain howitzers, and a 6-pounder field gun—which were stationed at three of the fort's corners. Gere had earlier dispatched a message to Governor Ramsey requesting reinforcements. Meanwhile, frightened civilian refugees trickled into the fort all day, until more than 200 had sought protection.[30]

But the army would not be able to prevent the Dakota Indians from raiding throughout the countryside at will and slaughtering every white person that they encountered.

By the time stars had filled the night sky, at least 400 settlers had been butchered, countless others had been taken captive, and many Indian wagons had been loaded with plunder from farms and settlements. And the Dakota were not yet content with the devastation that they had inflicted on the whites.[31]

On August 19, while many of the Dakota warriors had resumed their reign of terror, chiefs Little Crow, Mankato, and Big Eagle, along with a sizable war party of about 300, held a council on the prairie within sight of Fort Ridgely. Little Crow was contemptuous of those who wanted to kill women and children, and proposed instead that they engage in battle against their real enemy—the army. He and the other older chiefs pointed out that Fort Ridgely was of vital strategic value and should be attacked at once. The younger warriors objected, arguing that their present force was too small to mount an effective assault on the fort. Besides, they were more interested in the plunder that they could accumulate from attacking farms and settlements. The council ended with Little Crow disgustedly returning home with his allies, while about 200 warriors rode off toward the town of New Ulm. The fort, which at that point would have been quite vulnerable, inasmuch as reinforcements had not yet arrived, had been spared for the time being.[32]

At about 3:00 P.M., a war party composed of at least 100 Dakota warriors approached the mostly German-speaking town of New Ulm, which was located sixteen miles below the fort. They dismounted and advanced on foot into the town, firing as they moved forward. While the terrified women and children huddled in buildings and behind barricades, militiamen under Jacob Nix returned fire. Small groups of warriors occasionally charged the buildings, but each time, they were repulsed by the rifles and shotguns wielded by the defenders, although several whites were killed during these brazen rushes. Unoccupied structures on the outskirts of town were put to the torch, but the Indians could not overwhelm the militia-men, who had taken to moving from building to building in an effort to force the Indians back.

The vicious fighting had lasted for about two hours when a severe thunderstorm commenced with sizzling lightning accompanied by a blind-ing, drenching downpour. At the same time, reinforcements—about twenty-three men—arrived in New Ulm. The warriors, apparently dis-couraged by their inability to gain the upper hand, decided to break con-tact. The Dakota had killed six people in the town, as well as another eleven that they happened upon on the nearby prairie, but they had taken no loot or captives. After dark, groups of farmers and displaced townspeo-ple rode to the rescue, until New Ulm boasted about 300 defenders, who hurriedly made preparations in the event of another attack.[33]

Meanwhile, Little Crow held a council in his village that night and gained assurances that at least 400 warriors would be available in the morn-ing to attack Fort Ridgely. He correctly surmised that about 175 soldiers defended the fort—Lt. Timothy Sheehan and his 50 men, as well as two other units, had arrived during the day to bolster the garrison to about 153 soldiers, in addition to 25 armed civilians. Little Crow was confident that his warriors, who outnumbered the soldiers by more than a two-to-one margin, would easily prevail. The Indians held a celebration feast that night, with the young men bragging about their killing and torturing exploits, and everyone was in high spirits with the certainty that the whites would be defeated.[34]

In the early afternoon of August 20, Little Crow, riding a black horse, led his warriors toward Fort Ridgely. The chief, accompanied by three companions, rode to a spot just out of rifle range and waved some uniden-tifiable object as if inviting a parley. This diversion gave his warriors the opportunity to creep into various assigned positions around the fort within the cover of deep, wooded ravines. When all was ready, three volleys were fired. Hair-raising war cries split the air. The attacking force rose as one and threw itself at the fort, firing arrows and bullets as it charged.

The Indians quickly breached the northeast corner of the post, occu-pied some outlying log huts, and stampeded the army horses, mules, and cattle. A number of warriors were able to reach the parade ground but were cut down by a barrage from Lieutenant Sheehan's men. Two how-itzers, under Ordnance Sgt. John Jones, were then turned on those Indians who had taken cover in the huts. The blasts of cannon shot successfully forced the warriors from their refuge and back to the ravine.[35]

The big guns discouraged the Dakota from exposing themselves en masse, but occasionally small groups would summon the courage and charge—only to be pushed back by the defenders. Little Crow's warriors poured a constant, blistering fire into the fort for a period of five hours but could not penetrate the defenses. The Indians shot flaming arrows at the wooden buildings but failed to ignite any major fires. Each time Little Crow mounted a concerted offensive, the artillery opened up, and the bursting shells sent the Indians running for cover. At dusk, the frustrated Dakota decided to abandon the fight and go home. They had not captured any provisions or prisoners, and the howitzers, which they had never before faced, were simply too effective a deterrent.

Little Crow was discouraged but not defeated. He returned to his village and contemplated his next move. Many of the warriors, however, instead of heading for home, rode from the fort to join brethren who were carrying out raids on isolated farms and settlements all over southwestern Minnesota.[36]

Heavy rain commenced at midnight and continued through the following day, which offered a respite for the beleaguered fort and the town of New Ulm. Both places made good use of the time by strengthening defenses—with good reason. The Indians had by no means given up the idea of removing the whites from those two strongholds.

Little Crow, his force now doubled in size by the arrival of 400 Sisseton and Wahpeton warriors, decided to immediately attempt another assault on Fort Ridgely. On August 21, the Dakotas once again crept into positions encircling the post. At the appropriate time, the warriors sprang from the tall grass and ravines and charged, shooting as they closed in on the complex of buildings. The defenders returned fire from behind barricades and through windows, while Sergeant Jones brought his howitzers into action.[37]

The warriors bravely pushed forward in spite of the violent artillery explosions, one group managing to occupy the sutler's house and the stables, all the while firing barrages of arrows and bullets at the soldiers. Other Indians shot flaming arrows at the buildings, but the roofs were still damp from the rain and failed to ignite, although great plumes of smoke engulfed the area, obscuring the vision of those on both sides. The Indians executed one assault after another, and only the devastating discharges of the howitzers kept them at bay. "The hail of bullets, the whizzing of arrows, and the blood-curdling war-whoop were incessant," Lieutenant Gere wrote in his report.[38]

The vicious battle waged throughout the afternoon, as the Indians closed in time and again, only to be beaten back by the resolute defenders. At one point, Little Crow was standing too close to a bursting shell and was sent reeling from the concussion. Although not seriously injured, he required assistance to leave the field. Chief Mankato later led a large group of warriors on one final, dramatic charge directed at the southwest corner of the fort, but Jones and his guns—the 24-pounder in particular—once again stopped the Indians in their tracks. "The ponderous reverberations" of the howitzers, Lieutenant Gere reported, "echoed up the valley as though twenty guns had opened, and the frightful explosions struck terror to the savages." Not only terror—many were killed or wounded by the explosions. After six hours of what Lieutenant Sheehan described as "one of the most determined attacks ever made by Indians on a post," the demoralized Dakota Sioux withdrew.[39]

Little Crow was incensed, and perhaps to some measure humiliated, by this second failure to capture the fort—and by the fact that only six soldiers had been killed and less than twenty wounded in both assaults, while Indian casualties had been considerable. He gathered up about 650 warriors that night, deciding to vent his frustration on the town of New Ulm.

It was about 9:30 the next morning, Saturday, August 22, when the war party assembled along the bluff above the town.

Judge Charles E. Flandrau, who had arrived in New Ulm from St. Peter during the first battle, had assumed command of the town's citizen-soldiers. The thirty-five-year-old Flandrau had directed the construction of a series of barricades improvised from wagons, logs, and rocks. His 300 volunteers were hunkered down in these defensive positions on the edge of town when Little Crow gave the order to charge. Judge Flandrau described the scene:

> Their advance upon the sloping prairie was a very fine spectacle, and to such inexperienced soldiers as we all were, intensely exciting. When within about one mile and a half of us, the mass began to expand like a fan and increase in the velocity of its approach, and continued this movement until within about double rifle-shot, when it had covered our entire front. Then the savages uttered a terrific yell and came down upon us like the wind.[40]

The sudden appearance of the warriors, combined with the horrific war cries, was too much for the untrained citizen-soldiers to withstand. Flandrau's unnerved men broke and ran to the rear toward another set of barricades inside the town, while the Indians quickly occupied the abandoned outer buildings. Flandrau and his officers calmed down the men to some degree and directed their fire well enough to hold off the encroaching Indians. In an effort to improve fields of fire, the volunteers then commenced setting fire to buildings in front of their position, which created a large, open space that the Indians were hesitant to cross.[41]

The fighting raged throughout the morning and into the afternoon, with skirmishes taking place from house to house as ground was alternately taken and lost by both sides. At about 3:00 P.M., a large group of Indians had gathered along the river, near the ferry landing, with intentions of mounting a major assault. Flandrau realized what was about to take place and sent sixty men forward with guns blazing. This unexpected assault succeeded in dispersing the Indians and prevented any further concentrated effort. Sporadic fighting continued until sundown, when the Indians conceded that the town's defenders were too stubborn to be dislodged and headed back to their villages.[42]

New Ulm, however, had suffered 32 killed and 60 wounded, with one-third of the town—190 houses—destroyed. Six days later, Flandrau evacuated the town and moved about 2,000 people and 153 wagons to Mankato, thirty miles downriver.

While heading home to St. Peter, Judge Flandrau happened upon Col. Henry Hastings Sibley, with a command of hundreds of state militia troops who had been dispatched by Gov. Alexander Ramsey as a rescue force. Both Sibley and Ramsey, who had become governor when Sibley had declined to run for reelection, bore a large share of the blame for the uprising. Regardless, as many as 800 bodies of white massacre victims were strewn over the Minnesota countryside, and the responsibility for quelling this uprising rested on the shoulders of the fifty-one-year-old Sibley.

Sibley, a Michigan native, had built the first private residence within the borders of Minnesota while employed by the American Fur Company. In 1849, he had been elected as a territorial delegate to Congress, and in 1858, he had become the state's first elected governor. Sibley had returned to private life until the summer of 1862, when he was commissioned a colonel and placed in charge of the state militia.

By August 26, when Colonel Sibley departed his staging area at St. Peter, his force totaled about 1,400 well-armed men. Reinforcements— about 200 troopers—were immediately sent to shore up defenses at Fort Ridgely.[43]

On August 31, Sibley dispatched two detachments on reconnaissance missions to determine where the Indians had gone. Maj. Joseph R. Brown was ordered to visit the area around the Redwood Agency, while Capt. Hirum P. Grant scoured the eastern side of the river.

Brown, a former Indian agent who was familiar with the territory, had a personal stake in this operation—his family had been taken captive by the

Sioux. Brown's command halted now and then to bury bodies of settlers. It arrived at the Lower Agency villages to find the area abandoned.

Reports of Sibley's arrival with a large force of soldiers had reached the ears of the Indians. Little Crow had held a council on August 25 and thought it prudent that they withdraw from their villages. The chief, with captives in tow, led the Dakota up the valley northward toward a traditional hunting ground known as the Big Woods. Along the way, Little Crow and sixty warriors raided the town of Hutchinson, which caused settlers throughout central Minnesota to flee their homes.[44]

Dakota Sioux scouts had been following the movements of the soldiers and were watching when the two commands under Brown and Grant bivouacked together on the night of September 1 near the mouth of Birch Coulee, not far above the Lower Agency. While the soldiers slept, more than 200 warriors, led by Chiefs Mankato, Gray Bird, Red Legs, and Big Eagle, stealthily occupied the bluffs and coulees to surround the camp.

At dawn, the Indians broke from their hiding places and, with war cries echoing in the still air, charged toward the camp. The ferocity of this surprise assault nearly allowed the Indians to overrun the position and resulted in twenty-two soldiers killed and another sixty wounded. The shocked soldiers who had dodged the initial onslaught scrambled to seek refuge beneath wagons and behind carcasses of horses, more than eighty of which had been shot down. According to participant James Egan, they returned fire "without aim or other object than to give evidence that there were survivors of their murderous fire, and to prevent a charge on the camp. . . . It looked as if our last hour had come on earth."[45]

But the soldiers regrouped and desperately fought for their lives. After an hour of close-range combat, they managed to push back the attackers. The Indians assumed positions surrounding the camp but were hesitant to mount another charge. The men hurriedly dug defensive positions in preparation for an impending assault, all the while exchanging long-distance fire with their enemy.[46]

Faint sounds of this battle had carried all the way to Fort Ridgely, sixteen miles downstream. Colonel Sibley dispatched a rescue party under Col. Samuel McPhail, composed of fifty mounted rangers, three infantry battalions from the 6th Minnesota, and an artillery section—250 troops in all. The detachment was within sight of Brown's camp when the Indians closed in from all sides, and only thunderous blasts of artillery kept them from overwhelming the column.

Brown and his men had been cheered by the comforting sounds of approaching reinforcements, but that emotion soon turned to consternation when the distant firing faded away. Instead of fighting his way to rendezvous with Brown and Grant, McPhail had deemed it necessary to retreat and establish a defensible position. The rescue party, while fighting off the Indians with rifle fire and shots from their howitzer, then dispatched a courier to the fort requesting that another rescue party be sent out to save them as well as Brown's men.[47]

Colonel Sibley rode to the rescue with his entire command and relieved McPhail just after midnight. The troops waited until morning to move toward Brown's location and arrived at about 11:00—thirty-one hours after the attack—to find that the Indians had vanished, leaving behind at least two dozen dead and more than sixty with disabling wounds.[48]

Sibley chose not to pursue the warriors, a decision that evoked bitter criticism from the populace. He defended his position by pointing out that his troops were raw and untrained, his supplies of food and ammunition were insufficient, and he feared that an aggressive movement at that time would cause the execution of the prisoners held by the Indians.

To be fair, Sibley was correct in his assessment. After Birch Coulee, citizen volunteers had departed for their homes, leaving him an undermanned, unmounted force. And with the future of Minnesota at stake, he could not risk defeat. He therefore set about reorganizing and training his army. The state adjutant general provided rations, ammunition, and other vital supplies. Governor Ramsey, as well as governors of neighboring states, petitioned Secretary of War Stanton in Washington for assistance.[49]

President Abraham Lincoln responded to the crisis by creating the Military Department of the Northwest. He placed in command Maj. Gen. John Pope, who had recently been ingloriously relieved of duty after his defeat at the second battle of Bull Run. Pope arrived in St. Paul to assume his new command on September 16.

Colonel Sibley, in the meantime, had been in contact with Chief Little Crow. A message had been left in a split stake at Birch Coulee, with an offer by Sibley to negotiate an end to hostilities. The Dakota chief responded with a list of grievances and reminded Sibley that he held a great number of captives, which he would use as bargaining chips for peace or as a shield to ensure the safety of his people. Sibley demanded that Little Crow release the prisoners, but he received no answer.[50]

The Dakota Sioux, however, were anything but unified. The upper bands accused the lower bands of starting a war without consulting them. Dissension among the two factions steadily increased, and finally a feast was held to discuss the future of the war. It was decided, with much grumbling by the peace faction, that war would continue.[51]

Sibley was not about to wait for negotiations to settle the conflict. By September 19, he had assembled the 3rd, 6th, 7th, and 9th Minnesota Infantry regiments and assorted other troops—1,619 in all—and marched up the valley from Fort Ridgely in pursuit of Little Crow. Three days later, the army camped for the evening on the eastern shore of Lone Tree, or Battle, Lake—not Wood Lake, which was three and a half miles west and has incorrectly received credit as the location of the battle.

Little Crow's Dakota, with their white captives, were presently camped near the mouth of the Chippewa River, just a few miles north of the army's position. The Indians had been observing Sibley's movements and held a council to determine a course of action. After a heated debate, it was decided that they would ambush the soldiers at daybreak—although many members of the peace faction refused to participate.[52]

When the eastern sky burst into light on that morning of September 23, 700 Sioux warriors were secreted in the tall grass along the road that they presumed the soldiers would follow. At 7:00 A.M., however, a small forage detail from the 3rd Minnesota, who had decided without permission to raid a nearby pumpkin or potato patch, stole out of camp. The troopers ignored the road and instead headed across the prairie—directly toward the spot where many of the Indians were hiding.

Two hundred anxious warriors in the vicinity rose up and fired at the forage detail. This sudden noise aroused the camp, and other members of the 3rd rushed to the rescue. Maj. Abraham K. Welch quickly formed his men as skirmishers and charged into the fray. The Indians initially retreated, then regrouped and deployed in a fan-shaped fashion, threatening the army's flank. Sibley ordered the 3rd Minnesota, which was in the center, to pull back. The order was issued twice before the men complied with much confusion, while sustaining a number of casualties, including Major Welch, who was shot in the leg. The 3rd, with the Renville Rangers rushing to their aid, managed to form an adequate line of defense on a plateau.

The Indians in the ravine had started moving toward the army camp but were repulsed by canister shot from a 6-pounder. By this time, the 3rd, 6th, and 7th Minnesota had reached the field, and Sibley ordered a charge. After about two hours of heavy fighting, the Indians withdrew, and the army held the field. Sibley had lost seven killed and thirty wounded in what became known as the battle of Wood Lake. Indian casualties were estimated at about thirty, including Chief Mankato, who was killed when struck in the back by a cannonball.[53]

Sibley's victory had been decisive. A majority of the Dakota Indians had lost their will to fight. And during the battle, the peace faction of the tribe had taken possession of most of the white captives. On September 25, Sibley arrived at the camp of the peaceful chiefs to liberate 269 white and mixed-blood captives. He established a bivouac nearby, which he called Camp Release, and began rounding up Dakota people, until eventually over 2,000 Indians had surrendered.[54]

Chief Little Crow and a band of about 200 Mdewakanton renegades and their families, however, had escaped and were en route to Devil's Lake in present-day North Dakota, with intentions of seeking allies who would join the chief in his fight against the whites in Minnesota.[55]

In a twist of irony, the annuity money from Washington—$71,000 in gold coin—had arrived at Fort Ridgely on Monday, August 18, just a few hours too late to prevent the rampage of the angry Dakota. The money had remained at that location throughout the attacks—a fact of which the Indians were not aware, but one that gave the soldiers added reason to protect the post.

The battle had been won, hostilities had decreased, but this war was far from over.

CHAPTER FOUR

Carleton, Carson, and the Apache

WHILE MINNESOTA CONTENDED WITH ITS UNREST AMONG THE SIOUX, A large force of Californians, commanded by Col. James H. Carleton, was on the march in the spring of 1862 from the West Coast toward the Southwest for the purpose of assisting Union brigadier general Edward R. S. Canby in his effort to drive Confederate brigadier general Henry Sibley's Texans out of New Mexico. Sibley had ambitious plans for the Confederacy in that region, and Canby was his only obstacle.

The forty-three-year-old Canby was a tall, judicious, somewhat reserved Kentuckian who had grown up in Indiana. After graduating from West Point, he had served in the Seminole War in Florida and was cited twice for gallantry during the Mexican War. Canby had assumed command of the Department of New Mexico in June 1861.

Canby and his enemy, Brig. Gen. Henry Hopkins Sibley (not to be confused with the Union's Henry Hastings Sibley), were well known to each other. The two men had been classmates at West Point, and Canby not only had been best man at Sibley's wedding, but also was married to a cousin of Sibley's wife. They had recently served together in the U.S. Army during the previous winter's campaign against the Navajo Indians.[1]

Sibley, a debonair Louisianan with a reputation as a man who enjoyed a frequent alcoholic beverage, had been stationed in New Mexico Territory at the outbreak of the war and had resigned from the army to accept a commission in the Confederacy. On June 17, 1861, Sibley was promoted to brigadier general by President Jefferson Davis. He was given orders to recruit a brigade of Texans and drive the Union soldiers out of present-day Arizona and New Mexico, which would clear the way to California for the South.

71

The forty-four-year-old Sibley was an experienced officer who had served in the Seminole War and the expedition into Utah against the Mormons, and he had received a brevet for bravery in the Mexican War. He also was the inventor of the Sibley tent, which had become regular army issue in 1856 and continued to be a mainstay until the 1890s.

Sibley recruited his Army of New Mexico from Texans eager to fight for the South and, in early 1862, headed up the Rio Grande River Valley from San Antonio toward his first objective, Fort Craig, New Mexico, which was commanded by his friend, then-Colonel Canby.

On February 19, Sibley led 2,600 men across the Rio Grande to Valverde Ford, six miles north of Fort Craig. Sibley understood that he could not mount a successful assault of the fort, but he was nonetheless depending on seizing its supplies. He decided to feint to the north in an effort to convince Canby that supply lines would be cut in that direction, thereby drawing out the Union forces where they could be engaged under more advantageous circumstances.

After waiting out a sandstorm for two days, Colonel Canby met this perceived threat by Sibley on February 21 with more than 3,800 troops—including Col. Kit Carson and his New Mexico volunteer regiment—who tore into Sibley's outnumbered force with small arms and artillery and managed to push the Confederates back into a defensive position in an old river channel. Rather than attack this position head-on, Canby attempted to envelop the Confederate left flank. Sibley countered with a frontal assault by his main force, which, in bloody hand-to-hand fighting, eventually caused the Union ranks to collapse and retreat. The Texans pursued, but they magnanimously withdrew when Canby raised a white flag in order to remove his dead from the field.

The day's fighting had cost the Union 68 killed, 160 wounded, and 35 missing; the Confederates suffered 36 killed, 150 wounded, and 1 missing. Figures reported by both sides were likely somewhat lower than actual losses. Sibley had won the battle, but in the process, he lost quite a number of wagons loaded with supplies and equipment, and gained nothing in the way of provisions from the fort.

Sibley demanded that Canby surrender the fort but was curtly rebuffed. Due to the lack of supplies, Sibley had no choice but to bypass Fort Craig and head north to resupply his troops from Albuquerque, where the Union was said to have stored $250,000 worth of goods. The Confederates arrived in that city to discover that the Union defenders had fled after learning about Canby's defeat. Much to Sibley's chagrin, the valuable supplies had been either removed or destroyed, but his troops did manage to occupy the

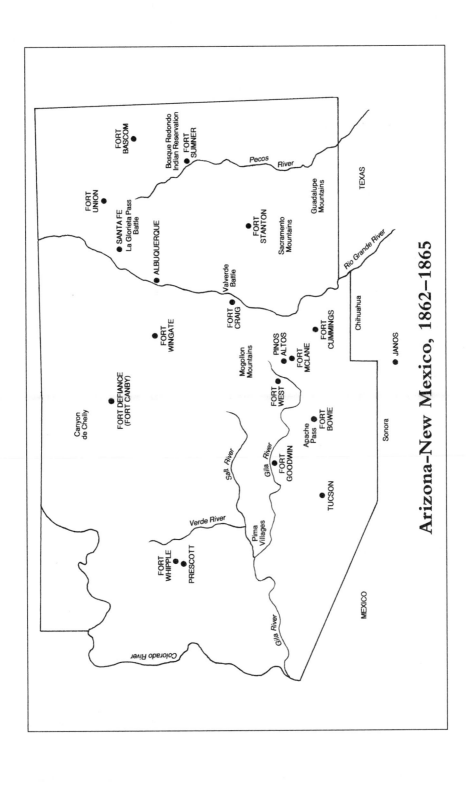

Arizona–New Mexico, 1862–1865

city. In his search for provisions, Sibley dispatched a detachment under Maj. Charles L. Pyron to Santa Fe, but the stores there had met with the same fate. Pyron's troops could accomplish little more than terrorize the citizenry and raise the Confederate flag over the 250-year-old Palace of Governors. Sibley's Southerners for all intents and purposes were in control of New Mexico Territory.

Inasmuch as Colonel Carleton's column was still bogged down in Southern California and could offer no assistance, Maj. Gen. David Hunter, the commander of the Department of Kansas, ordered Colorado Territory's acting governor Lewis Weld to reinforce Canby in New Mexico. The 1st Colorado Volunteer Infantry Regiment marched immediately for the purpose of uprooting the occupying Confederates.

In the meantime, Major Pyron received word that troops from Fort Union were on their way to Santa Fe. He decided to head eastward to engage those Union troops with about 400 men and two 6-pounder field guns.

The Colorado volunteers had been reinforced by a number of Regulars on their march south and were now about 1,340 strong. When they were within fifty miles of Santa Fe, Maj. John Chivington, a fire-and-brimstone Methodist preacher, was sent forward in advance of the column with 418 soldiers, under orders to move against the Confederates occupying Santa Fe.

These two detachments, commanded by Pyron and Chivington, were headed on a collision course that would culminate in a battle near La Glorieta Pass, a part of the old Santa Fe Trail that twisted through the southern tip of the Sangre de Cristo Mountains, about twenty miles southeast of Santa Fe.

On the night of March 25, Chivington, who was camped at a ranch owned by Polish immigrant Martin Kozlowski, learned from several captured Confederates that Major Pyron was bivouacked at Johnson's ranch, located at the far end of the pass. At dawn, Chivington moved toward that location, captured a thirty-man Rebel advance guard, then engaged Pyron's main force just west of Pigeon's ranch—six miles northeast of Johnson's ranch.

The surprised Pyron countered Chivington with artillery that sent the Union troops reeling. Chivington, however, rallied his men and divided his force into two detachments, which he deployed in positions along the slopes, catching the Confederates in a crossfire. Pyron pulled back about a mile and a half and established a strong defense.

Chivington followed and once again gained the high ground to pour devastating fire into his enemy. Within an hour, the Confederates broke and retreated. The Union troops chased after them and captured sixty to seventy prisoners. Chivington withdrew to Kozlowski's ranch, while Pyron regrouped at Johnson's ranch and dispatched couriers to Sibley demanding reinforcements. The Federals had lost nineteen killed, five wounded, and three missing in the day's fighting. Confederate losses totaled sixteen dead and thirty to forty wounded, in addition to those captured.

Col. William R. Scurry arrived to reinforce Pyron on March 27, which brought Confederate strength to about 1,100. Inasmuch as Chivington had not attacked, Scurry decided to take the offensive. On the morning of March 28, he headed toward Pigeon's ranch, leaving behind his train of seventy-three wagons, guarded mostly by those men who had been wounded.

Chivington had also received reinforcements with the arrival of Col. John P. Slough and the main force of Colorado volunteers. While Scurry was on the move, Slough led about 900 men toward the Pigeon ranch.

The two armies met about midmorning, and a battle of charges, countercharges, and dueling artillery commenced. It lasted until late afternoon, when Slough and the Federals finally retreated to Pigeon's ranch. Confederate losses were listed as thirty-six killed, sixty wounded, and twenty-five missing. The Federals lost thirty-one killed, more than fifty wounded, and thirty missing.

Scurry, who held the field, believed that he had gained a smashing victory—and it would have seemed so, except for the fact that Major Chivington had visited Johnson's ranch while the fighting raged. There he had burned the Confederate supply wagons, killed 500 to 600 horses and mules, and captured seventeen prisoners.

The destruction of nearly all of the Confederates' supplies became the turning point of the war in New Mexico Territory. The destitute Rebels returned to Albuquerque, only to find Edward Canby, recently promoted to brigadier general, waiting for them with 1,200 men. Sibley, who also had learned that Carleton's California Column was on the way, had no choice but to retreat back to Texas, barely escaping Canby's clutches by sneaking off under the cover of darkness.[2]

Fortunately for Canby, the Coloradans had ridden to the rescue, inasmuch as the California Column was still plodding its way en route across the desert toward Arizona.

That column, which numbered 2,350 officers and enlisted men when it had departed California, was composed of the 1st California Infantry Regiment, elements of the 1st and 2nd California Cavalry and the 5th California Infantry, with support from the 3rd U.S. Artillery. A great number of these men had joined the army after failing to strike it rich in the California and Colorado gold fields, and could be described as ruthless, ragtag soldiers.[3]

The brigade was commanded by Col. James Henry Carleton, who was destined to remain in New Mexico for more than three years and would become a dominant figure in shaping the tragic history of the Indians of the Southwest.

The forty-eight-year-old Carleton had the reputation as a power-hungry, tough-as-saddle-leather soldier, a mercenary of sorts. He had aspired to be a writer as a young man in Maine—corresponding with Charles Dickens about his career—and successfully published a number of professional and scientific articles. Carleton abandoned his writing for the time being in 1839, when he received a Regular army commission as a second lieutenant in the 1st Dragoons. He went west to serve under Brig. Gen. Stephen W. Kearny on an expedition to the Rocky Mountains. He then fought in the Mexican War and earned a brevet as major for gallantry at Buena Vista, a battle about which he wrote a book.

Now Carleton was returning to the Southwest, the place where he had campaigned against the Jicarilla Apaches in the mid-1850s, and the place where he had met Christopher "Kit" Carson, the man whom he would depend upon as his principal field commander in the near future.[4]

Carleton, in spite of his recognized ability and accomplishments, was known as a tyrannical, overbearing man whose demanding, unscrupulous leadership style and harsh disciplinary techniques occasionally bordered on cruelty toward his men. His autocratic attitude and abrasive temperament were betrayed by the perpetual frown that furrowed his forehead above sunken eyes, a visage that had gained him the nickname the "Great Mogul." C. L. Sonnichsen, the respected Apache historian, characterized Carleton thusly: "He had intelligence and foresight, driving energy, and a consuming ambition to do well. . . . His trouble was that he could not admit an error, change his mind, or take a backward step."[5]

Colonel Carleton's blustery, self-righteous attitude toward subordinates and those civilians who dared cross him could be considered relatively benevolent, however, when compared with his opinion of the Indian, whom he characterized as being nothing less than wild game to be hunted down. His philosophy for stalking the red man was summarized in this passage of instructions given to a subordinate:

The troops must be kept after the Indians, not in big bodies, with military noises and smokes, and the gleam of arms by day, and fires, and talk, and comfortable sleeps by night; but in small parties moving steathily to their haunts and lying patiently in wait for them; or by following their tracks day after day with a fixed purpose that never gives up. . . . If a hunter goes after deer, he tries all sorts of wiles to get within gunshot of it. An Indian is more watchful and a more wary animal than a deer. He must be hunted with skill; he cannot be blundered upon; nor will he allow his pursuers to come upon him when he knows it, unless he is stronger.[6]

On March 15, Carleton, while leading his column across the dusty, desolate desert, dispatched a small advance unit, commanded by Capt. William McCleave, toward Tucson with orders to chase away the Confederates under Capt. Sherrod Hunter, who presently occupied the city. Hunter, however, managed to capture McCleave in the Pima villages near present-day Phoenix.

Meanwhile, some of Hunter's men were moving down the Gila River and raided a number of Federal supply depots. At Stanwix Station, about eighty miles from the Colorado River, these raiders happened upon a detachment of Carleton's troopers. In the ensuing skirmish, one California volunteer was wounded, but Hunter's men were forced to run for their lives. This confrontation became a footnote in history as the westernmost engagement of the war between Union and Confederate troops.[7]

Carleton, in the meantime, had sent out another advance unit of 272 men under Capt. William Calloway with orders to capture Tucson and liberate Captain McCleave. A detachment of Calloway's force, led by Lt. James Barrett, had an encounter with Confederates at Picacho Peak, north of Tucson. Barrett was killed, and Calloway withdrew westward until reaching a large advance unit from Carleton's main column.

On June 7, Carleton and his California Column marched triumphantly into Tucson in the not yet officially established Territory of Arizona. At that time, Carleton received word that he had been promoted to brigadier general and promptly proclaimed himself military governor. He set out to clean up the town and, to that end, had his men round up undesirables, such as gamblers, outlaws, and Southern sympathizers—including one irate wealthy mine owner—who were then imprisoned at Fort Yuma.[8]

The object of the general's military mission, however, would not be to corral gamblers, outlaws, or Confederates, but to make Arizona and New Mexico safe for travelers and army supply convoys. And his primary obstacle would be the Apache Indians.

The Apaches, known as courageous fighters and shrewd tacticians, had proven themselves formidable enemies to both whites and rival Indian tribes. The tribe was divided into small, independent bands that roamed a large territory in the rugged mountains and deserts of present-day Arizona and south-central New Mexico, raiding ranches, settlements, and supply trains, and selling their captives into slavery. From the outbreak of the Civil War, the Apaches had relentlessly attacked settlers, miners, stagelines, and Confederate army troops in an effort to rid their territory of all outsiders. Carleton's recently arrived Californians now became their primary target, and it was not long before they made their presence known.

On June 15, General Carleton dispatched three couriers with a message informing Colonel Canby in New Mexico that the California Column was on its way. These men were riding through the San Simon Valley, a few miles east of Apache Pass, when they unwittingly stumbled onto a group of secreted Chiricahua Apache led by Chief Cochise.

The thirty-eight-year-old Cochise, of all the Apache leaders, traditionally had been most tolerant, even accommodating to whites. During the 1850s, he had graciously granted safe passage to Americans headed to California. Some of his people had supplied wood to the stage station in Apache Pass, and use of the spring by Overland Mail coach passengers and livestock had been permitted there.

That all changed, however, in February 1861, when Lt. George N. Bascom held a parley with Cochise at Apache Pass and accused the chief of stealing cattle and kidnapping a six-year-old boy, crimes of which Cochise was innocent. Bascom, who apparently was convinced of Cochise's guilt, attempted to seize the Indian delegation as hostages, and a fight broke out. One Apache was killed, and the rest were taken prisoner. Cochise was severely wounded in the fray and grabbed by the soldiers, but he subsequently slashed his way out of a tent and escaped. He responded by capturing a Butterfield Overland Mail employee and two hapless travelers, and offered them in exchange for the Indian hostages. Bascom refused unless the cattle and the boy were included in the trade. When negotiations broke down, both sides killed their hostages. Cochise then went on the warpath, killing, burning, stealing livestock, and virtually shutting down all traffic through Apache Pass and the surrounding area.[9]

This one act by an inept, inexperienced army officer made Cochise an enemy of all Americans and incited twenty-five years of warfare. Now Colonel Carleton's couriers were going to pay the price for Lieutenant Bascom's lack of judgment, when Cochise and his Chiricahua warriors ambushed the soldiers east of Apache Pass on June 15. Two were killed, and a third escaped to the Rio Grande, only to be captured by the Confederates under Sibley who were being routed by Canby's troops. Carleton, by the way, was at that time unaware that Sibley had decided to retreat to San Antonio upon learning that the California Column was approaching and had fully intended to engage the Rebels.[10]

Several days later, Carleton ordered Lt. Col. Edward E. Eyre, with 140 men from Companies B and C of the 1st California Cavalry, to make an advance reconnaissance to the Rio Grande between Tucson and Mesilla. These troops had halted at Apache Pass to water the horses when they were confronted by Cochise and about seventy-five warriors. Eyre had been ordered to avoid any conflict with Indians, if possible, and although his men heard several rifle shots nearby, he held a parley with Cochise to profess his peaceful intentions. Cochise was perhaps amused by the officer's naivete but nonetheless did not attack. The shots that had been heard earlier, however, had killed three of Eyre's troopers who had wandered away from the column. Their stripped and scalped bodies were located within an hour of Cochise's departure. Eyre made camp outside of Apache Pass, but for reasons known only to himself, he did not report the incident to Carleton.[11]

Meanwhile, Cochise gathered his warriors and began preparations to ambush the next party of soldiers that appeared at Apache Pass.

Carleton had decided to send his troops eastward in detachments, separated by an interval of a day or two. On July 10, he dispatched a twenty-two-team wagon train with 242 head of stock escorted by 126 infantry, cavalry, and a battery of two howitzers, under the command of Capt. Thomas L. Roberts of the 1st Infantry. Roberts, like Eyre, received orders to refrain from fighting unless absolutely necessary.

By early morning on July 12, Captain Roberts had reached the San Pedro River and, according to orders, left a detachment of men, under Capt. John C. Cremony, with the train to establish a supply base for the troops that would follow. Roberts, with about eighty infantrymen, eight cavalrymen, three wagons with five or six civilian teamsters, and the howitzers, then proceeded to Dragoon Springs. The soldiers rested at the springs for a day, then, at about 5:00 P.M. on July 14, resumed their eastward march toward Apache Pass, forty miles distant. Roberts, at that time, had not received any information about Captain Eyre's losses at that location.[12]

Hidden in the dark recesses along the route Roberts traversed were Apache scouts, who informed Cochise about every move made by the soldiers. Allied with Cochise was Mangas Coloradas, the elderly but fierce leader of the eastern band of Chiricahua. Mangas, who was in his early seventies, was the father-in-law of Cochise. The two chiefs had assembled a group of warriors estimated at anywhere between 100 and 800 at Apache Pass, the likely destination of the soldiers, and waited to spring an ambush.[13]

The Californians marched all night across Sulphur Springs Valley in an ordeal remembered by participant Sgt. Albert Fountain to have been "one never forgotten by those who made it; all night long the burdened infantry marched over the forty miles of dusty road, the heat was oppressive and the pace fast enough to test the muscles of men who had become hardened by their march from the Pacific coast."[14]

Roberts and his men approached along the Butterfield mail route through ravines and canyons that led to the abandoned mail station near Apache Pass. An advance unit of cavalry had arrived at that location and unsaddled to rest. The main body of troops, hot, thirsty, and in dire need of water, began arriving about noon on that July 15.

The Apache commanded the approaches to the spring at Apache Pass and had devised a two-pronged strategy for their attack. Mangas Coloradas and his warriors were positioned in an ambush site behind rocks on the steep slopes along the trail, while Cochise's men were posted on hills behind rocks and breastworks south and north of the spring.

When the soldiers, with nothing but the thought of water on their minds, passed Cochise's position, the order was given, and the Chiricahua opened fire on the rear guard. The initial volley killed one man and wounded one or two teamsters.

Roberts immediately wheeled up the two light howitzers and commenced firing into the hillsides. The Apache answered this tactic by leaving their positions and closing with the soldiers to fight in vicious hand-to-hand combat. Infantry troops managed to drive back the Indians, who then stubbornly dug into their positions, denying the soldiers access to the water. Roberts divided his command into two platoons, one of which was deployed with instructions to secure the spring and hold it no matter the cost. The second platoon, with the howitzers, maintained fire on the hillside. The platoon that dashed for the water, however, was within fifty yards of the prize when the Apache unleashed a tremendous volley that forced them to retreat. The two sides, both determined to control the precious water resource, then began taunting and cursing at each other, while Captain Roberts formulated another plan.[15]

Within minutes, twenty volunteers, under Sgt. Albert Fountain, broke from the line to storm the highest hill near the springs and eventually managed to dislodge the enemy. Meanwhile, the remainder of the command dashed to the water and hastily filled their canteens, while the howitzers were moved to the high ground. Roberts then dispatched six cavalrymen to warn the supply train. These men were soon overtaken by a group of fifteen or twenty Indians, led by Mangas Coloradas. The Indians quickly shot most of the horses and wounded one trooper.[16]

During this brief action, Mangas Coloradas was severely wounded— shot in the chest—and thought to be in desperate condition, perhaps near death. The elderly chief was carried from the field by his warriors and transported to the town of Janos, Chihuahua, to seek medical aid from a doctor there.[17]

One of the troopers in the party, Pvt. John Teal, who had allegedly shot Mangas, escaped and—carrying his saddle and gear—began walking. Eight miles and four hours later, Teal arrived at the supply train camp near Ewell's Spring and reported to Captain Cremony.

Roberts, unaware of Teal's heroics, deployed half of his troops in a defensive position and rode with the remainder to alert the supply train. After resting for several hours with the train at Ewell's Springs, the entire 150-man command returned to Apache Pass to discover that the Indians had reoccupied the spring. The howitzers were brought into play, the infantry was deployed as skirmishers, and a vicious fight ensued, with the Indians eventually being driven back. By 4:00 P.M., the battle for control of the springs at Apache Pass ended when Cochise broke contact and led his warriors toward Sonora.[18]

Captain Roberts reported two killed and two wounded in the engagement. Indian casualties were estimated at nine dead, although an Apache eyewitness later set that number at more than sixty.[19]

Brig. Gen. James H. Carleton, escorted by two companies of cavalry and one of infantry, arrived at Apache Pass on July 27. Capt. Thomas Roberts, whose bravery under fire had been duly noted by his commander, recommended that a fort be established near the springs in order to avoid further conflicts over the water. Carleton agreed and issued General Order No. 12, which decreed that Fort Bowie—in honor of Col. George W. Bowie, commander of the 5th California Infantry, whose men would be occupying the post—be established near the abandoned stage station. The stone and adobe fort, with its garrison of one company, would be charged with not only protecting the spring, but also keeping communications open on both sides of the Chiricahua Mountains. This post would remain operational until 1894.[20]

At that time, Carleton vowed to make Cochise and Mangas Coloradas pay dearly for having the audacity to attack his command, an act that he considered a personal affront.

It was mid-August by the time the entire column of Carleton's troops had reached the Rio Grande in a march that greatly impressed Maj. Gen. Henry W. Halleck, who said in Washington: "It is one of the most creditable marches on record. I only wish our Army here had the mobility and endurance of the California troops."[21]

Carleton, however, was disappointed that Sibley's Rebels had been chased out of the territory before he had arrived, saying that "it would be a sad disappointment" for his men to march back home without having fought the enemy. General Canby authorized Carleton to ride into Texas in search of Confederates, an excursion which, after about 200 miles, yielded no resistance from the enemy.[22]

In September, Brig. Gen. Edward Canby was ordered East for reassignment. He would serve two years as assistant adjutant general in Washington, then command troops in the 1863 draft riots. In May 1864, he was promoted to major general and assigned command of the Military Division of West Mississippi. Canby captured Mobile in April 1865 and accepted the surrender of the last Confederate army in the field. After the war, Canby was given the rank of brigadier general and command of the Department of the Columbia. In 1878, he was murdered by Modoc Indians in California while leading a peace mission.

After Canby's departure, Brig. Gen. James H. Carleton assumed command of the Military Department of New Mexico on September 18, 1862. Leadership of the California Column was handed over to newly appointed Brig. Gen. Joseph R. West, who would be assigned leadership of the new District of Arizona, which included the Mesilla Valley and surrounding territory. Carleton had for all intents and purposes become the absolute ruler of New Mexico, and he intended to make his presence known.[23]

Inasmuch as the Confederate threat had been for the time being alleviated, the general turned his attention to ridding the territory that skirted the Rio Grande of those troublesome Indians, who had increased their raids of settlements and travelers. The disposition of the Mimbres and Chiricahua Apache was left to General West, and Carleton decided to focus on the Mescalero. He embraced the anger of the local New Mexicans, who pointed out that this tribe had made a treaty with the United States but had taken advantage of their recent vulnerability to resume hostilities.

The Mescalero lived in the mountain ranges of southeastern New Mexico, between the Rio Grande and Pecos River. Their basic subsistence came from hunting and gathering the mescal plant, from which their Spanish name was derived. The Mescalero had a tradition of raiding neighboring tribes and white settlements, which made them a target for retaliation by the U.S. Army. In 1854 and 1855, campaigns by Ewell, Sturgis, and Miles had resulted in a treaty that granted the Mescalero a reservation in the area of Sierra Blanca, where Fort Stanton had been established to guard them. Government-supplied rations had been few and far between during the preceding six years, and the Mescalero had eked out a meager living by hunting game, which was sparse; farming, which was relatively unsuccessful; and the occasional raid of livestock from nearby settlements. But when Fort Stanton was abandoned in July 1861 and rations were cut off, the chiefs lost control of the young men. Aggressive warriors increased their attacks on whites from the vicinity of Fort Union in the north to the settlements on the Rio Grande around Mesilla and Las Cruces. The Mescalero had stolen large numbers of horses, mules, donkeys, cattle, and sheep, and in the process wantonly killed those whom they encountered—during August 1861 alone, forty men had been killed and many other whites taken captive.[24]

Carleton wasted little time in planning his campaign or selecting a leader. He summoned the man whom he had come to trust and admire when they had campaigned together against the Jicarilla Apache in northern New Mexico in 1854—Christopher "Kit" Carson.

Carson had been born in 1809 in Madison County, Kentucky, but spent most of his early life in the Boone's Lick district of western Missouri, where he was apprenticed as a saddler and harness maker. That profession, however, did not suit young Kit, and in 1826, he ran away from home on a wagon train to Santa Fe, New Mexico. He eventually settled in Taos and soon earned a solid reputation as a fur trapper, mountain man, and guide on three of John C. Frémont's expeditions. His bravery during the Mexican War as a member of Frémont's Battalion of Mounted Riflemen made him nationally famous, and he spent the last year of the war as a personal courier for President James K. Polk, carrying messages to commanders in the Far West. After 1849, Carson settled with his wife, Josefa, on a ranch near Taos and raised sheep. He was appointed Federal Indian agent for Northern New Mexico in 1853. Carson resigned that post at the outbreak of the Civil War and helped organize the 1st New Mexico Infantry, for which he served as a lieutenant colonel. He further distinguished himself in the February 1862 battle at Valverde, and again the following month at La Glorieta Pass.[25]

General Carleton dispatched Carson, with five companies of the 1st New Mexico, to reoccupy Fort Stanton. On October 12, the general issued orders to Carson for the conduct of the campaign against the Mescalero:

All Indian men of that tribe are to be killed whenever and wherever you can find them. The women and children will not be harmed, but you will take them prisoners and feed them at Fort Stanton until you receive other instruction about them. If the Indians send in a flag and desire to treat for peace, say to the bearer that when the people of New Mexico were attacked by the Texans, the

Mescaleros broke their treaty of peace, and murdered innocent people, and ran off their stock; that now our hands are untied, and you have been sent to punish them for their treachery and their crimes; that you have no power to make peace; that you are there to kill them wherever you can find them; that if they beg for peace, their chiefs and twenty of their principal men must come to Santa Fe to have a talk there.

You will keep after their people and slay them until you receive orders to desist from these headquarters; that this making of treaties for them to break whenever they have an interest in breaking them will not be done any more; that that time has passed by; that we have no faith in their promises; that we believe if we kill some of their men in fair, open war, they will be apt to remember that it will be better for them to remain at peace than to be at war. I trust that this severity, in the long run, will be the most humane course that could be pursued toward these Indians.[26]

Some historians have interpreted these as "extermination orders." On closer examination, however, the fact that Carleton made a point that the women and children be spared tends to discount much of that theory. The orders were certainly harsh but can be construed as an indication of Carleton's determination to make an impact on the minds of his enemy. He intended to put an end to this conflict, one way or another, and it was the choice of the Mescalero as to which course of action would be taken by the army—a peace treaty or all-out war. That was not to say that Carleton did not desire to punish them for past transgressions, for he did not believe that the Indians could be trusted to keep their word in the future any more than they had in the past.

Colonel Carson, who had enjoyed periods of friendship with certain Mescalero leaders and understood their culture, was said to have had mixed emotions about these orders. He knew that the tribe had turned to violence as an act of desperation due to their poor conditions. They were an impoverished people, lacked adequate weapons, and had been placed by treaty in an area where daily life was a hardship. The raids had been about the only way in which they could find food for survival. Nonetheless, Carson, the obedient soldier, marched with elements of his regiment to reactivate Fort Stanton.

The presence of Carson and his fighting New Mexicans had an alarming affect on the Mescalero, many of whom fled south to seek sanctuary in the Sacramento and Guadalupe Mountains. Other tribe members gathered at the fort, perhaps out of fear or simply seeking something to eat. Carson, at this point, likely believed that a protracted military operation could be avoided in favor of diplomacy.

Violence, however, was inevitable. Soon after the regiment had taken to the field, one of Carson's companies, commanded by Capt. James "Paddy" Graydon, a veteran of Valverde, located a group of Mescalero, led by two prominent chiefs, the elderly Manuelito and José Largo. The chiefs were said to have been taking their people to Santa Fe in an effort to secure peace.

Upon seeing the soldiers, Manuelito raised his hand to indicate his peaceful intentions. Graydon apparently ignored the gesture and ordered his men to open fire. In the ensuing volley, Manuelito, José Largo, nine warriors, and one woman were killed. The frightened Mescaleros fled but were ridden down by the troops, who killed five and wounded several more before the others escaped. Graydon's troops then rounded up the Mescalero's stock, selling some of the animals along the way to defray expenses, and reported back to Fort Stanton.

This incident greatly disturbed Kit Carson and led Carleton to instruct the colonel to investigate the matter. "If you are satisfied that Graydon's attack on Manuelita [*sic*] and his people was not fair and open," Carleton told Carson, "see that all the horses and mules . . . are returned to the survivors of Manuelito's band." There was no mention, however, of a reprimand for Graydon, who professed that it was the Indians who had initiated hostilities.

Meanwhile, California troops commanded by Capt. William McCleave—who had been liberated from the Confederates when Carleton arrived in Tucson—were patrolling southwest of Fort Stanton and managed to sneak up on a band of about 100 Mescalero warriors at a stronghold in the Sacramento Mountains at Dog Canyon, above the White Sands. McCleave's men killed several of the Indians and captured a number of others; the remaining members of the band hurried to the fort and surrendered to Kit Carson.[27]

Carson subsequently sent three chiefs—Cadete, Chato, and Estrella—to Santa Fe with their government agent for a peace parley with General Carleton. Cadete maintained his dignity when he surrendered to the general with these words:

> You are stronger than we. We have fought you so long as we had rifles and powder; but your weapons are better than ours. Give us weapons and turn us loose, and we will fight you again; but we are worn out; we have no more heart; we have no provisions, no

means to live; your troops are everywhere; our springs and water-holes are either occupied or overlooked by your young men. You have driven us from our last and best stronghold, and we have no more heart. Do with us as may seem good to you, but do not forget that we are men and braves.[28]

Carson, rather than obey to the letter Carleton's standing order and resume his campaign to shed more blood, suspended operations and remained at the fort. After all, most of the hostile Mescalero were already in custody. And Graydon's actions of cutting down the Indians under the flag of truce had soured Carson, and perhaps Carleton, on the prospects of igniting further hostilities that would make it more difficult to secure the surrender of the remaining Indians.[29]

Carleton had established a new post, named Fort Sumner—in honor of Col. Edwin Sumner—near the Pecos River in a stand of timber on the grasslands of eastern New Mexico known as Bosque Redondo, or Round Grove. This place, which offered excellent wood, grazing, and water resources, had long been a favorite camping place of the Mescalero whenever they ventured onto the plains. Carleton viewed Bosque Redondo as an ideal location at which to resettle all those members of the Mescalero tribe who had surrendered. The garrison that manned the post would be responsible for feeding the people until they were able to grow their own food. These Indians would also be protected; their brethren who chose to remain at large would be hunted down and killed.

Carson was ordered to continue operations against the Mescalero, sending any band that surrendered to Bosque Redondo. "The result of this will be that, eventually," Carleton wrote, "we shall have the whole tribe at the Bosque Redondo, and then we can conclude a definite treaty, and let them all return again to inhabit their proper country." Unfortunately, that would not be the case.[30]

While Carson entered the final stages of his campaign against the Mescalero, General Carleton became concerned about reports that Mangas Coloradas and his Chiricahua, or Mimbreno, Apache had resumed raiding in their old haunts around southwestern New Mexico.

Gold had been discovered in the summer of 1860 in the foothills of the Mogollon Mountains at Pinos Altos—near present-day Silver City—and thousands of miners had flooded the area to prospect in the old Spanish copper mines. This intrusion into the domain of the Gila Apache had been met with fierce opposition. The Indians, taking advantage of the collapse of Federal authority in the area at the outbreak of the Civil War, commenced a campaign of terror to rid the area of the miners. Led by Chiricahua chief Mangas Coloradas, the Apache had chased off or killed most of the miners and settlers by the summer of 1862, with perhaps only thirty or so remaining who were presently desperate for relief. To be fair, some accounts have questioned whether the culprit in these attacks was actually Mangas Coloradas. Other Apache bands, under Geronimo, Victorio, and Nana, were operating in that area, and it has been said that Mangas had by that time lost his zeal for war.[31]

Nonetheless, Carleton vowed to deliver this region of valuable mineral deposits from the clutches of the dangerous Mangas Coloradas. He promptly ordered Brig. Gen. Joseph R. West to establish a post in the vicinity of Pinos Altos, which would become known as Fort West, and wage war on the Chiricahua in the same manner as Kit Carson had with the Mescalero. West was told to "immediately organize a suitable expedition to chastise what is known as Mangas Colorado's [*sic*] Band of Gila Apaches. The campaign to be made by this expedition must be a vigorous one and the punishment of that band of murderers must be thorough and sharp."[32]

The army's new public enemy number one, Mangas Coloradas, or Red Sleeves, had been born in New Mexico, perhaps in the Mimbres Mountains, about 1791, which made him more than seventy years old. His early life had been occupied with raids into Chihuahua and Sonora, Mexico, a practice that continued through the years as a normal way of life for the Apache. He quickly earned a reputation for intelligence, wisdom, and physical prowess, the last in part attributed to his extraordinary size. Mangas was well over six feet tall at a time when the average Apache stood five feet, six inches. By his twenties, he was made war chief of the Mimbres band. He married only one woman, Carmen, when others of his tribe customarily took several brides. Carmen bore him three sons and three daughters.

Eventually, in retaliation for this raiding by Mangas and his warriors, the Mexican government placed a $100 bounty on Apache scalps. In 1837, Mangas and some members of his tribe were invited by a group of trappers to attend a great feast. Instead of feeding the Indians, however, the trappers attempted to kill them in order to redeem the bounty on their scalps. Mangas and his people fought back and managed to kill most of the trappers, then commenced raiding nearby mining settlements.

In 1846, the United States assumed possession of New Mexico, and Mangas signed a treaty of friendship with Gen. Stephen W. Kearny. A dispute over captives taken by the Chiricahua, however, led to a resumption of hostilities. Mangas signed another treaty in 1852, but a few days later, he was beaten by some miners at Pinos Altos and began raiding again. He eventually joined forces with his son-in-law, Cochise, and the two chiefs embarked on a reign of terror against the whites.[33]

Carleton's troops had already encountered Cochise and Mangas Coloradas at Apache Pass the previous July. During that battle, Mangas had been severely wounded by a bullet in the chest. His people had carried him more than 100 miles to a doctor in the town of Janos. The doctor had been warned that if Mangas died, the town would also die. Both Mangas and the town were spared.[34]

Perhaps old age, not to mention the serious wound, had mellowed the defiance that Mangas had displayed throughout his life. Although Cochise entertained no such thoughts, Mangas, while recuperating in September 1862, had decided that his best course would be to make peace with the army. He had always considered himself peaceful toward the United States, believing that violations of the treaties he had signed had been the fault of the other party.

At Acoma, Mangas dispatched an intermediary, a prominent member of that pueblo, to ascertain whether entreaties for peace would be welcomed. The messenger relayed the chief's request to Capt. Julius C. Shaw, who in turn wrote General Carleton:

> At present Mangas lives at Mogoyon [Mogollon Mountains], formerly lived at Cuero [more likely Santa Lucia] where himself & people used to till the land and were at peace with the world until the troops attacked & killed many of his people. After the third assault he states he armed himself in self-defense but is now anxious for peace and wishes to return to his former home and pursuits, and to live like a Christian. He would have come himself in person but was afraid of the Mexicans killing him.[35]

Carleton responded to the request in a note to General West: "Mangas Coloradas sends me word he wants peace, but I have no faith in him." Further, Carleton ordered West to begin gathering intelligence about the whereabouts of Mangas in order to mount an offensive against the chief and his band of Chiricahua, who were said to be committing outrages against travelers and settlers in the Pinos Altos mining district.[36]

In early 1863, Mangas returned to the Pinos Altos area and petitioned local citizens and the few soldiers there for peace and food. The Chiricahua were issued some beef, blankets, and other supplies. Mangas at that time promised to return within two weeks and said that if the whites were at that time sincere about wanting peace and would provide adequate rations, he would bring in his entire band. His beleaguered people were desperate for peace and wanted nothing more than to settle at their former home of Santa Lucia and return to planting crops.[37]

By this time, General West had departed Mesilla with 250 men headed for Fort McLane, which was presently unoccupied and would serve as a temporary headquarters for his expedition against Mangas Coloradas. Rumors reached the column that Mangas had been seen around the Pinos Altos area. An advance guard of twenty soldiers from the 1st California Cavalry, under Capt. Edmund D. Shirland, guided by Juan Arroyo, New Mexico's best Apache scout, was dispatched in pursuit of the Chiricahua chief.[38]

Upon arrival at Fort McLane, the soldiers encountered a group of about forty prospectors under the leadership of Joseph R. Walker. This legendary mountain man and adventurer, who was a mountain of a man at six feet, four inches tall and weighing more than 200 pounds, was one of the few frontiersmen whose actual deeds equaled or surpassed his legend. He had roamed the West since 1825 and was presently returning with his party to Arizona after a trek that had taken him gold hunting in California, east through the Grand Canyon to Colorado, and southward along the Continental Divide to prospect in the Pinos Altos area.

Along the way, Walker's party had skirmished several times with local Apache, and they sought a manner in which to assure their safety for the remainder of their trip. A scheme was hatched that called for the capture of an Apache chief. If they could hold this tribal leader until they departed the mining district, they believed, the party would be able to venture freely anywhere they wished.[39]

This devious idea fit very nicely into the mission of Captain Shirland, and it was decided that the target of the prospectors would be none other than Mangas Coloradas. On January 16, a number of Walker's men, led by Jack Swilling, a local man who had recently joined the party, accompanied the command as it marched for Pinos Altos and, they hoped, a rendezvous with Mangas. The column arrived shortly after sunrise, hoisted a white flag, sent out word that the army wanted to talk peace, and settled in to wait for the appearance of the Chiricahua chief.[40]

While the soldiers were secreted in the chaparral and old shacks within the mining community, Mangas Coloradas was meeting with other tribal leaders to plead his case for peace. Geronimo, Victorio, and Nana attempted to dissuade Mangas from this risky peace overture, but the elderly chief, a veteran of signing treaties with the United States, was resolute in his belief that peace could be attained.[41]

It was about noon on January 17 when Indians were noticed approaching the outskirts of Pinos Altos. One of them was considerably over six feet tall, broad-shouldered and muscular, with hair that fell to his waist. He was wearing a straw hat, checked cotton shirt, breechcloth, and a pair of moccasins that rose to his knees. This impressive Apache was none other then Chief Mangas Coloradas.

Daniel Ellis Conner, a member of Jack Swilling's party, described the scene:

> Suddenly Swilling issued a war whoop that might have made an Apache ashamed of himself. There was only a short delay when Mangas, a tremendously big man, with over a dozen Indians for a bodyguard following, was seen in the distance walking on an old mountain trail toward us, evidently observing us intently. A precipace [sic] broke down the mountain between the two parties and the trail bent up to cross it at a shallow place, probably 150 yards from us. Jack left us and walked to meet Mangas, who, with his bodyguard slowly but decisively crossed the ravine. Swilling, though six feet tall, looked like a boy beside Mangas.
>
> They both could speak broken Spanish. We could not hear what they said, but Swilling looked back at us. We interpreted the look to mean that he wanted to be covered. When our squad suddenly leveled our guns upon the party, for the first time Mangas showed appreciation of his serious position. Swilling went up to him and laid his hand on the chief's shoulder and finally convinced him that resistance meant destruction of the whole party. They came walking toward us, bodyguard and all. When Swilling told Mangas that his bodyguard wasn't wanted, he stopped with some gutturals and finally instructed them in Spanish, "Tell my people to look for me when they see me!" When we passed back over the summit the soldiers came out of their concealment, disgusting Mangas beyond measure.[42]

The capture had been perfectly executed without a shot fired—and without the assistance of the army troops, although Captain Shirland claimed credit for the deed in his report dated January 22, 1863.

On January 18, Mangas was spirited away to Fort McLane, escorted by the soldiers and Swilling's men. Along the way, one of Mangas's sons approached the column and was permitted to speak to his father. From all accounts, this meeting was quite emotional, for Mangas apparently understood that his situation was grave. His son was said to have departed with tears in his eyes.[43]

At Fort McLane, the prisoner was turned over to Brig. Gen. Joseph R. West for a private interrogation. Mangas towered over West, who, according to eyewitness Clark Stocking, "looked like a pigmy next to the old chief."[44]

Mangas had expected West to entertain his peace entreaties, but instead, the general blamed the chief for every depredation that had been committed in southern New Mexico. "You have murdered your last white victim, you old scoundrel," West raged. He added that "the remainder of [Mangas's] days would be spent as a prisoner in the hands of the United States authorities; that his family would be permitted to join him and they would be well treated."[45]

West apparently was less than sincere in his description of Mangas's fate and instead had decided to assume the role of both judge and jury. Clark Stocking claimed to have overheard West's instructions to the guard: "Men, that old murderer has got away from every soldier command and has left a trail of blood for 50 miles on the old stage line. I want him dead or alive tomorrow morning, do you understand? I want him dead."[46]

January 18, 1863, was a bitterly cold night, and the only fire that burned was the one maintained by the soldiers who guarded Mangas in an open adobe building. One of those guards was Daniel Ellis Conner, who wrote: "About 9 o'clock I noticed the soldiers were doing something to Mangas, but quit when I returned to the fire and stopped to get warm."

At about 1:00 A.M. on January 19, Conner walked leisurely back from the far end of his beat and observed the sentinels' pranks:

> I could see them plainly by the firelight as they were engaged in heating their fixed bayonets in the fire and putting them to the feet and naked legs of Mangas, who from time to time would shield his limbs from the hot steel. When I came up to the fire each time they would become innocent and sleepy and remain so until I departed on my beat again, when they would arouse themselves into the decided spirit of indulging this barbarous pastime.
>
> I was about midway of my beat and approaching the firelight. Just then Mangas raised himself upon his left elbow and began to expostulate in a vigorous way by telling the sentinels in Spanish that he was no child to be playing with. But his expostulations were cut short, for he had hardly begun his exclamation when both sentinels promptly brought down their minnie [*sic*] muskets to bear on him and fired, nearly at the same time through his body.

The chief fell back off his elbow into the same position in which he had been lying all the forepart of the night. This was quickly followed by two shots through the head by each sentinel's six-shooter, making in all, six shots fired in rapid succession. The old chief died without a struggle in the precise position that he had occupied continuously since dark.[47]

Another version of the story, related by Clark Stocking, claimed that Sgt. Henry Foljaine rushed into the room and shot Mangas in the head. This story was corroborated by New York phrenologist Orson Squire Fowler, who later examined the old chief's skull and found only one wound in the back of the head.[48]

The entire camp was roused by the sound of shots, but the men returned to their blankets when informed that it had only been an attempted escape by an Apache, who had been shot and killed. General West appeared and, after confirming that Mangas was dead, relieved the guard and told them to get some sleep.[49]

West then dispatched two patrols—one under Capt. William McCleave, the other led by Capt. Edmund Shirland—with intentions of attacking Mangas's band before they could receive word of their leader's execution.

McCleave and twenty cavalrymen rode for Pinos Altos. Later that day, a group of Mangas's people peacefully approached the town. McCleave ordered his men to attack, and accompanied by a number of local miners, they tore into the band of vulnerable Indians. When the firing had ceased, at least eleven Chiricahua Apache had been killed, including Mangas's wife and one of his sons, and many others had been wounded.

Meanwhile, Shirland's fifty cavalrymen happened upon a camp of Victorio's band "located on one of the most rugged, high, and difficult mountains to ascend and pass" that they had ever seen. Shirland accepted the offer by the Indians to surrender and gave them some food to eat as a goodwill gesture. He then ordered his men to open fire on the eating Apache. The volley killed nine and sent the others in a desperate flight for their lives. Shirland also captured thirty-four head of stock, which included government mules stolen the previous year.

Both patrols later rode triumphantly into Fort McLane with scalps "dangling from their saddles."[50]

At noon on the day of Mangas's murder, his body was unceremoniously dumped into a shallow grave. His scalp had been removed, and a few days later his head was severed, then boiled, the skull sent to that noted New York phrenologist. The skull, which was said to have been larger than that of Daniel Webster, was added to the collection at the Smithsonian Institution and placed on public display.[51]

General West defended his actions in his official report, the veracity of which must be questioned. He claimed that he had detailed seven men, including a noncommissioned officer, to guard Mangas, who had already made two escape attempts, "and he was killed at midnight while he was rushing his guard to escape." West professed that he had done everything possible to protect the chief: "I have thus dwelt at length upon this matter in order to show that even with a murderous Indian, whose life is clearly forfeited by all laws, either human or divine, wherever found, the good faith of the U.S. Military authorities was in no way compromised." He also failed to mention the conspiracy with Walker's adventurers at Pinos Altos, saying that Mangas had been caught "red-handed in a fight with the soldiers," or any torture inflicted on Mangas that might have encouraged him to resist.[52]

The cold-blooded murder of Mangas Coloradas was a reprehensible act to the Apache, but worse was the fact that he had been mutilated. According to Apache beliefs, Mangas's body would now be destined to go through eternity in its butchered condition.

Brig. Gen. Henry Carleton was predictably elated upon hearing the news from Fort McLane. "Mangas Coloradas," he gloated in a dispatch to Washington, "doubtless the worst Indian within our boundaries and one who has been the cause of more murders and torturing and burning at the stake in this country than all together—has been killed."[53]

The execution of Mangas Coloradas, the one Indian in the Southwest who had truly desired peace with the whites, and perhaps could have convinced others to follow suit, without question prolonged hostilities between the whites and Apache. The Indians could have accepted his death had it occurred honorably in battle. But they were incensed that he had been grabbed under a flag of truce and brutally murdered, then horribly mutilated. Other chiefs—Victorio and Cochise, in particular—made plans to intensify their raiding. In future acts of revenge, the Apache would apply the same treatment to the bodies of their victims—including decapitation.

On February 3, 1863, Col. Kit Carson submitted a letter of resignation to General Carleton. He had joined the army to fight Confederates, and in the event of another invasion, he wrote, it would be his "pride and pleasure" to serve. But, he continued, "at present I feel that my duty as well as my happiness, directs me to my home & family and trust that the General will accept my resignation."

Carleton, however, set out to persuade Carson to remain in the army. He showered the colonel with praise for Carson's remarkable achievement in effecting the surrender and deportation to Bosque Redondo of nearly the entire Mescalero tribe within a period of only three months. There were other Indian enemies to fight, Carleton assured him, and Carson fit into the general's plans for the future. Therefore, Col. Christopher Carson would remain on active duty until his services were no longer required.[54]

By March 1863, more than 400 Mescalero had been settled at Bosque Redondo; another 100 or so had taken to the hills and resumed raiding. These were aggressively pursued. The Indians who had submitted were put to work digging irrigation ditches and planting, in what turned out to be a futile effort to raise crops. Carleton had made a mistake frequently made by government treaties—he had ignored the culture of the hunter Apache and attempted to transform them into farmer Pueblo Indians.[55]

In the future, the Mescalero would not be the only inhabitants of Bosque Redondo. As Carleton continued his efforts to subdue the Apache, he also prepared for operations against the tribe that he considered the greatest threat to New Mexico—the Navajo.

And as for Joe Walker and his band of prospectors, they would resume their search for gold in Arizona—without an Apache chief to guarantee their safety.

CHAPTER FIVE

Sibley, Sully, and the Sioux

THE VICTORY IN THE SEPTEMBER 23, 1862, BATTLE OF WOOD LAKE against the Dakota Sioux by Col. Henry Hastings Sibley had been an unqualified success.

In the month or so prior to the battle, the uprising by the Indians in western Minnesota had destroyed thousands of acres of crops, burned hundreds of homes, killed some 800 whites of all ages, subjected many girls and women to savage forms of rape and torture, and made captives of many whites and mixed-breeds. Sibley's victory at Wood Lake, however, had marked the end of organized warfare by that tribe in Minnesota. The hostiles had been driven from the state, and the prisoners were about to be rescued. The fact that Little Crow remained at large was of little consequence. Six days after Wood Lake, Sibley, although denounced at times for his patience, or extreme caution, in pursuing his enemy, was rewarded with a promotion to brigadier general.

Perhaps the most satisfying—and heartrending—aspect of the operation for Sibley and his men was the rescue of the white and mixed-blood captives. This occurred at about noon on September 26, 1862, when the troops finally reached the camp of the friendlies, where the prisoners were being held. By that time, the hostiles had scattered across the countryside.

Captive Samuel J. Brown, the seventeen-year-old mixed-blood son of Maj. Joseph Brown, described the reaction of the camp when the army was observed approaching:

> When the troops suddenly appeared on an eminence a mile away and there was no doubt that they were coming to our rescue the captives could hardly restrain themselves—some cried for joy, some went into fits or hysterics, and some fainted away. It was a joyful

95

scene, yet most sad and gloomy. No grander sight ever met the eyes of anybody than when the troops marched up with bayonets glistening in the bright noon day sun and colors flying, drums beating and fifes playing. I shall never forget it while I live. We could hardly realize that our deliverance had come.[1]

Isaac V. D. Heard, a St. Paul lawyer who was with Sibley's column, wrote:

The poor creatures wept for joy at their escape. They had watched for our coming for many a weary day, with constant apprehensions of death at the hands of their savage captors, and had almost despaired of seeing us. The woe written in the faces of the half starved and nearly naked women and children would have melted the hardest heart.[2]

Not all of these captives, however, were relieved or even joyful over their liberation from their Indian captors. Sibley wrote to his wife about one "rather handsome" white woman:

[She] had become so infatuated with the redskin who had taken her for a wife that although her white husband was still living at some point below and had been in search of her, she declared that were it not for her children, she would not leave her dusky paramour. . . . She threatens that if her Indian, who is among those who have been seized, should be hung, she will shoot those of us who have been instrumental in bringing him to the scaffold, and then go back to the Indians. A pretty specimen of a white woman she is, truly![3]

Sibley liberated a total of 107 whites and 162 mixed-breeds—269 prisoners in all. Most of the whites were women and children, with accounts varying from one to four as the number of white men, ages unknown, among them.[4]

These captives were indeed fortunate that they had remained alive by the time Sibley arrived to rescue them. They owed their safety to the "friendly" Dakota, who had taken custody of them after the hostiles had chosen to flee rather than resume the battle. According to captive Samuel J. Brown, Little Crow had other ideas for the captives two days after the battle, as the chief prepared to flee:

On Wednesday, the 24th, Little Crow called all his warriors together and told them to pack up and leave for the plains and save the women and children, the troops would soon be upon them and no time should be lost. "But," he said, "the captives must all be killed before we leave. They seek to defy us," he went on, "and dug trenches while we were away. They must die."

The camp of the friendlies, where trenches were dug and earth works thrown up, and where the captives had been secreted, was pitched a little way from the main or hostile camp, and was rapidly increasing in numbers so that the captives felt comparatively safe. Indeed, when the friendlies had threatened to take Little Crow and his whole camp and turn them over to the troops and several hundred of the hostiles had come over into our camp with their captives and vowed they would stand by us, we simply laughed at Little Crow's bombastic talk.[5]

Many of the released captives were taken by wagon to Fort Ridgely, while orphaned children were sent to various settlements for care. Some of the women would remain at Camp Release in order to point out those Indians who had committed crimes against the whites. Sibley was determined to punish in some manner those individual warriors who were responsible for the murders, rapes, and other atrocities that had rendered Minnesota a state of terror during the previous month.

Of course, it would be quite a task to ferret out the guilty parties from the nearly 2,000 Indians who finally had surrendered or been captured by the soldiers. These prisoners had been disarmed and placed under guard at Camp Release, a bivouac Sibley had established nearby, and a second compound near Yellow Medicine. Many of the Indians had remained peaceful throughout and had willingly surrendered. Sibley had deceived others by enticing them into his grasp with the promise that their annuities were about to paid but first they had to be counted. And yet others, entire extended families and small bands, had been wandering the prairie in near starvation and viewed submission to the soldiers as blessed relief from their miserable plight.[6]

The people of Minnesota echoed Sibley's sentiments with respect to the fate of the captured Indians and called for harsh punishment, without necessarily separating the guilty from the innocent. The editor of the *Goodhue County Republican* wrote, "They must be exterminated, and now is a good time to commence doing it." The Mankato *Semi-Weekly Record* stated, "The cruelty perpetrated by the Sioux nation in the past two weeks demand [*sic*] that our Government shall treat them for all time to come as outlaws, who have forfeited all right to property and life." And a letter to the editor of the Faribault *Central Republican* said, "Extermination, swift, sure, and terrible is the only thing that can give the people of Minnesota satisfaction, or a sense of security."[7]

On September 28, Colonel Sibley appointed a five-man military commission at Camp Release to gather evidence and conduct trials of those Dakota who had participated in the uprising. The members of this tribunal were Col. William Crooks; Maj. George Bradley; Capt. Hirum P. Grant; Capt. Hirum S. Bailey; Lt. Rollin C. Olin, who would serve as judge advocate; and recorder Isaac Heard.

This body of military officers, who would sit in judgment over the Dakota Sioux, became known by various unofficial names. Generals Pope and Sibley called it a "military commission." Gov. Alexander Ramsey referred to it as a "military court." Judge Charles E. Flandrau preferred to describe the proceedings as either a "court-martial" or "military tribunal." Inasmuch as neither military nor civilian law provided for such a procedure with respect to Indians, it could be regarded as an invention or creation of Sibley's.[8]

Rev. Stephen R. Riggs, who had founded a mission at Hazelwood and had accompanied Sibley on the campaign as chaplain and interpreter, was instrumental in gathering much of the evidence used to identify the perpetrators. The best source of information was twenty-seven-year-old Joseph Godfrey, or Otakle, an articulate mulatto who was married to an Indian woman. Godfrey had been the first prisoner tried, convicted, and sentenced to death, but he turned state's evidence and testified against his former comrades-in-arms. Godfrey, as a reward for his cooperation, later received a commuted sentence of ten years in prison, of which he served only three years.[9]

In the beginning, the work of the commission was slow and deliberate, and only about 120 cases had been disposed of by late October, with another 300 remaining on the docket. Missionary Stephen Riggs explained that the procedure was then altered:

> Instead of taking individuals for trial, against whom some specific charge could be brought, the plan was adopted to subject all grown men, with a few exceptions, to an investigation of the commission, trusting that the innocent could make their innocency appear. This was not possible in the case of the majority, as conviction was based on admission of being present at the battles.

Lawyer Isaac Heard went on to say that the logic of the white man at that time could be summed up as follows:

> The fact that they were <u>Indians</u> . . . would raise the moral certainty that, as soon as the first murders were committed, all the young men were impelled by the sight of blood and plunder . . . to become participants in the same class of acts.[10]

This procedure would appear to have contradicted the time-honored constitutional principle of law that forms the basis of the U.S. justice system, in which a person is considered innocent until proven guilty. Perhaps it was noted that the Dakota Sioux were not American citizens, and therefore such rules of law could be suspended—particularly when taking into consideration the pressure brought to bear on the tribunal by the outraged people of Minnesota.

Regardless of such technicalities, justice was dealt more speedily from that point in time. The tribunal measured guilt and innocence by the testimonies of the defendants, none of whom were represented by lawyers or permitted to present witnesses on their behalf. Those Indians who admitted to merely being in the vicinity of a battle, or bearing arms, were judged guilty. The commission—sometimes accommodating up to forty trials a day—completed its work on November 5. Isaac Heard explained: "The trials were elaborately conducted until the commission became acquainted with the details of different outrages and battles. Then, the only point being the connection of the prisoners with them, five minutes would dispose of a case."[11]

In total, 392 Dakota Indians were tried during the proceedings, with 323 convicted of complicity—307 of them sentenced to death by hanging and 16 handed lengthy prison terms. It can be safely assumed that most of the actual murderers and rapists were not included in this number, but had escaped Sibley's pursuit and remained at large, having fled for their lives. A high percentage of those who were convicted had made the mistake of being in the wrong place at the wrong time and apparently would pay for the crimes of their guilty brethren.[12]

On November 9, the condemned Indians were shackled together and, along with their dependents, transported by wagon from Camp Release downriver to Camp Lincoln, a hastily improvised prison at South Bend, west of Mankato. The caravan was greeted in New Ulm with a violent reaction from the angry townspeople, who descended upon the helpless prisoners with revenge on their minds.

Gabriel Renville, a mixed-blood raised by a full-blooded father, later told about the march of the condemned:

> On the way, when they were passing through the town of New Ulm, the whites were very much excited. Both men and women, coming with stones, bricks, and pitchforks, and anything they could lay their hands on, and rushing through the ranks of the soldiers who were guarding them, attacked the chained prisoners in the wagons, and knocked many of them senseless. The guards, striking these whites with their sabers, drove them back. Finally, with much difficulty, they were brought through the town.

In addition to the weapons mentioned above, the townspeople assaulted the Indians with pots full of scalding water, scissors, hoes, and knives. Sibley, in a letter to his wife, singled out the women of New Ulm when he wrote, "The Dutch she-devils were as fierce as tigresses." Fifteen Indians and several guards were injured in the melee.[13]

Those captive Sioux who had not been convicted—about 1,700, mostly old men, women, and children—were sent, in a four-mile-long procession, to an encampment near Fort Snelling, where it would be easier for the army to feed them. Along the way, they suffered the same fate as the convicts. The people of Henderson assaulted them with guns, clubs, and other weapons, injuring several, including a baby who later died. These Indians endured a miserable winter, living under guard in a fenced camp of tepees on the north bank of the Minnesota River. In spite of the high fence, settlers came and stole their horses and oxen. The older people were given bread to eat, and the children crackers. Measles broke out—the first time the Dakota had ever experienced this disease—and many died.[14]

The people of Minnesota welcomed the verdict of the military commission and were anxious for the executions to commence. President Abraham Lincoln, however, had been visited by Bishop Henry B. Whipple, the Episcopal bishop of the Missionary District of Minnesota, who interceded on behalf of the Dakota Sioux. The president said that Whipple, who blamed the white man as much as the Indian for hostilities, "talked with me about the rascality of this Indian business until I felt it down to my boots."[15]

Gen. John Pope telegraphed the names of the condemned Indians to Washington, at a cost of $400, which the *New York Times* suggested should be deducted from the general's paycheck. Lincoln responded: "Please forward as soon as possible the full and complete record of the convictions; if the record does not fully indicate the more guilty and influential of the culprits, please have a careful statement made on these points and forward to me. Send by mail."[16]

Lincoln appointed two men, George Whiting and Francis Ruggles, to carefully examine each case. During this process, the administration came under intense pressure from humanitarians, who urged leniency, and the military and citizenry of Minnesota, who wanted revenge for the atrocities committed on their soil.

Governor Ramsey wrote to the president with a warning:

> I hope execution of every Sioux Indian condemned by the military court will be at once ordered. It would be wrong upon principle and policy to refuse this. Private revenge would on all this border take the place of official judgement.

Gen. John Pope added this perspective:

> It is to be noted that the horrible outrages were not committed by wild Indians, whose excuse might be ignorance or barbarism, but by Indians who have been paid annuities for years, and who committed these crimes upon people among whom they had lived, at whose homes they had slept, and at whose tables they had been fed.

President Lincoln was also inundated with appeals from the usual parties who pay attention to such matters—those who had never seen one but asked for mercy for the poor Indian, those opposed to the death penalty, and certain frontier people, missionaries in particular, who believed that an injustice was taking place. Indian Commissioner William P. Dole said that the "indiscriminate punishment of men who have laid down their arms and surrendered themselves as prisoners would be a stain upon our national character and a source of future regret."[17]

After the trial records of the condemned had been carefully scrutinized, it was determined by Lincoln's two examiners that most of them were far from full and complete, and therefore the majority of the convictions could be regarded as unsubstantiated by the evidence. The president ignored the pressure put on him by Minnesota officials and, in an act of fairness, reduced the number to be executed from 303 to 39. He reported to Congress that only 2 prisoners had been proven guilty of violating women, and only about 40 had been involved in the "wanton murder of unarmed citizens." The others had perhaps participated in battles, which was not enough evidence for conviction.

In other words, the tribunal had judged the other Indians guilty for hundreds of murders and rapes because they had merely participated in battles, when most of the actual murderers and rapists had fled before being rounded up by the army. President Lincoln wrote the names of the 39 condemned Indians in his own hand on executive mansion stationery. This document became part of the collection of the Minnesota Historical Society in 1868.[18]

Predictably, this edict from Washington was not well received by the frustrated people of Minnesota, who insisted that all of the condemned be made to pay for their treachery. General Sibley predicted that thousands of residents would rebel against the army and attempt to lynch the prisoners, acts that would result in the loss of many lives. General Pope also voiced his fears that it would be impossible for the army to prevent citizens from taking matter into their own hands and indiscriminately killing innocent Indian men, women, and children.[19]

One incident of attempted vigilante justice did occur on the evening of December 4, when a band of armed citizens from Mankato marched to Camp Lincoln, picking up recruits along the way, with intentions of lynching the guilty parties. This mob numbered at least 150 by the time it arrived at the stockade shortly before midnight. The vigilantes were quickly surrounded by a large force of guards and taken prisoner. The men were released when they promised to return home—or more likely, to the nearest tavern, which had been the place where they hatched their plan. The Indians subsequently were removed from Camp Lincoln and placed in safer quarters in a log structure in present-day downtown Mankato. Otherwise, the citizenry watched and waited for the executions of those judged guilty.[20]

The execution date for the 39 guilty Indians was set for December 26, on a large scaffold being built near the river across the street from where the prisoners were confined. In order to ensure the safety of all concerned, martial law had been declared within a ten-mile radius surrounding the gallows, liquor sales were banned, and a large number of soldiers were stationed around town with orders to maintain the peace.[21]

The task of informing the condemned Indians of their fate fell onto the shoulders of Rev. Stephen Riggs. The missionary entered the stockade four days before the execution date and read the list of names. Those Indians were separated from the others and moved to a stone structure, where they began chanting the Dakota wail of death.[22]

During the week preceding the execution, missionaries Thomas Williamson, Father Augustin Ravoux, Riggs, and others spent many hours visiting the condemned men. The clergymen listened to confessions, and all but two of the Indians accepted Christian baptism. Relatives were permitted to visit on Christmas and the day before. Personal items—knives, money, rings, and other mementos—were given away, and good-byes were said. Most of the doomed men, in the tradition of the Dakota, retained their composure and faced death stoically.[23]

At 10:00 A.M. on December 26, 38 prisoners—one had been spared at the last moment—were marched toward the wooden gallows and up the steps. The Indians had been bound at the wrists by cord, and the white muslin caps that had been placed on their heads were pulled down over their faces. More than 1,400 soldiers closed ranks around the gallows to keep order among the hundreds and hundreds of spectators who crowded rooftops, windows, streets, and riverbanks to witness the much-anticipated event.

As the nooses were placed in position, the Sioux warriors began their mournful death chant, punctuated by an occasional scream and the shout of their names. A drum pounded out three rolling beats as the executioner, William J. Duley, father of two victims of the Dakota rampage, stepped forward with knife in hand. On the third beat, Duley cut the rope. The platforms dropped, and 38 Indians danced in the air. An eyewitness reported that "as the platform fell, there was one, not loud, but prolonged cheer from the soldiery and citizens . . . and then all were quiet and earnest."

The dead Indians were covered with blankets and buried in a shallow mass grave on a slope near the riverfront. That night, however, several doctors from Mankato, St. Peter, and Le Sueur exhumed the bodies to use as study subjects.

Thus concluded this country's largest public mass execution.[24]

Conspicuously missing from that list of 38 Indians who had been hanged was Little Crow, the Dakota chief who had led the bloody uprising. Little Crow had disappeared with perhaps 150 to 200 followers, journeying far to the north, out of reach of the soldiers. Most accounts report that his band ended up that winter of 1862–63 in the vicinity of Devil's Lake, 500 miles northwest of St. Paul, near the northeast corner of Dakota Territory, not far from Canada. This area, which offered plentiful game and fish, had for generations been a popular summer hunting base for many tribes—the Dakota, Chippewa, and Arikara among them—and would now serve as a comfortable headquarters for Little Crow to winter.[25]

Devil's Lake was also an ideal location for Little Crow to contact nearby tribes that could assist in his plans to resume the war against the army. Convincing these people, however, could prove to be most difficult.

Such an alliance would not be entered into lightly by any tribes without strong reasons being presented by the Dakota chief.

The Chippewa, for example, were sworn enemies of the Sioux. The Yankton Sioux were receiving annuities from the government and had much to lose if they participated. Other tribes, the Cree, Assiniboin, and Ojibwa, regarded the Dakota as competitors for the buffalo, which was their major source of subsistence. The Mandan and Arikara were agriculturally oriented and had little in common with the Dakota. And, it must be remembered, Little Crow had even failed when trying to persuade those of his brethren among the Sisseton and Wahpeton to join him in the first fight against Sibley.[26]

An early attempt at reviving loyalty from a band of Sisseton led by Standing Buffalo went for naught. Many of these warriors had participated in attacks on Forts Abercrombie and Ridgely, and had also fled to the north. Little Crow understood that if he could recruit Standing Buffalo, it would strengthen his plea for other bands and tribes to join him.

In the meantime, General Sibley had dispatched a Dakota scout to find Standing Buffalo's band, which was camped twenty miles from Big Stone Lake, not far from Little Crow. Sibley requested that Standing Buffalo refuse aid to Little Crow and, in addition, surrender his tribe without delay. Standing Buffalo rebuffed Sibley's request to surrender, and in anger, he told Little Crow: "You have already made much trouble for my people. Go to Canada or where you please, but go away from me and off the lands of my people."[27]

Little Crow was disappointed by Standing Bear's rejection but nevertheless dispatched emissaries to his current neighbors, asking for their help in fighting the white man. The various tribes received these messengers with guarded interest—only the Mandan displayed any outward contempt and chased the Dakota visitor from their camp. When the word had been passed around the region, many tribes—most notably the Yankton and Yanktonai, and the Oglala, Hunkpapa, and Minneconjou of the Lakota Sioux from the Great Plains—voted to send representatives to Devil's Lake, not with intentions of planning a war, but only to listen to what Little Crow had to say.[28]

Little Crow and a delegation of about eighty Sioux visited Fort Garry—now present-day Winnipeg—and other Canadian trading posts in late December and early 1863. The Indians met at Fort Garry with William McTavish, the governor of the Red River Colony, and Alexander G. Dallas, the governor of Hudson's Bay Company.

These officials were reminded by Little Crow that the British in Canada and the Sioux had long-standing ties of friendship, beginning with the assistance of the Indians in the War of 1812, and should strengthen that alliance. The Canadians, however, stated that they were under no obligations from any fifty-year-old treaty. Little Crow then requested ammunition—only for hunting—which was also refused. He asked for a grant of land in western Canada where he and his band could peaceably settle. The officials told him that such grants were beyond their authority.

Concerned that the Indian war could spread onto their soil, the Canadians politely requested that Little Crow leave their country, which had vowed to remain neutral in all aspects of the Civil War.[29]

During that winter, perhaps as many as 30,000 curious Indians from around the western plains—including 6,000 warriors—visited Little Crow's camp at Devil's Lake. The Dakota chief, known for his eloquence, outlined his grievances against the whites, calling them swindlers, liars, and cowards, and spoke about a summer campaign to drive away these invaders. He made his best pitch for uniting the tribes, saying that together they would gain a great victory that would restore the land to the Indian.

His impassioned words were received with sympathy, but most of the tribes were not provided annuities like the Dakota, and therefore had no animosity about being cheated. Those who were recipients of annuities did not want to jeopardize their arrangements. One by one, the tribes wandered back to their homelands without committing to war. As spring approached, Little Crow had failed to gain aid and comfort from Canada or in his effort to recruit the allies necessary to resume his fight against the whites in Minnesota.[30]

Meanwhile, the people of Minnesota remained greatly concerned—perhaps hysterical would be a better word—about the prospects of further hostilities. In an effort to pacify some of these fears, Congress voted in February and March 1863 to void all treaties with the Dakota Sioux. This ended any and all claims to a reservation and annuities, and also ordered the removal of the four bands from the state.

To this end, General Sibley, who in late November had been named head of the newly created Military District of Minnesota at St. Paul, prepared to transport his 1,700 prisoners from the stockade at Fort Snelling to Crow Creek, about eighty miles above Fort Randall on the open plains of Dakota Territory. The Dakota would be accompanied by about 2,000 Winnebago Indians, who were suspected of having ties with the Sioux.[31]

This hard line when dealing with the Indians extended to army operations as well. Maj. Gen. John Pope, commander of the Military Department of the Northwest, along with Gov. Alexander Ramsey, made the mistake of informing Washington that the war against the Sioux was over. This statement was greeted with vehement protests from residents of Minnesota and its border states, who were keenly aware that hundreds of hostile Dakota Sioux were still at large. There had been sporadic raids throughout the countryside during the winter, and rumors had spread that Little Crow was assembling an alliance of Indians and securing arms from a British trader. Besides that, the Lakota Sioux were said to be gathering along the Missouri to resist the presence of those whites traveling through their country to the Idaho mines.

The St. Paul *Press* served as spokesman for the citizenry when it wrote: "The war is not over! What the people of Minnesota demand is . . . that the war shall now be *offensive*. In God's name let the columns of vengeance move on. . . . until the whole accursed are crushed."

General Pope, who needed little prodding to take the offensive, responded to the outcry by preparing to dispatch two columns of soldiers—one led by Brig. Gen. Henry Sibley, the other by Brig. Gen. Alfred Sully. They would execute an ambitious sweep through the area, with the mission of killing or capturing every hostile Indian within their reach.[32]

Inasmuch as Little Crow's plans for another uprising had been dashed, his ambitions centered on self-preservation. He decided that he would seek refuge for his wives and children in some remote area west of the Missouri or in the vast wilderness of western Canada, where he could ponder the prospects of another war. He would, however, need horses before embarking on such a trip and could think of no better place to procure them than by raiding in Minnesota.

Another bloody trail followed Little Crow's return to the Big Woods of Minnesota. Whether these acts were committed by Little Crow himself or bands sympathetic to him cannot be determined. On June 11, a detachment of the 11th and 8th Minnesota Regiments was ambushed near Lake Elizabeth in Kandiyohi County, and Capt. John S. Cady was killed. Later that month, searchers found the lifeless, mutilated remains of the Amos Dustin family, which had been traveling across the prairie in their wagon forty-five miles west of St. Paul. On July 1, homesteader James McGannon was killed seventy miles west of Minneapolis, his horse and gray coat stolen.[33]

On the afternoon of July 1, Little Crow and his sixteen-year-old son, Wowinapa, could be found about six miles northwest of Hutchinson, where berry bushes were abundant. The chief and his son contentedly set about stripping the bushes and eating the fruit.

At the same time, a settler named Nathan Lamson and his oldest son, Chauncey, were nearby rounding up their horses. The Lamsons observed the two distant Indians, whose identities were unknown to them. They dropped to the ground and crept slowly forward. Nathan Lamson eventually paused behind a tree, steadied his rifle, and fired at the nearest Indian.

The bullet struck Little Crow just above the hip. He stumbled backward, grasped his weapon, and fired at Lamson, but missed. The settler backed away to reload, as both Indians then fired a load of buckshot. Lamson was struck in the shoulder and knocked flat. Chauncey Lamson returned fire at Little Crow, the bullet striking the chief in the chest.

Chauncey Lamson believed that his father was dead and that other Indians may be close by. He ran to Hutchinson and returned later that night with a party of soldiers and townspeople. They found only one body in the clearing, that of Little Crow, who was wearing a gray coat that he had stolen from the dead body of James McGannon two days earlier. Nathan Lamson had only been stunned by the shotgun blast and had returned home. Wowinapa, after crossing the dead chief's hands over his body, had fled.

The body of Little Crow, still as yet unidentified, was transported to Hutchinson. The scalp was removed, and the mutilated body was thrown to a pit in which rotting beef entrails were customarily disposed. Several observers swore that the body was that of Little Crow, pointing out that the corpse had a double set of teeth, a withered left arm and wrists that had been crippled—the latter injuries had occurred when the young Little Crow had fought for the position of chief of his tribe. Inasmuch as Little Crow was said to have been far from Hutchinson, these statements were ridiculed.

The mood of the people at that time with respect to the treatment of Indians can be determined by the fact that no charges were filed and nothing was ever said about the fact that the Lamsons had fired upon two unidentified Indians who were simply picking and eating berries.

Twenty-six days after Little Crow had been killed, his son was captured by a party of half-breed hunters. Wowinapa then related the story about his father's death at the hands of the settlers near Hutchinson. This confirmation erased all doubt about the identity of the dead Indian. Little Crow was indeed dead—not in heroic fashion in battle against soldiers, as he would have preferred, but, in an act of poetic justice, by a settler, a member of that group of people that he had brutally tormented and killed.

A military commission later found Wowinapa guilty of participating in the Sioux uprising and other assorted charges, and sentenced him to death by hanging. That sentence, however, was eventually commuted, and he was set free. Nathan Lamson collected the $500 reward from the state for killing Little Crow. Chauncey received only a small bounty for the chief's scalp.[34]

Little Crow's skull, scalp lock, and forearm bones were donated to the Minnesota Historical Society, where they were placed in a display case and became a featured attraction until the early twentieth century. In 1971, the remains were removed from storage and buried in a family plot in South Dakota.[35]

By now, most of Little Crow's Mdewakanton had scattered across the plains, and the stronghold at Devil's Lake was mainly populated by Standing Buffalo's Sisseton, who wished to avoid any conflict with the whites and were only interested in hunting buffalo.

But roaming to the south were hostile bands of other Sisseton and Yanktonai, who had allied themselves with the outlaw and outcast Inkpaduta. The Wahpekute chief had been a fugitive ever since he and his band had murdered those settlers at Okooji in 1857. These Indians were rumored to have been supplied with weapons and ammunition by Canadian traders from Fort Garry—present-day Winnipeg. In addition to those hostiles, many Lakota Sioux, with young Hunkpapa warriors Sitting Bull, Black Moon, and Gall in attendance, had entered the area following the buffalo and were always interested in protecting their territory from whites who were traveling to the mines in Idaho.

During the winter, these Indians had participated in many raids against settlers in Minnesota and Dakota, and the route along the upper Missouri River Valley to the western mines was under constant threat. If America was to succeed in its quest of fulfilling manifest destiny—"to overspread the continent allotted by Providence for the free development of our multiplying millions"—it would mean driving away the Indians from their traditional hunting grounds.

And that indeed was the destiny that General Pope had in mind for those roving bands of hostile Indians. He vowed to eliminate them, or at least render them benign, when he planned a two-pronged operation for the spring of 1863. Pope informed General Halleck that he would vigorously pursue the Indians wherever they went—even into Canada. This plan did not sit well with Halleck, who let Pope know in no uncertain terms that he was not authorized to cross the border without permission from President Lincoln.[36]

Pope's plan called for Brig. Gen. Henry Sibley to march northward from Camp Pope, which recently had been established on the Minnesota River between the two Indian agencies, to the Devil's Lake area, where he would rendezvous with the other column, then head across eastern Dakota Territory toward the Missouri River. He and his troopers would ride under orders to either kill every hostile Indian they found or drive them out of the area.

Sibley would command a brigade of almost 3,000 troops, composed of the 6th, 7th, and 10th Minnesota Infantry; the 1st Minnesota Mounted Rangers; and the 3rd Minnesota Battery of Light Artillery—commanded by Capt. John Jones, the hero of the Fort Ridgely battles. In addition, a 225-wagon train would transport the brigade's ninety-day supply of provisions.[37]

The second column would be commanded by forty-three-year-old Brig. Gen. Alfred Sully, the son of well-known artist Thomas Sully. Sully was a graduate of West Point and had distinguished himself in the Peninsula campaign, as well as the battles at Antietam and Fredericksburg. He was, to say the least, less than enthused about being shipped west. The general believed that his talents could be better utilized in the East and regarded his transfer as an exile. Sully had been chosen to command this brigade after Secretary of War Stanton denied Pope permission to lead, which caused Pope to resent the presence of Sully. This rift between the two officers was exacerbated by the fact that Sully had helped protect the bumbling Pope's rear during the disastrous defeat at second Bull Run and regarded his superior as incompetent.

Sully would command about 1,200 cavalrymen from the 6th Iowa, 2nd Nebraska, a company from the 7th Iowa, and a battery of four howitzers. His troops would ascend the Missouri River Valley from Fort Randall, drawing supplies from riverboats, in a movement designed to cut off any escape by Indians that Sibley drove west.[38]

Pope was confident that the hostiles would be trapped within this pincer movement that extended through the Sioux hunting grounds of Dakota Territory.

Sibley's column—which measured five miles long—marched out of Camp Pope on June 16 and, after enduring the dust and heat of the prairie, arrived a month later at a point some forty miles southeast of Devil's Lake. Sibley established a field base called Camp Atchinson at that location. He soon learned that hundreds of Indians had departed Devil's Lake and were presently heading toward the Missouri River. These Indians were Standing Buffalo's relatively peaceful Sisseton who, along the way, had happened upon Inkpaduta's hostiles. The two groups had decided to join forces to hunt buffalo and were now traveling together.[39]

On July 20, Sibley moved out with 2,300 men. Four days later, he received reports that about 1,500 Indians were camped ahead near Big

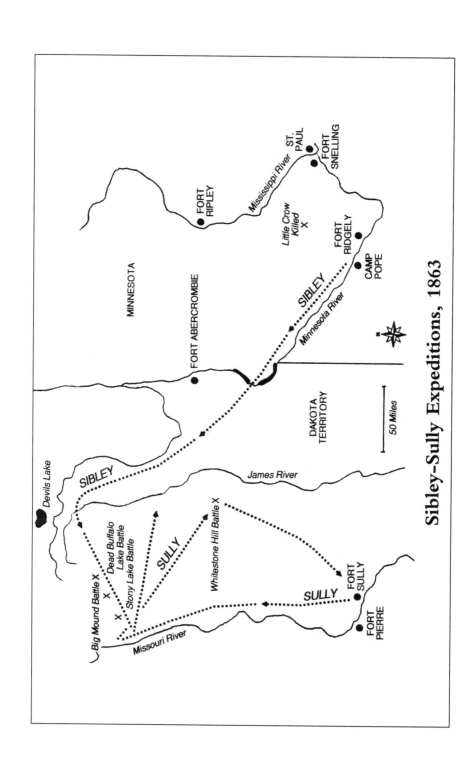

Sibley-Sully Expeditions, 1863

Mound, forty miles northeast of present-day Bismarck. Sibley probably was not aware of Inkpaduta's presence when he sent out entreaties to the village for a parley. The invitation to talk, however, greatly appealed to Standing Buffalo, whose people had no desire to fight and perhaps realized that they had made a mistake by being found in the company of the hostiles.[40]

Sisseton participant Iron Hoop recalled:

> General Sibley had sent word to Standing Buffalo that he had brought him his goods, and that he wanted him to be sure and separate himself from the Mdewakantons. I saw a number gathered about Standing Buffalo's lodge and I went over there and saw him and all the old men sitting together and talking. The understanding was that Sibley and Standing Buffalo were to meet on friendly terms. Shortly afterwards they all got up and started towards Sibley's command, but, before they got there this man was shot.[41]

The plan for a peaceful meeting was ruined when a hot-headed member of Inkpaduta's band fired a shot that killed Dr. Josiah S. Weiser, a surgeon with the Minnesota Rangers. This irresponsible act touched off an eruption of violence, as both sides commenced shooting at each other. The Indians gradually retreated, delaying long enough to allow time for their families to flee, before finally returning to their village to make a stand. Sibley attacked the camp and, supported by his artillery, steadily drove the Indians from that position and chased them through the nearby hills and ravines. At nightfall, the Indians withdrew, retreating in a westward direction.[42]

Standing Buffalo's Sisseton soon altered their course and hastily fled toward the northwest in an effort to remain out of the army's reach. Inkpaduta's band, however, continued heading westward, where they joined a large group of Hunkpapa and Blackfeet Lakota Sioux on the eastern side of the Missouri River.

Sibley had paused to burn everything within the abandoned village, then resumed his march. On July 26, shortly after the army column had halted to camp at Dead Buffalo Lake, it encountered about 1,600 warriors of the newly united hostile Sioux band. The Indians attacked the Minnesota brigade but were repulsed by howitzers and vigorous counterattacks by the soldiers.

Sibley followed the trail of those Indians for twenty-seven miles to Stony Lake, northeast of present-day Driscoll, North Dakota, where he bedded down his troops for the night. On the morning of July 28, as the column formed for the day's march, the Sioux warriors charged. The 10th Minnesota stepped forward to greet the wild rush by the determined Indians with blistering volleys of rifle fire. The Indians, now split into two groups, then took to the flanks and threatened the baggage train in the rear until artillery forced them back. From that point on, the warriors probed the lines for any weakness, but they soon realized that they could not overwhelm Sibley's men and broke contact.[43]

Sibley resumed his pursuit and reached the banks of the Missouri River on July 29. His advance elements approached the bluffs overlooking the river to observe an assemblage of Indians below at water's edge. Evidently the will of these warriors to engage the troops had diminished, and they instead were hurriedly constructing bullboats in an attempt to cross the Missouri before the army could stop them.

Frank Jetty, a mixed-blood Dakota who claimed to have been a reluctant member of Inkpaduta's band, described the scene:

> The Indians fled again, and the soldiers followed with intention of overtaking them at the Missouri River. When the Indians arrived between Mandan and Bismarck, N. Dak., below the hills of the river shore, they camped. Sibbly [sic] and his soldiers watched them four miles from the encampment to encircle them the next morning. When the Indians perceived that they were discovered, they started to improvise boats with small trees on which they tied buffalo hides. All during the night the Indian swimmers guided these boats across the river with ropes held between their teeth. Thus, all who could not swim and the women, children and belongings were carried across.[44]

At dawn the following day, some Indian stragglers were still crossing. Sibley's men fired on them and watched as a number of Indians, including women and children, drowned before reaching the opposite bank. The troopers also burned about 150 wagons and carts that had been abandoned by the Sioux prior to their crossing.

Sibley estimated that in the three engagements with the hostiles, his men had killed 120 to 150 Indians, while suffering less than a dozen casualties. In addition, he had destroyed large quantities of food and other vital supplies—and, perhaps more importantly, had driven the Sioux from eastern Dakota Territory, which ended their threat to those settlements. Sibley spent three days in a futile search for General Sully's column, then turned his column for the march back to Minnesota.[45]

The column commanded by Brig. Gen. Alfred Sully had not departed his advance base near Fort Pierre until August 21. The northern plains had been suffering from a severe drought, and water levels on the Missouri River had fallen too low for the steamboats carrying Sully's provisions to safely navigate through the numerous snags, sandbars, and muddy shallows. When the column finally located the sites of Sibley's battlegrounds in late August, the Lakota Sioux had already returned to their normal range near the Black Hills.

Sully, however, learned from some captured Indians that Inkpaduta had recrossed the river to hunt buffalo near the headquarters of the James River. The general directed his Iowa and Nebraska troops to the southeast with intentions of tracking down Inkpaduta's hostile band, which might help him save face. General Pope, who sought any manner in which to criticize his subordinate, had blamed Sully personally for his failure to rendezvous as planned with Sibley and trap the Indians.

Three days later, on September 3, Sully's forward battalion, which consisted of four companies of the 6th Iowa commanded by Maj. Albert E. House, arrived at Whitestone Hill—twelve miles northwest of present-day Ellendale, North Dakota. The troopers rode down a ravine and suddenly found themselves face-to-face with perhaps as many as 4,000 Sioux from Inkpaduta's band. Trooper E. A. Richards later wrote, "Can you imagine our feelings . . . many miles from civilization with a little band of 300 men pitted against 5,000 savages . . . we couldn't retreat if we could, nor would if we could."[46]

The surprised Indians reacted instantly to the threat and attempted to surround the detachment. Fortunately for the soldiers, a courier managed to escape before the trap completely enclosed around them and rode to inform Sully and the main column, which was ten miles to the north. The Indians quickly succeeded in encircling the soldiers, but Inkpaduta declined to immediately close in and destroy his greatly outnumbered prey.

Instead, the chief believed that he had plenty of time to dispatch the trapped soldiers at his leisure and decided that the men should paint themselves and the women should prepare a feast for them to eat before commencing the slaughter. Some of the Indians, claiming that they were friendly, engaged in an informal parley with Major House, who believed that the act was simply a delaying tactic to allow time for the women and children to be removed from the line of fire. The major demanded that the

Indians surrender, which was greeted by a refusal, then silence, as the two sides simply remained at a distance and stared at one another.[47]

Inkpaduta had made a grave mistake by not attacking House's detachment without delay. Two hours later, at sunset, General Sully and his column arrived at the Indian camp and thundered into the midst of Inkpaduta's surprised warriors with rifles and pistols blazing. The entire band of Indians, once again caught with their breeches down by the sudden appearance of troops, hastily assumed positions in the nearby ravines and mounted a fierce resistance.

The soldiers managed to turn the tables, encircling the camp and trapping most of the Indians within a nearby ravine. The Sioux warriors desperately fought back while seeking an escape route, but were held in place by the steady stream of fire from the soldiers. Within an hour, however, dusk turned to darkness, and the soldiers were compelled to hold their fire for fear of hitting a comrade on the other side of the ravine. This afforded the Indians an opportunity to finally escape, and those who were able vanished into the night.

At daybreak, Sully entered the village and took possession of 156 prisoners—124 women and children and 32 warriors. His troopers had killed an estimated 200 Sioux, while the army had suffered 22 dead and 38 wounded. In addition to taking prisoners and routing his enemy, Sully destroyed a huge amount of property belonging to the Indians, including more than 400,000 pounds of dried buffalo meat. It would take a party of 100 men two days to gather all the bounty and burn it.

The Sioux prisoners were then subjected to a torturous march, later called a "death march" by their descendants, to Crow Creek, where they were placed with those Dakota who earlier had been moved to that location from Fort Snelling. Those Indians who managed to escape would fare little better than their brethren, inasmuch as all their possessions had been left behind, and they would face a bleak winter without food, shelter, or clothing.[48]

The dangerous Inkpaduta, who had been exiled from his own tribe, was one of those who had escaped with his Lakota Sioux allies. He remained around Dakota Territory and was said to have been present in Sitting Bull's village on June 25, 1876, when the Sioux encountered the 7th Cavalry, led by Lt. Col. George Armstrong Custer, at the Little Bighorn River in south-central Montana Territory. Inkpaduta journeyed with Sitting Bull to Canada after that battle, then vanished from the pages of history, his death speculated as occurring sometime between 1878 and 1882.

This ambitious campaign that General Pope had intended to rid the area of the Indian forever could not by any means be termed a success. True, many Indians had been killed, and great amounts of possessions had been destroyed. But the number of Indians who died, either in battle or as a result of their incarceration, never came close to avenging the total number of whites who had lost their lives since that initial uprising in 1862. In addition, a large number of the Indian participants who had committed the heinous crimes had taken refuge in Canada or had spread across the Great Plains and remained a threat for years to come. Those red men who had been pushed out of Minnesota and Dakota Territory eventually crossed the Missouri once more to hunt buffalo, and the army was forced to march against them time and time again as settlers filed land claims that encroached on traditional Indian hunting grounds.

Generals Pope and Sully would contend with that problem in 1864, when it was decided to build military forts to establish control over the eastern half of Dakota Territory.

Little Crow had been shot by Chauncey Lamson; Mankato had gotten in the way of a cannonball at Wood Lake; and Cut Nose had been hanged at South Bend. Of those Dakota who had taken an active part in the uprising in 1862, Chief Big Eagle was one of the few ever to return to Minnesota. Big Eagle had been tried by the military tribunal and sentenced to death. He received a reprieve and was sent to prison in Davenport, Iowa, where he was issued a pardon by President Lincoln in 1864. Big Eagle, who added the first name Jerome, lived for forty years on a farm near Granite Falls, near the site of the former Upper Agency, until his death on January 5, 1906.[49]

William Duley, the man who had cut the rope to hang the thirty-eight presumed guilty Dakota, returned to his farm at Lake Shetek to discover that someone else had taken up residence there. He apparently had lost interest in the area anyway and subsequently moved his surviving family members to Beeson, Alabama.

Charles E. Flandreau, the Minnesota Supreme Court justice who had taken command at New Ulm, moved to Nevada. He lived there for two years before returning to Minnesota to establish a successful law practice in St. Paul.

Henry Hastings Sibley did not actively participate in future campaigns in Minnesota, but sat out the remainder of the war, commanding his district in St. Paul. He was breveted major general for "efficient and meritorious service" in November 1865 and was mustered out of the army on

April 30, 1866. After the war, Sibley became a successful businessman in Minnesota, heading the St. Paul Gas Company, an insurance company, and City Bank, and was a director of the First National Bank and the Sioux City Railroad. He also served in the state legislature, held a seat on the Board of Regents of the University of Minnesota, and became president of the state historical society. Sibley died at the age of eighty in St. Paul on February 18, 1891.

There can be no way of determining exactly how many civilians, soldiers, or Indians were killed in the Minnesota fighting. At one point, Indian agent Thomas Galbraith made an area-by-area tally and arrived at 634 civilians and 93 soldiers—a total of 737. Fifty years later, an effort was made to list all the names of those whites who had been killed, and only 447 names could be remembered. But by then, many of the shallow graves had been plowed over or the remains blown away in the winds of time.[50]

The conflict of 1862–63 left the Dakota, or Santee, Sioux tribe in ruins. Most of the 6,500 inhabitants of the two reservations had been scattered across the plains, imprisoned, executed, or killed in battle. Only several hundred mixed-bloods and their full-blooded relatives were spared in Minnesota. Those who had escaped eventually settled in Dakota Territory, Nebraska, or Canada, with some gradually returning to live in their homeland, where they established small villages. Over the years, the population of the tribe has varied, and by the 1960s, the Dakota numbered less than 5,000. But as was the case with many tribes at that point in time, they became conscious of their identity and revived many traditions, such as holding powwows and recovering their lost arts, crafts, and other cultural distinctions. Perhaps about the same number of Dakota Sioux who had populated those Minnesota reservations in 1862 are alive today.

PATRICK E. CONNOR. Adventurer Connor led his regiment of California volunteers to Utah in Fall, 1862, and received a less-than-enthusiastic welcome from the Mormons in Salt Lake City. Connor's massacre of the Shoshones at Bear River in early 1863, however, led to the removal of that tribe from the territory claimed by the Mormons. UTAH STATE HISTORICAL SOCIETY

HENRY HASTINGS SIBLEY. Sibley rose from clerk in a fur company to become the first elected governor of Minnesota. In 1862 during the Sioux uprising, he was assigned the command of the state's volunteers, and defeated Little Crow's warriors at the Battle of Wood Lake. MINNESOTA HISTORICAL SOCIETY

LITTLE CROW. This Santee Sioux was the principal leader of his tribe's violent protest of their concentration camp–like conditions, which resulted in the slaughter of hundreds of people throughout the Minnesota countryside in what has become known as the Sioux Uprising of 1862. MINNESOTA HISTORICAL SOCIETY

JAMES H. CARLETON. This power-hungry, tyrranical officer became the absolute ruler of New Mexico and Arizona and, with Kit Carson as his primary field commander, was a dominant figure in shaping the tragic history of the Indians of the Southwest during the early 1860s. LIBRARY OF CONGRESS

CHRISTOPHER "KIT" CARSON. Appointed colonel of the 1st New Mexico Infantry in 1861, Carson distinguished himself against the Confederates, but the famous trapper, guide, and mountain man would assume a larger role in campaigns against the Indians.

MANGAS COLORADAS. This fierce Mimbreno Apache alternately waged war and spoke for peace as a solution to the problem of the miners who had invaded the traditional territory of his people. He was eventually lured into custody and killed, an act that ignited what has come to be known as the Apache Wars of the Southwest.

KING S. WOOLSEY. This wealthy rancher's land and stock outside of Prescott, Arizona, was the target of frequent raids by the Apache tribe. He formed several Indian-hunting expeditions for the purpose of subduing the hostiles and recapturing his property and that of his neighbors. SHARLOT HALL MUSEUM PHOTO, PRESCOTT, ARIZONA

JOHN MILTON CHIVINGTON. Known as "The Fighting Parson," Chivington became a hero for his actions during the La Glorietta Pass battle against the
Confederates. The political ambitions that motivated this arrogant commander
of the Colorado Volunteers, however, led to the massacre of Southern
Cheyenne and Arapaho Indians at Sand Creek. COLORADO HISTORICAL SOCIETY

BLACK KETTLE. This prominent Southern Cheyenne chief was a well-known advocate of peace between his people and the white man. Assurances of safety from the army for his people camped at Sand Creek, Colorado Territory, were ignored by Col. John Chivington, a betrayal that resulted in one of the most notorious massacres on the frontier. COLORADO HISTORICAL SOCIETY

CHAPTER SIX

The Navajo Long Walk

AT THE OUTBREAK OF THE CIVIL WAR, MOST OF THE NAVAJO BANDS IN New Mexico were inclined to embrace peace with the whites. This decision by the Indians, however, could not be considered one of free will; rather, it had been greatly encouraged by a recent vigorous military campaign waged against them by then-Maj. Edward R. S. Canby.

The Navajo Indians, numbering perhaps 12,000, lived in small, related bands in an area of thousands of square miles within the rugged landscape of canyons, buttes, mesas, and high desert in northwestern New Mexico and northeastern Arizona. They had established farming communities, growing gardens and orchards, and raising herds of goats and flocks of sheep.

That Navajo farming lifestyle certainly differed from that of other western tribes, who were known as great hunters, and could present the impression that these Indians were rather passive. The Navajo, however, also had a tradition of being fierce warriors, with a long history of raiding throughout the territory. Following several rather bloody incidents in 1853, a concerted effort was made by authorities to find a solution that would end hostilities. The governor, David Meriwether, at that point decided that "the government must either feed and clothe these Indians to a certain extent, or chastise them in a decisive manner." Meriwether, in a rare act of selecting the best man for the position, appointed as Navajo agent Henry L. Dodge, who had lived with the tribe and was known to care deeply about their welfare.

Dodge, who came from a distinguished Iowa family—his father and brother were both U.S. senators—had taken an Indian wife and settled into a cabin in the Chuska Mountains. The fact that Dodge lived in Navajo country and traveled extensively throughout without a military escort, unlike the agents before him, greatly influenced his charges.

For the next several years, Dodge, working with Maj. Henry Lane Kendrick, earned the trust of the Navajo by dealing honestly with them, a trait that could be called uncommon in those days. The Navajo called their agent "Red Shirt" because of the red flannel shirt that he had a custom of wearing. His fairness and hard work for their benefit, which quickly gained him the friendship of many previously skeptical tribal leaders, eventually elevated him to the lofty status of somewhat of a living legend among the Navajo Indians.

In November 1856, however, the popular Henry Dodge vanished while hunting deer near Zuni Pueblo. It was speculated that perhaps the local Apache had a hand in the disappearance. Mangas Coloradas was employed as an intermediary in an effort to ransom the Navajo agent from the Indians, but the Chiricahua chief's inquiries failed to confirm his disposition among them—even whether Dodge was dead or alive. The mystery was finally solved in February 1857, when a detachment of soldiers from Fort Defiance happened upon what remained of Henry Dodge. He had been shot and scalped, his naked body left in the snow for scavengers to prey upon. No person or tribe was ever brought to justice for the crime.[1]

The Navajo Indians had lost the only man who had truly cared about their well-being, the man whose level-headed efforts had prevented a major conflict between the tribe and the military during the preceding three years. Dodge, according to a member of the 1st Cavalry of New Mexico, "possessed unbounded influence over the Navajo Chiefs, and was fairly worshipped by them . . . had he lived, I am of the opinion that the subsequent Navajo Wars would never have occurred."[2]

But with Dodge gone, the Navajo stepped up raids on settlements and neighboring tribes, stealing livestock and taking captives. An incident at Fort Defiance in July 1858, when a hot-blooded Navajo warrior killed a black servant with an arrow, set in motion a retaliatory campaign led by Lt. Col. Dixon S. Miles. The initial clash of this operation took place at Canyon de Chelly. An army column of 300 or so soldiers was greeted by 600 armed Navajo warriors, who lined the steep cliff walls of the canyon. Although the advantage was clearly with the Navajo, the brief skirmish resulted in only minor casualties being sustained on both sides. Miles continued his campaign throughout October and November, with the fighting escalating—twenty-five Navajo were killed in one October battle—until finally a peace treaty was negotiated in December. The treaty outlined specific boundaries that kept the Navajo from approaching settlements, released all prisoners, and made the chief responsible for the actions of his tribe—as well as providing for the return of stolen livestock.

It could be said, however, that the Navajo likely did not fully understand the treaty. Certain provisions moved them farther west, relinquishing valuable land that had been given them by Governor Meriwether in 1855.[3]

The Navajo agent, David Yost, protested the treaty on the grounds that the Indians would lose some of their best planting and grazing land. He wrote in the *Santa Fe New Mexican* that the provisions would "transpose the Navajos from the pursuits of industry and agriculture . . . to robbers and plunderers."[4]

Yost's assessment was correct. The Navajo soon realized that they had been taken advantage of and resorted to raids by hit-and-run war parties to supplement their meager government-issued rations. Only the efforts of Col. Benjamin L. E. Bonneville at Fort Defiance for the time being prevented an outbreak of war. Bonneville had beefed up the garrison to include four companies of infantry, and he deployed six other infantry companies on the Rio Grande for support. He then frequently dispatched columns to march through Navajo country as a vivid reminder to the Indians of the army's might and willingness to fight.[5]

This rather fragile relationship continued throughout most of 1859, but violence erupted in November. At that time, a Navajo raiding party stampeded a large herd of government horses and made off with nearly all of them. The following day, the soldiers captured an unarmed Navajo warrior, who likely had nothing to do with the incident of the previous day, and made him the object on which to vent their embarrassment and anger over losing the horses. The soldiers lured the lone warrior into their camp, stripped him, tied him to a post, and viciously whipped him. The Navajo chiefs were shocked and outraged by this brutal act and vowed revenge on the culprits.[6]

The counterstroke by the Indians was initiated in January 1860, when a war party of about 200 Navajo warriors attempted, without success, to steal a large herd of horses that grazed near Fort Defiance. The warriors subsequently attacked a wagon train carrying supplies to the fort. A running battle ensued, which lasted for three days, with forty soldiers bravely managing to ward off each determined assault by an overwhelming number of their enemy. On February 8, about 500 Navajo struck a herd guard of twenty-eight soldiers seven miles north of the fort. In the ensuing firefight, ten warriors were reported killed and another twenty wounded.

What was intended as the coup de grace by the Indians came in the predawn hours of April 30. Navajo warriors gathered in force and surprised Fort Defiance with a three-pronged assault. The Indians and soldiers furiously battled for more than two hours, before a brazen foot charge executed by members of the 3rd Infantry managed to drive the stubborn Navajo away and into the hills. The soldiers, moving cautiously forward with trees and rocks for cover, eventually cleared the area. Remarkably, only one soldier had been killed and two wounded in the fierce action. Indian casualties were estimated at perhaps a dozen warriors killed. The soldiers considered themselves fortunate that the Indians had been armed with only bows and arrows and not with rifles, or the result might have been vastly different.[7]

It was now apparent to military authorities that the Navajo would have to be dealt with severely. The time for compassion and humanitarian aid had passed, and war was the only solution. On July 9, 1860, Secretary of War John B. Scott decreed, "Active operations will be instituted against the Navajoes as soon as the necessary preparations can be made." Scott also reinforced the Department of New Mexico with the 5th and 7th Infantry Regiments, three companies of the 10th, and two from the 2nd Dragoons. Capable Maj. Edward R. S. Canby of the 10th Infantry, in the brevet rank of lieutenant colonel, was chosen to command the offensive.[8]

Canby, who was known as a colorless yet prudent soldier, had graduated from West Point in the class of 1835 and subsequently served in the Florida Seminole Indian Wars and the Mexican War. He would go on to distinguish himself in the Civil War battles of Valverde and La Glorieta Pass and chase Henry Sibley's Texans out of New Mexico. But for now, Canby was obliged to contend with the Navajo.[9]

Canby organized his command—more than 600 soldiers and a large force of Ute, Pueblo, and Mexican volunteers—at Fort Defiance in September. He separated his troops into three columns: one under Bvt. Maj. Henry H. Sibley, his brother-in-law and future rival; another led by Capt. Lafayette McLaws; and the third under his own direct command. The three columns marched in November with intentions of scouring the Chuska Mountains. Sibley had orders to head west from Fort Defiance toward Granado, then north to the mouth of Canyon de Chelly, where they would rendezvous with Canby, who had marched to the mouth of the gorge. The column led by Captain McLaws headed north from the fort with orders to cut off any attempted escape by the Navajo who fled from the approaching columns.

The execution of the campaign, however, was soon affected by the drought that had gripped the region. Usually dependable water holes had dried up; forage became quite sparse, which caused the cavalry horses to eventually break down; and the delivery of supplies could not be depended upon to arrive with enough frequency to maintain the march. Adding to the difficulty was the fact that the Navajo, who were familiar with the terrain in their homeland, could easily evade the soldiers.

Nonetheless, the army did have some success as they swept through Navajo land along the Chuska Mountains and north along the San Juan River. In a series of skirmishes, the Navajo lost thirty-four warriors, 1,000 horses, and 7,000 sheep. These losses, combined with the threat of an active army, encouraged a number of chiefs to petition for peace. Canby, however, refused to entertain peace overtures until the chiefs could guarantee that all Navajo would cease raiding, a demand that at that time could not be met.[10]

Colonel Canby went back to the drawing board and, with guidance from Secretary Floyd, decided that, inasmuch as humanitarian warfare had failed, the only manner in which to subdue his foe would be a continuous campaign, waged in all seasons. The strategy would call for what later became popularly known as "total war." This tactic had been initially used by Brig. Gen. William S. Harney in 1854 against the Sioux at Ash Hollow; it would be employed throughout the Plains Indian wars of the 1860s and 1870s. Generals Sheridan and Sherman would also put the strategy to use in the Shenandoah and March to the Sea Civil War campaigns in 1864.

Total war called for the army to relentlessly pursue the Navajo and not only strike bands of warriors, but also destroy the tribe's homes and crops, and capture their livestock. This would render them impoverished and helpless, and thereby dependent on the government for their daily subsistence.[11]

Canby carried out his orders with great zeal, unyieldingly chasing the Navajo during the fall and winter of 1860. His scouts located camps and hiding places, and the troops initiated surprise attacks. The effectiveness of the army's campaign eventually forced the tribe to split into small bands, each fighting for survival against the inclement weather and the threat of an unexpected appearance by the army.[12]

The pressure exerted by Canby's troops became too much for the Indians to withstand, and the chiefs petitioned in earnest for relief. By early 1861, Canby was convinced that the overtures were sincere and believed that the circumstances had created the proper atmosphere for a favorable negotiation. In February 1861, more than 2,000 Navajo—including twenty-four chiefs—camped near Fort Fauntleroy for a council of peace. The chiefs were ordered to assemble their peaceful warriors at the fort and promise to make war against those of their tribe who continued to raid. In return, the U.S. Government would "render them assistance that may be necessary to place them in the same condition with other nations under the protection of the government."[13]

Canby and his superiors, certain that peace had at long last come to Navajo country, commenced withdrawing troops from the territory. By the end of April, every soldier had been removed from Fort Defiance.

Peace may have been initiated between the Navajo and the army, but the woes of the tribe and the instability of the region were increased by another dangerous threat. Traditional enemies of the Navajo—Ute and Pueblo Indians, and particularly self-styled New Mexican volunteers—prepared to take advantage of the tribe's vulnerability and inability to properly defend itself. These savage bands of vigilantes began raids into Navajo land, swooping down on small camps, killing warriors while taking women and children captive to sell as slaves.

The army was spread very thin and therefore was powerless to protect the Indians against these raiding parties, one of which "openly avowed their intentions to disregard the treaty made with the Navajo, and on their return to home, to organize a new expedition to capture Navajos and sell them." These renegades did not discriminate between hostile and friendly Indians—on one occasion killing and scalping a Navajo army scout who was wearing his uniform.[14]

Meanwhile, Fort Sumter had been fired upon, and the now-Colonel Canby rushed to Santa Fe to prepare for an invasion by Confederate troops from Texas, led by former subordinate Henry Hopkins Sibley, now a brigadier general in the Rebel army.

With the army assembling in the Santa Fe area, their presence virtually nonexistent in the remainder of the territory, the Navajo people were left to fend for themselves in the worst of conditions. Most of their homes and crops had been destroyed, and the brutal raids by their traditional enemies and the New Mexican volunteers were incessant. The tribe resorted to the only practical remedy in their struggle for survival: They mounted their ponies and vowed to die fighting. To that end, warriors resumed raids on ranches and settlements to steal livestock and take captives to sell as slaves, which was said to be a dilemma for the average Navajo. Navajo expert Frank McNitt wrote that "a state of constant warfare was contrary to Navajo nature and totally disruptive of normal Navajo life. Stock raisers and farmers could not live as raiding nomads or fugitives." That was perhaps true, unless the alternative was annihilation by their enemies and a life of despair and starvation.[15]

The confounding situation gnawed at Colonel Canby, who wrote in December to headquarters:

The depredations of the Navajoes are constant. . . . Between the Navajoes and the people of New Mexico a state of hostilities, with occasional intervals of peace, has existed almost since the first settlement of the country. Each party claims that the treaty of peace has been broken by the other, and it is impossible now, even if it were profitable, to inquire which is right. Each successive war has reduced the Navajoes strength and wealth, and has, by reducing them to poverty, added to the strength of the ladrones, or war party. There is no doubt that many of these difficulties, if not caused, have at least been greatly aggravated, by the illegal acts of the Mexican people, and in some cases have been the direct cause of the difficulties that immediately followed them. The consequences of these acts have almost invariably fallen upon the portion of the Navajoes known as the peace party and upon those inhabitants who have property to lose, while the aggressors profit by the sale of their booty and captives. These acts are not restrained by the moral sense of the community, and so long as these marauders find a ready sale for their plunder and for their captives, it will be impossible to prevent these depredations and the consequent retaliation by the Indians.

Recent occurrences in the Navajo country . . . have so demoralized and broken up that nation, that there is now no choice between their absolute extermination or their removal and colonization at points so remote from the settlements as to isolate them entirely from the inhabitants of the Territory.[16]

But Edward Canby would not be in command to finish the campaign that he had begun against the Navajo. He was appointed brigadier general a week after his heroic action in the March 1862 Glorieta Pass battle, and he soon thereafter received orders to report to Washington, D.C., to become assistant adjutant general. He would command troops during the New York City draft riots of July 1863 and be appointed major general in May 1864, when he assumed command of the Military Division of West Mississippi. Canby's troops would capture Mobile in May 1865, and he would also become notable for being the general who received the surrender of the last Confederate army—under the command of Lt. Gen. E. Kirby Smith—more than six weeks after Lee surrendered to Grant. In April 1873, as commander of the Department of the Columbia, he would be killed while attempting to negotiate a treaty with the Modoc Indians in northern California—thus becoming the only active-duty U.S. general in history to be killed by Indians.

In September 1862, Brig. Gen. James H. Carleton became head of the Military Department of New Mexico. Carleton turned his immediate attention to subduing the Mescalero and Chiricahua Apache. Then, with those successful campaigns behind him, he decided to aim his army at another target—the Navajo.

Carleton, who was called a humanitarian in his day, believed that he could direct the Navajo to the ways of civilized whites, which included conversion to Christianity. It was likely that Carleton, who embraced the doctrine of Manifest Destiny, also desired to clear the way for exploration of the vast resources in the territory. Then there was the ongoing war of attrition between the New Mexican and the Navajo—a war that the 12,000 Navajo against 80,000 New Mexicans would be destined to lose. By that time, the Navajo tribe had divided into war and peace factions, but there was no distinction between the two in the eyes of the military authorities. Those who called for peace and protection by the army were being made to pay for the atrocities committed by those warriors who had continued raiding the countryside.

Carleton prepared for his campaign by building Fort Wingate, near present-day San Rafael, at the eastern edge of Navajo country, as a base for his operations. This construction activity and the presence of troops served to greatly disturb the Navajo people. In December 1862, eighteen inquisitive Navajo chiefs traveled to Santa Fe to meet with Carleton to determine his intentions for this new post. The general told them in no uncertain terms that "they could have no peace until they would give other guarantees than their word that the peace would be kept . . . that we had no faith in their promises; that if they did not return we should know that they had chosen the alternative of war; that in this event the consequences rested on them."[17]

The "other guarantees" referred to total surrender and the agreement by the Navajo to move the entire tribe to Bosque Redondo, the place 400 miles distant where the Mescalero Apache had been confined near Fort Sumner. This outrageous demand without question angered the chiefs, but perhaps another emotion affected them even more—the fear that this could actually happen. The Navajo had a profound religious attachment to their land, which they believed was located between four sacred mountains and had been provided for them by their creator. To move from this sacred land would be a violation of their deepest religious beliefs. Not only that, but it would mean abandoning their traditional lifestyle to reside in a confined area.[18]

In April, Carleton sent for Degadito and Barboncito, two of the prominent peace chiefs with whom he had met in December. He reiterated his demand that the tribe move to Bosque Redondo and received the predictable reply—the Navajo would not voluntarily move. Barboncito declared that he would remain peacefully near Fort Wingate, but even under the threat of death, he would not move to the Pecos.

Carleton had lost patience with the Navajo. On June 23, he issued an ultimatum to them, which stated

> that all those Navajoes who claimed not to have murdered and robbed the inhabitants must come in and go to Bosque Redondo, where they would be fed and protected until the war was over; that unless they were willing to do this, they would be considered hostile and would be proceeded against accordingly . . . that we have no desire to make war upon them and other good Navajoes; but that the troops cannot tell the good from the bad, and we neither can nor will tolerate their staying as a peace party among those whom we intend to make war. Tell them they can have until the twentieth day of July of this year to come in . . . that after that day every Navajo that is seen will be considered as hostile and treated accordingly; that after that day the door now open will be closed.[19]

To be fair, word of this edict could not have traveled throughout Navajo country in a period of one month. Not that it would have mattered—Carleton was not about to wait for the Navajo to comply. He had already set the wheels in motion for a campaign to force the submission of the Navajo. On June 15, he issued the following General Order No. 15:

> For a long time past the Navajoe Indians have murdered and robbed the people of New Mexico. Last winter when eighteen of their chiefs came to Santa Fe to have a talk, they were warned,—and were told to inform their people,—that for these murders and robberies the tribe must be punished, unless some binding guarantees should be given that in the future these outrages should cease. No such guarantees have yet been given: But on the contrary, additional murders and additional robberies have been perpetrated upon the persons and property of our unoffending citizens. It is therefore ordered, that Colonel CHRISTOPHER CARSON, with a proper military force proceed without delay to a point in the Navajoe country known as Pueblo Colorado, and there establish a defensible Depot for his supplies and Hospital: and thence to prosecute a vigorous war upon the men of this tribe until it is considered at these Head Quarters that they have been effectually punished for their long continued atrocities.[20]

Once again, Carleton had charged his trusted subordinate and friend Kit Carson with the responsibility of carrying out a campaign against the enemy.

Carson assembled his regiment, 760 men—260 of whom were infantry composed mainly of the 1st New Mexico Volunteers—at Fort Wingate to prepare for the march to Pueblo Colorado (Red Town). This wash, which was located twenty-eight miles southwest of the abandoned Fort Defiance, would be established as the base of operations and called Fort Canby in honor of the former commander of the Department of New Mexico. At the same time, another detachment, led by Lt. Col. J. Francisco Chavez, who commanded Fort Wingate, would depart that location with a force of 326 and patrol the area in coordination with Carson.[21]

On July 7, 1863, Col. Kit Carson and part of his command—221 men—left Los Lunas, on the Rio Grande. He marched northwest and arrived three days later at Fort Wingate. After three days of rest, Carson led his men to Ojo del Oso, a lush, green valley bounded by colorful cliffs, which was a major watering place for the eastern Navajo. He paused for two days to feed his stock in the ripening Navajo wheat fields, an act that demonstrated to the Indians that destruction of their resources would be instrumental in the success of the campaign. The column reached the abandoned Fort Defiance on July 20. Carson was joined at that point by a band of Ute scouts, who were anxious to fight their traditional enemy.[22]

On July 22, Carson, accompanied by those people appointed to select the site for the new fort, about seventy troops, and the Ute scouts, headed for Pueblo Colorado. Their route took them south past Window Rock, then west, before gradually moving up the Fort Defiance Mesa and descending into the valley near the place called Pueblo Colorado, where Fort Canby was to be established.

Carson and the scouts rode ahead of the column and, on Rio de Pueblo Colorado, encountered a small party of Navajo. In the skirmish that followed, Carson's men killed three of the enemy. A Paiute woman who had been taken captive by the Navajo informed them that a large herd of sheep, cattle, and horses could be found watering at a pond about thirty-five miles to the west.

After a brief rest, Carson started out after the livestock, riding all night across the barren landscape—only to find that the Navajo had already departed the pond. Carson reported:

> I followed their trail for two hours, and until many of the horses had given out, and only returned on my own conviction . . . that it would be impossible to overtake them, without having to travel some ninety miles without water, and this my horses could not do.

On my return route the Ute Indians killed eight Navajos, making a total of twelve since my arrival in this country.[23]

Carson and his men reached their camp on July 23, after having been in the saddle for nearly thirty-six hours. This arduous ride across the wasteland had convinced Carson that Pueblo Colorado—an area lacking in adequate food, water, timber, and forage—was not an ideal site for a fort. Instead, he suggested that old Fort Defiance be revitalized and renamed Fort Canby. General Carleton readily agreed with his request. Carson embarked on the task of rebuilding the ramshackle fort, which likely had been destroyed by the Navajo, and made preparations for a summer of chasing his enemy.[24]

Carson's troops were dispatched in small detachments on a series of scouts in search of the Navajo, with orders to burn every hogan (traditional Navajo log-and-mud dwelling), field, and storehouse of supplies that could be located—in addition to capturing herds of livestock and killing on sight every Navajo male. On July 25, during one such scout in the Canoncito Bonito area, a group of Indians was spotted, and the soldiers set out after them. Maj. Joseph Cummings foolishly "left the command alone and proceeded up the canyon" and was killed—shot in the stomach—by Navajo warriors, who escaped without detection. Cummings was the only officer to become a casualty of the campaign. Oddly enough, the major was found to be carrying $5,301 in cash on his person, the reason for which never became known. A fort later established by General Carleton at Cook's Canyon on the main road from Mesilla to Tucson in southwestern New Mexico was named Fort Cummings in honor of the major.[25]

On August 5, Carson took to the field with 16 officers and 333 men, and headed south toward Zuni Pueblo, then east and south near Window Rock, with an initial objective of recruiting Indian guides. Along the way, he encountered a number of corn and wheat fields. The men fed their horses on the Navajo crops, then burned what was not consumed. The soldiers also gathered up twenty-five horses and 100 sheep, and took thirteen women and children as prisoners. Seven of these captives were sent to Fort Defiance; the others were handed over to the Ute as slaves.[26]

Carson had earlier addressed this practice of turning over Indian prisoners to the Ute, who would ultimately sell them as slaves, in a letter to Carleton:

> It is expected by the Utes, and has, I believe, been customary to allow them to keep the women and children, and the property captured by them, for their own use and benefit; and as there is no

way to sufficiently recompense these Indians for their invaluable services, and as a means of insuring their continued zeal and activity; I ask it as a favor that they be permitted to retain all that they may capture. I make this request the more readily as I am satisfied that the future of the captives disposed of in this manner would be much better than if sent even to the Bosque Redondo. As a general thing the Utes dispose of their captives to Mexican families, where they are fed and taken care of and thus cease to require any further attention on the part of the government. Besides this, their being distributed as Servants thro' the territory causes them to lose that collectiveness of interest as a tribe, which they will retain if kept together at any one place.[27]

On the one hand, some merit must be given to the idea of saving these captives from the misery associated with confinement at Bosque Redondo. On the other hand, however, it would require not only the approval of detribalization, the loss of any sense of tribal identity, but also the justification of the practice of slavery.

Carleton, to his credit, responded:

I have the honor to acknowledge receipt of your letter in relation to the disposition to be made of captured Navajoe women and children—and to say in reply, that all prisoners which are captured by the troops or employes [sic] of your command will be sent to Santa Fe, by the first practicable opportunity. . . . There must be no exception to this rule.[28]

Perhaps the issue of not turning over captured women and children to the Ute, if Carson had indeed obeyed Carleton's orders, would explain why many of the scouts subsequently abandoned the army column.

By mid-August, Carson reported from the field that three Indians had been killed, fifteen captured, and one wounded. In addition, twenty horses, two mules, 100 sheep, and a few goats had been taken. Carleton, however, was less than impressed by those numbers. In an effort to "stimulate the zeal" of the troopers, the general offered to pay $20 for "every sound, serviceable horse or mule and $1 per head for every sheep" delivered to Fort Canby. Inasmuch as the soldiers made less than $20 a month in pay, this offer was extremely attractive. Unfortunately, they could not capture what they could not find.[29]

On August 20, Carson moved north toward Canyon de Chelly, where the soldiers discovered fields resplendent with corn, pumpkins, and beans. Some of this bounty was eaten by the hungry troops; another portion was packed up for later use; and the rest was destroyed. The presence of the crops, however, indicated to Carson that Indians were surely nearby, and he decided to set a trap for them.

He led his main column from the area, leaving behind five men under Capt. Albert H. Pfeiffer secreted at an ambush site. Sure enough, two curious Indians approached the fields as soon as Carson had passed out of sight. The soldiers lying in wait opened fire, but the Indians, both perhaps badly wounded, nonetheless escaped.[30]

Three days later, Carson reached the west entrance of Canyon de Chelly, the famous Navajo stronghold, but determined that there probably were not enough Indians within those walls to warrant an exploration. There was a likelihood that his assumption at that time was correct. No doubt the soldiers had been under the wary eye of the Navajo, and word would have been passed detailing the route of the soldiers. Those Indians in the pathway would have hidden or remained distant until the threat had passed.[31]

Carson's column returned to Fort Canby on August 31, 1863, after a twenty-seven-day, 490-mile march under a scorching sun that had yielded little in the effort to subdue the Navajo. On the bright side for the army, however, they had destroyed about 187 acres of corn and 15 acres of wheat, taken over 1,000 animals, killed three Navajo, and captured another twenty-four. Carson placed a positive spin on the operation when he wrote to headquarters in Santa Fe:

> In summing up the results of the last month's scout, I congratulate myself on having gained one very important point Viz; a knowledge of where the Navajoes have fled with their stock, and where I am certain to find them. I have also gained an accurate knowledge of a great portion of the country, which will be of incalculable benefit in our future operations.[32]

Meanwhile, the other column of New Mexican volunteers under Lieutenant Colonel Chavez, which Carleton had dispatched from Fort Wingate, reported moderate success. One company, led by Capt. Rafael Chacon, had killed eight Navajo, captured another fourteen, and rounded up 1,500 sheep and goats and seventeen horses and mules. At the same time, Ute warriors who were out hunting their traditional enemy were said to have killed thirty-three Navajo, captured sixty-six, and grabbed 2,000 sheep and thirty horses.[33]

One controversy that faced Colonel Carson upon his return to Fort Canby—in addition to numerous incidences of drinking, fighting, and prostitution—was a matter concerning a California volunteer named Maj. Thomas Blakeney, the acting post commander, who was a personal friend of Gen. James Carleton. According to an officer at the fort, Blakeney's conduct during Carson's absence had been "overbearing and unbecoming to an officer." Blakeney had on one occasion ordered the commissary department to throw away "a lot of fresh potatoes" and ordered the men to "turn out and police around the Commissary Corrall." This was particularly insulting, because Colonel Carson had exempted commissary personnel from control of the post commander. A series of other petty clashes between the tyrannical Blakeney and his subordinates had occurred throughout the month.

Blakeney's actions in the treatment of several Navajo who had come in to surrender, however, was much more serious and threatened to undermine the entire campaign.

On August 4, an elderly Navajo man arrived at the fort to give himself up. Six days later, he was shot dead in what was dubiously noted as an escape attempt. On August 26, four Navajo, who represented a group of perhaps 100 who were poised to surrender, appeared at the fort to talk peace under a flag of truce. They were grabbed and dragged off to prison as soon as they had approached within reach of the guards. Two of these men were subsequently sent out to police the parade ground and bury "offal and dead dogs" outside the post. The men escaped while engaged in this degrading assignment. The soldiers gave chase, shooting and killing one instantly and wounding the other, who later died from his wounds.

Charges were brought against Blakeney by his men, who claimed that the major had ordered the killing of the Navajo and had told the officer of the guard to write up a fraudulent report of the incident. Blakeney had retaliated by confining several soldiers on disciplinary charges.

Kit Carson was greatly disturbed by Blakeney's actions and placed him under arrest, while freeing those men whom the major had placed in confinement. Carson disgustedly remarked that he could not "blame these people [the Navajo] for distrusting the good faith of the troops at this Post, from the manner in which their Messengers have been received at it on more than one occasion."

Blakeney was sent to Santa Fe to explain his side of the story to his friend General Carleton. The major complained about the men at Fort Canby, saying: "I am subjected to the organized hostility of the officers of the Navajo Expedition; which hostility seems prompted by a natural hatred and jealousy of officers hailing from the state of California."

On September 13, while Colonel Carson was out on another scout, fellow Californian James Carleton dropped all of the charges against Maj. Thomas Blakeney and transferred him to Pinos Altos.[34]

Carleton then answered Carson's concerns about the treatment of those Indians who desired to surrender by writing:

> You are right in believing that I do not wish to have those destroyed who are willing to come in. Nor will you permit an Indian prisoner once fairly in our custody to be killed unless he be endeavoring to make his escape. There is to be no other alternative but this: say to them "Go to the Bosque Redondo, or we will pursue and destroy you. We will not make peace with you on any other terms. You have deceived us too often and robbed and murdered our people too long—to trust you again at large in your own country. This war shall be pursued against you if it takes years, now that we have begun, until you cease to exist or move. There can be no other talk on the subject."[35]

Carleton had chosen not to address the possible consequences of Blakeney's behavior with respect to peaceful Navajo people who desired to surrender, and again reiterated his intention to either confine or exterminate the tribe. There was no telling how many Indians changed their minds about voluntarily coming in when word of Blakeney's treatment passed through the Navajo nation.

Col. Kit Carson, in obedience of the general's orders, set aside the matter and continued his relentless pursuit of the Navajo.

On September 9, he departed Fort Canby with just over 400 troopers and moved southeast toward Zuni Pueblo. The Zuni professed that they had killed several Navajo and captured some sheep and goats. In a show of their friendliness to (or fear of) the whites, the governor of the pueblo provided Carson with a number of scouts to assist in the operation.[36]

The column did not encounter any sign of their enemy until late September, when they discovered a small, recently abandoned village. The troopers burned everything—hogans, saddles, bridles, and blankets—and captured nineteen animals. The warriors had been watching the soldiers from a concealed location and were soon afforded an opportunity to exact some measure of revenge. Three soldiers had ridden away from the main column to chase down several horses that had bolted. The Navajo ambushed these isolated men, killing one and wounding another. Carson gave chase, and about eight miles away, a detachment of six soldiers came upon a lone Indian. In the ensuing skirmish, that Indian was wounded at least three times but escaped—after managing to wound one of the bluecoats.

Upon his return to the fort in early October, Carson was disappointed to report that his scout "was a failure as regards to any positive injury inflicted on the Navajoes."[37]

Carson personally remained at Fort Canby throughout the month of October and into mid-November, while regularly dispatching scouting expeditions. These patrols, which explored the area south of the fort between Zuni and Pueblo Colorado, failed to locate any enemy. But as winter set in, the Navajo became more desperate. The scorched-earth policy enacted by the army had destroyed many villages and acres of crops, which forced the Indians to become bolder in an effort to survive. They raided military horse herds with great success, much to the embarrassment of the army. In early November, however, a party of New Mexican civilians engaged a Navajo war raiding party. They killed fourteen Indians, captured sixty, and took twenty horses and mules and twenty-five goats and sheep.[38]

On November 15, Carson departed Fort Canby with five dismounted companies and a detachment of Zuni scouts, and headed toward the Hopi villages "for the purpose of exploring the country west of the Oribi villages and, if possible to chastise the Navajoes inhabiting the region." The column marched for three weeks and destroyed two small Navajo villages, killing four warriors and wounding three others, until the poor condition of the animals forced a return to the fort.

The prolonged campaign could not be called a total success for Carleton's army, but it had produced some encouraging results. To that point in time, almost 200 Navajo—including Chief Degadito—had surrendered at Fort Wingate for transfer to Bosque Redondo. A total of 301 Indians had been killed, 87 wounded, and 703 captured. The army had lost seventeen soldiers killed and twenty-five wounded.[39]

Colonel Carson applied for a two-month leave of absence on December 15. He was anxious to see his wife, Josefa, who was expecting their sixth child. Besides that, the army animals would require time to recuperate, and the Navajo had been quite elusive, as they apparently had found a shelter from the cold and snow. And Carson was of the opinion that a winter campaign on foot would be highly impractical, whereas by February, the weather would have improved enough to resume operations. Carleton, however, responded, "I have not authority to grant you leave." The general had been making plans that would not allow Carson and the troops to rest for the remainder of the winter.[40]

General Carleton wanted Carson to mount an expedition to invade Canyon de Chelly, the traditional Navajo stronghold located some forty miles northwest of Fort Canby in northeastern Arizona. This mysterious canyon—thirty miles long and shaped like a Y, with red-rock walls rising to a height of 1,500 feet—was relatively unknown territory to whites. The Anasazi, or "Ancient Ones," were said to have been the first inhabitants of the canyon, building rock, adobe, and plaster homes along the sheer ledges above a fertile floor through which flowed a pleasant waterway. The Anasazi at some point, for reasons unknown, abandoned the canyon, and it became home to the Navajo, who lived along the rims and constructed their hogans on the sandy floor, where they planted gardens and peach orchards. Many sites and rock formations within the walls of Canyon de Chelly were considered sacred to the Navajo.

The canyon had long been deemed almost impregnable. The Spanish had located it in 1805 and were said to have at that time killed a number of Navajo. In 1849, army colonels John M. Washington and Edwin V. Sumner had marched twelve to fourteen miles into the western end, under a vicious attack of arrows, musket balls, and rocks, until forced to retreat. Lt. Dixon S. Miles had entered Monument Canyon in 1858, and Capt. John G. Walker had first traversed the central gorge the following year. Miles warned that "no command should ever again enter" Canyon de Chelly.[41]

On January 6, 1864, Col. Kit Carson departed Fort Canby with an expedition force of 14 officers and 375 enlisted men, consisting of New Mexico volunteers and a few California troops, and marched across the high, snow-covered landscape, headed for the western entrance of Canyon de Chelly. The troops struggled through deep snow on foot, carrying overcoats and blankets along with their normal gear, while the officers were mounted.

Carson's spirits during this difficult march were most likely quite low. He longed to be at home with his wife and considered the expedition a waste of time. He did not believe that significant numbers of Navajo would be found in the canyon, an opinion that he had voiced to Carleton to no avail. In addition, he was aware of the toll the march would have on his animals at that time of year. Nevertheless, Kit Carson, the good soldier, would carry out his mission to the best of his ability.

Carson had dispatched the supply train three days earlier and also sent out a second column of thirty-three men from the 1st New Mexico Cavalry—under Capt. Albert Pfeiffer, whose zeal as an Indian fighter resulted from the murder of his wife at the hands of Apache the previous year—toward the canyon's east entrance.

Carson's column, hampered by deep and drifting snow, reached Pueblo Colorado in three days—normally a one-day march—where he picked up the wagon train. The expedition finally arrived at the west entrance of Canyon de Chelly on January 12.[42]

Carson and his staff embarked on a preliminary reconnaissance that took them some four to five miles along the south rim of the canyon. They were seeking a pathway down but found the "heights of the sides averaging about one thousand feet and nearly perpendicular." The detail did, however, observe several Indians out of rifle range on the opposite side of the canyon.

Carson returned to camp and was greeted by Sgt. Andres Herrera, who had been in charge of a fifty-man patrol that had been combing the area since the previous night. At daylight, Herrera had overtaken a group of Indians just as they were about to enter the canyon and attacked them. His men had killed eleven Navajo and captured two women and two children, along with 130 sheep and goats.

Carson was growing anxious about Captain Pfeiffer's command, from which nothing had been heard. On the morning of January 13, he decided to send out two commands of two companies each, with three days' rations, which would operate on opposite sides of the canyon to search for Pfeiffer. Capt. Joseph Berney of the 1st New Mexico Cavalry would reconnoiter the north side, and Capt. Asa B. Carey, with Carson accompanying, would march along the south rim.[43]

Carson and Carey arrived at the site of Sergeant Herrera's encounter and found the bodies of the eleven dead Navajo. Nearby lay five wounded warriors, two of whom soon died. The others were treated by Dr. John H. Shout, who determined that they would survive. The following morning, the men arrived at a point from which they believed that they had an unobstructed view of the eastern entrance, but they were unable to discern any sign of Pfeiffer or Indians. They did, however, pass by many striking adobe ruins built by the Anasazi, which had been constructed from materials and colors taken from the canyon walls. Those landmarks, as well as others on their route, such as a pair of 800-foot natural pinnacles known as Spider Rock, were sacred places to the Navajo. The patrol also encountered some Navajo waving a flag of truce, "requesting permission to come in with their people and submit." Carson gave them until 10:00 the following morning to comply.

The discouraged patrol returned to the main camp, where, much to their surprise and gratification, they found Pfeiffer and his party waiting for them. Pfeiffer and his men had bypassed the main entrance to the canyon during a blinding snowstorm and entered through the northern branch. They had traveled along a frozen stream, taking a few starving prisoners along the way, and skirmished several times with groups of Navajo warriors. The detail had traversed the entire canyon from east to west, which was believed to have been an unprecedented feat. Pfeiffer reported that they had killed three warriors without losing a man, and he presented the relieved Carson with nineteen women and children they had captured.[44]

The next morning, about sixty ragged, emaciated Indians appeared at the camp, professing a willingness to emigrate to Bosque Redondo. These people were in various stages of starvation and nearly frozen to death. Carson noted that they "were agreeably surprised and delighted" when they realized that they would not be shot. The Navajo were given meat and blankets, and told to return to the canyon and collect the remainder of their people and report to the post within ten days. With that encounter, Carson believed that his mission had been accomplished and it was now time to return to Fort Canby.[45]

Meanwhile, Captain Carey requested that he be permitted to pass through the canyon on the return trip of this historic expedition. Carson agreed, and Carey departed on January 16 with two companies, seventy-five troopers, from the 1st New Mexico Cavalry. Carey traveled within the canyon from west to east, destroying Navajo property with abandon along the way, including a large number of expansive peach orchards. He also encountered large numbers of starved and near-naked Navajo, who asked to surrender. By the time Carey reached Fort Canby on January 18, over 100 Indians accompanied him, and many more followed along the trail.[46]

Colonel Carson arrived at Fort Canby with the main column on January 21. He reported the results of his expedition, which included 23 Navajo killed, 34 captured, over 200 who voluntarily surrendered, and an undetermined number of additional Indians who would be coming in to the post. Perhaps more telling, he had also captured 200 sheep and destroyed countless acres of crops, orchards, and property, which would render the Navajo impoverished. Carson stated:

> But it is to the ulterior effects of the "Expedition" that I look for
> the greatest results. We have shown the Indians that in no place,

however formidable or inaccessible, in their opinion, are they safe from the pursuit of the troops of this command; and have convinced a large portion of them that the struggle on their part is a hopeless one. We have also demonstrated that the intentions of the Government toward them are eminently humane; and dictated by an earnest desire to promote their welfare; that the principle is not to destroy but to save them, if they are disposed to be saved.[47]

The Carleton-Carson Canyon de Chelly expedition effectively brought the Navajo campaign to an end, with the principals being hailed as heroes by the people of New Mexico for ridding the territory of this red menace. At the same time, word spread throughout the Navajo nation that they would be fed rather than killed if they surrendered. By the end of January, nearly 3,000 cold and destitute Navajo had voluntarily surrendered. That figure had doubled by March, and altogether, some 8,000 Navajo—about three-quarters of the tribe—submitted and were taken in groups or awaited transport to Bosque Redondo.[48]

Thus commenced the most tragic chapter in Navajo history—the transport in large groups of thousands of the tribe a distance of 425 miles to their new home at Bosque Redondo. This episode, which would forever be known as the Long Walk, would—like the Cherokee Trail of Tears—become a symbol of the white man's injustice toward the Indians.

This arduous march on foot could be likened to a number of cattle drives, other than the fact that the cowboys perhaps respected their charges more than the army cared about the health and welfare of the Indians. Navajo accounts of this death march claim that people who lagged behind—the sick and the old—were shot, women and girls were raped by soldiers, and not enough food to eat was issued. Perhaps as many as 3,000 Navajo died from malnutrition, disease, exposure, and exhaustion during the course of the Long Walk.

Conditions at the forty-square-mile reservation at Bosque Redondo were not much of an improvement for the arriving Navajo refugees. There were barely enough rations to feed the 450 Mescalero who already lived there. Consequently, the Navajo continued to die of various illnesses related to malnutrition, as well as a measles epidemic into the year 1865. An estimated 2,000 were said to have succumbed during the first two years of captivity. Eventually, the outnumbered Mescalero, who resented the presence of the Navajo, fled the reservation and returned to their former hiding places in New Mexico.

In 1868, Gen. William Tecumseh Sherman visited Bosque Redondo and was horrified by the deplorable conditions. He informed President Grant, who took action by dispatching emissaries to negotiate a new treaty. In June 1868, the Navajo and the United States signed a treaty that allowed the Indians to finally escape Bosque Redondo and return to live on a reservation in their devastated homeland.

To emphasize the extent of the destruction left in the army's wake in 1864, a campaign to replant the orchards destroyed by the scorched-earth policy of Carson and his troops continues to this day.[49]

CHAPTER SEVEN

The Woolsey Expeditions

AFTER PARTICIPATING IN THE CAPTURE AND DEATH OF APACHE CHIEF Mangas Coloradas, mountain man Joseph R. Walker and his band of twenty-six adventurers resumed their search for gold in early 1863. The group departed Fort McLane and headed to Tucson, pausing only briefly to visit the Pima-Maricopa villages, then turned north and crossed the desert into an unexplored region of central Arizona.[1]

In February, Congress had separated Arizona from New Mexico, and it was now a territory in its own right, but for the time being, it remained under the authority of Brig. Gen. James H. Carleton's Department of New Mexico.

According to Daniel Conner, the company of men endured many hardships on this journey:

> The country from Tucson was nothing but one continuous desert. The only grass on the route of any consideration was coarse like wheat-straw and stood in bunches six or eight inches in diameter about the desert, with sand drifted against it. What little water we succeeded in finding was of a light mud color and is never known to become clear, nor even the least transparent.[2]

In May, Walker and his men began combing the terrain up Hassayampa Creek, a northern tributary of the Gila River, and were soon quite impressed with the prospects of finding gold in paying quantities in that area. They established a camp in the woods, which would become widely known as Walker's Diggings, or Walker's Camp, and erected the "stoutest corral ever built in Central Arizona." The men held a miners' meeting to establish boundaries for a mining district. Naturally, Joe Walker was elected governor of the district, but he declined the office, as did Daniel E. Conner. Finally, Thomas Johnson accepted the post. Fifty-two claims were then staked off along the Hassayampa up- and downstream from the camp, and the men drew numbers from a hat to determine ownership of two each.[3]

The prospectors were excited about having survived their arduous march through the desert and establishing a relatively comfortable base camp. Daniel Conner described the scene:

> We all now felt at home as the different messes were located around our heavy corral, with our stock safe within its stout high and rugged walls, and our mining property all divided off. There was no white population within hundreds of miles to be laying claims to our vast empire of deserts, whose capital was this camp in this splendid woods.[4]

One day in June, the miners buried "all the superfluous plunder" and set off across the Gila Desert to obtain supplies at a Pima Indian village.

On the return trip, Walker and his band encountered a body of mounted men on the trail and, thinking them to be Apache, prepared to engage in battle. These strangers, however, proved to be a party of Californians under the leadership of Pauline Weaver. This old mountain man and trapper from Tennessee, who was part Cherokee, had worked for the Hudson Bay Company, served as a guide for the Mormon Battalion in 1846, and discovered the pacer mines at La Paz, Arizona, in 1861. Joe Walker, an old acquaintance, informed Weaver about the prospects of gold around the Hassayampa. Weaver decided to investigate on his own and would eventually discover a strike that would be called the Weaver's Diggings in the Weaver Mining District.[5]

Walker and his men returned to their home in the "splendid woods" twenty days later, and preparations for mining operations commenced in earnest. The men constructed a rocker for washing gold from felled trees, and the search for rich deposits made progress. The diggings did not initially yield what they had expected, but there was enough color to convince them that it was only a matter of time before they would discover paying quantities. The only drawback was the occasional visits from Apache Indians, who became progressively troublesome. Violence was avoided, but the Indians were concerned about the presence of whites on their traditional land, which had the miners on guard.[6]

In the fall, the members of the party began prospecting in groups to enhance the odds of finding better diggings, which led them over a range lying at right angles to Hassayampa Creek, out of their organized district. Miner Sam C. Miller began prospecting about a mile up a creek on the eastern foot of this range. The twenty-three-year-old Miller had traveled to California from his home in Peoria, Illinois, to seek adventure. While working along this creek, Miller happened upon a lynx and shot and wounded the animal. Instead of running away, however, the lynx charged Miller, who was obliged to empty his six-shooter in order to dispatch the vicious beast. This incident gave the waterway its name of Lynx Creek.

And it was on Lynx Creek that the first strike of gold in paying quantities was found, likely by Sam Miller. The miners subsequently abandoned their old camp in the woods and established a new headquarters at the head of Lynx Creek.[7]

Word of Walker's discovery reached Santa Fe. It was welcome news to Brig. Gen. James H. Carleton, who boasted that with enough troops, he could "whip away the Apaches" and prove that the Southwest had "mines of precious metals unsurpassed in richness, number, and extent by any in the world." New Mexico surveyor general John A. Clark was dispatched to the mines, accompanied by an escort of Carleton's soldiers, who were instructed to seek a proper site for a new fort. Carleton promised to provide protection for this mining district, and on October 23, he created by general order the Military District of Northern Arizona, which encompassed everything in the new territory north of the Gila River. He ordered Maj. Edward B. Willis, with Companies C and F of the 1st California Infantry and Company D from the 1st California cavalry, to the mining district to establish Fort Whipple near the headwaters of the Verde River.

In January 1864, Arizona governor John M. Goodwin and other territorial officials, escorted from Santa Fe by a detachment of Col. Kit Carson's volunteers, arrived at Fort Whipple. The governor toured the area extensively and eventually came to the conclusion that the territorial seat would be located at the rollicking mining town of Prescott, which had grown near the place where Walker's adventurers had found gold.

This town of 500 people—and growing—was named for historian William Hickling Prescott, who had written extensively about Spanish conquests in the New World and was the favorite author of Territorial Secretary Richard C. McCormick. It was chosen as the capital not only because of the nearby bustling gold fields, but also because President Lincoln believed that Southern sympathizers dominated Tucson, the other logical place. Major Willis moved Fort Whipple, which had been twenty miles away, to Granite Creek a mile and a half northeast of Prescott to display a show of force to the Indians who roamed the area.[8]

And the presence of the army would indeed be required in an effort to maintain peace—perhaps as much among the whites as for protection against hostile Indians. The gold rush had brought to Prescott hordes of miners, opportunists, and merchants, as well as farmers and ranchers to feed them—typical mining town ingredients that at times combined to create an explosive mixture.

Prescott and the surrounding mines had been carved from territory inhabited by the Yavapai and Apache Indians. The Yavapai were a Yuman group commonly referred to as Apache, but although culturally similar to the Apache, they were actually unrelated to that tribe. The confusion might have been derived from the fact that the Yuma Indians gave the Yavapai the name e-patch ("men that fight"), which sounds a lot like the word Apache. The Yavapai and Apache, who upon occasion intermarried and were allies, responded at first to the white intruders by involving themselves in incidences of petty theft, but in time the Prescott area experienced its first recorded killing of a white by an Indian.[9]

A man from Missouri named George Goodhue and another called Sugarfoot Jack—a twenty-two-year-old who was said to have been an escaped convict from Australia who had enlisted in the California volunteers but had been cashiered for some unknown offense—had been occupying a cabin near Joe Walker's original corral. Goodhue and six companions were headed toward Prescott, when Sugarfoot Jack heard firing about a half mile away and ran in that direction to determine the source.

Unknown to Jack, the party had been ambushed by a band of Indians. George Goodhue was instantly killed, and several others, who dropped what they were carrying and ran off, were slightly wounded. The Indians then stripped and mutilated Goodhue's body and stole all the possessions left behind by the white men.

Sugarfoot Jack waited behind a large rock until fifteen Indians, loaded down with plunder, came down the pathway to within ten paces of his concealed position. Jack opened fire, killing one Indian and wounding another, and kept firing as the others fled, killing one more and wounding another.

By the time Goodhue's companions arrived on the scene, they found Sugarfoot Jack calmly smoking his pipe. The men retrieved Goodhue's clothing and other articles belonging to whites that the Indians had apparently stolen. Sugarfoot Jack, by the way, did not simply become a footnote in the pages of history for this incident, but later participated in one of the more controversial yet least known events that occurred in warfare with the Apache.[10]

This bloody skirmish coincided with another act of Indian-white violence, which occurred at Pauline Weaver's Diggings. Two Apache boys had visited the town, either to see the sights or trade, and were gunned down in cold blood by the resident miners. The miners had apparently panicked and allowed their fears to overrule common sense when they spotted these specimens of what they believed were a "warlike people, untamable, bloodthirsty, unconquerable."[11]

Perhaps this "shoot first, parley later" attitude was a direct result of the tension created by the ambush of George Goodhue and his companions. Or possibly it was provoked by Territorial Secretary McCormick's comment that "the sentiment here is in favor of an utter extermination of the ruthless savages who have so long prevented the settlement and development of the territory."[12]

As time passed, incidences of livestock theft by Indians became progressively worse, and the army was not prepared to adequately respond. The local citizens, therefore, decided to take matters into their own hands and organized an Indian-hunting expedition. This hunt into Indian country was intended to provide the miners and townspeople an opportunity to exact revenge and perhaps recover some of their lost animals, but it also held the prospect of exciting sport and a chance to explore new lands that might contain mineral deposits. The man who would assume command of this first Indian-hunting expedition was a Prescott-area rancher named King S. Woolsey.

Woolsey had been born in Alabama in 1832, raised in Louisiana, and arrived in Arizona in 1861 via California. One account claims that he had enlisted in the Confederate army but saw no service. Woolsey worked briefly as a freighter east from Yuma, then found a partner and established the Agua Caliente ranch about eighty miles up the Gila River. They built an irrigation canal on the ranch, set up a flour mill, and provided flour and hay to the army at Yuma, then furnished supplies to the California Column upon its arrival in Arizona in 1862.

Woolsey worked for a while wielding a pick and shovel with Joe Walker's band near Prescott, but he soon abandoned that endeavor and established another ranch, this one east of Prescott on the Agua Fria River near present-day Dewey. The ranch headquarters was constructed on the site of a prehistoric ruin, using rock from the ruin in the building of two structures and a shoulder-high wall that enclosed the compound.

Woolsey, a "dignified, full-bearded man," was certainly one of the Southwest's more colorful characters. He had a reputation as "a man of intelligence, of undoubted courage, but something of an opportunist and quite a rascal." One historian called King Woolsey "the most notable, the most enterprising and the most courageous of all the great host of trailblazers who first penetrated Arizona."[13]

Woolsey's Agua Fria ranch was located as far east of Prescott as any ranch at that point in time, and for that reason it was subjected to frequent Indian raids that cost him countless numbers of livestock. This constant danger that Woolsey faced from Indians engendered an intense hatred within him for that race.

In fact, Woolsey had already earned notoriety as an Indian fighter from an encounter near Burke's Station on the Gila River. He and two companions were returning to Agua Caliente ranch with a load of hay, when they found themselves surrounded by an overwhelming number of hostile Indians. The chief advanced toward Woolsey, who held a double-barreled shotgun—the only weapon the white men had. When the chief had approached within a few paces, Woolsey pulled the trigger, killing the Indian. The other hostiles hastily fled. Woolsey, who was aware of Indian superstitions, then hung the chief's body from a mesquite tree as a warning to other Indians who would dare to challenge him. The body dangled there for several years and became prey for passing scavengers.[14]

On another occasion, Woolsey was being menaced by a band of Apache while prospecting in the Bradshaw Mountains. He invited the Indians into his camp for a parley, then fixed some food—pinole, or cornmeal, which was a favorite of the Apache—and mixed into it a dose of strychnine. While he talked with the chief, the other Apache found the pinole and began to eat. One by one, they toppled over in pain. The sight had quite an effect on the chief, who, clearly frightened, dashed away with his remaining warriors. In an episode that became known as the "Pinole Treaty," as many as twenty-five Indians were said to have been victims of Woolsey's deadly concoction.[15]

King Woolsey volunteered to lead the first Indian-hunting expedition in early January 1864 in retaliation for the theft of twenty-seven head of horses and mules that belonged to Abe Peeples, one of his neighbors. Peeples was codiscoverer, along with Pauline Weaver, of the Rich Hill Mine and owned a ranch named Antelope Hill. In addition to the losses by Peeples, in the preceding two months nearly all the horses from the mines, about 300 to 400 head, had been taken, and Fort Whipple had lost about forty mules. And Woolsey was not merely being neighborly by helping Peeples; his own ranch also had been victimized on numerous occasions.

In the words of expedition participant John K. Simmons:

We are determined, if possible, to punish the guilty Indians. Otherwise, unless the government takes a hand, we have to leave this country and let the Indians have it. Many have already left on account of the Indians, and many more talk of leaving. The Indians are becoming more bold daily, and as soon as they steal the remnant of stock left, so as not to be followed, they will commence murdering small parties of prospectors and miners. . . . The whites have either to leave or the Indians have to be badly whipped.[16]

"Captain" Woolsey led a party of thirty to forty Indian hunters—miners, ranchmen, and traders from the vicinity of Antelope Hill and Weaver's Diggings—along the Agua Fria River through the Black Canyon to the plains of the lower Verde River, also known as the San Francisco, where they camped in a defensive position they jokingly referred to as Fort Badger. The group was running low on rations, so Abe Peeples and several others were dispatched to the nearby Pima villages to procure supplies and also, if possible, to recruit Indian reinforcements.

Peeples and his party returned with the supplies, accompanied by a group of forty-two Pima and Maricopa Indians, including noted Maricopa war chief Juan Chivaree and two white men, who had volunteered to join the expedition. These warriors were quite willing and anxious to fight against their age-old enemy, the Apache. One of the Indians, a young man they nicknamed Jack (not to be confused with Sugarfoot Jack), wanted to make certain that only the guilty Indians were punished, and volunteered to serve as guide and interpreter for the outfit. Jack, a Yuma Indian, had once been held as a captive by the Apache.[17]

The expedition, now totaling seventy-two men, headed out from Fort Badger on the afternoon of January 22 and traveled on the trail of the stolen horses for about five miles before camping on the Salt River, above the mouth of the Verde River. Scouts were dispatched to reconnoiter the mountainous terrain ahead, and the men settled in to rest. The white men, however, would not spend a restful night. After dark, the Maricopa and Pima formed a circle and, led by Chief Juan Chivaree, began making war speeches and singing and chanting, asking for protection from the spirits. This ceremony continued throughout the night. The scouts returned in the morning, having noticed fresh sign but nothing else of consequence.

Woolsey's outfit, perhaps somewhat frazzled and weary after listening to the night's entertainment, moved out with the Maricopa in the advance. They had gone about five or six miles when it was discovered that the Pima had vanished. These Indians calculated that they had journeyed far enough into Apache country and feared for their lives. With the loss of the Pima, the Indians who remained with the expedition numbered only seventeen Maricopa.[18]

The outfit halted at noon. Woolsey had decided that they would rest for the remainder of the day. They would resume their march late that afternoon and travel throughout the night. It was about 4:00 P.M. when they broke camp and began traversing terrain that John Simmons called "the worst and most dangerous trail I ever witnessed." They had found the Salt River, a winding, deep waterway with extremely high banks. The men moved cautiously through the river gorge, which they called Endless Canyon. In order to maintain their direction, they were compelled to frequently cross at deep-water fords and occasionally abandon the canyon floor and climb up the steep sides to avoid treacherous obstacles. Woolsey ordered a halt at about 2:00 A.M. on January 24 to permit the worn-out adventurers several hours to recuperate from the difficult march.[19]

Four hours later, the men were traipsing through rugged territory unknown to even the Maricopa. They had left the river to follow a creek bed, eventually coming upon a recently abandoned Indian rancheria. Apache sign in this area was plentiful, and they soon arrived at a location where the Indians had been camped the previous day with a large number of livestock. The scouts were dispatched in every direction but failed to find any Apache in the immediate vicinity. Inasmuch as they were near good water, Woolsey suggested that they camp and revive themselves with hot coffee.

John Simmons described what happened next:

Our fires had barely got under way before the war-whoop was heard in the distance. Soon signal fires were built on the tops of the highest mountains, and the wild Apaches were heard and seen coming from every point on the compass. In two hours they were in hailing distance; and, as they had seen us first, we knew unless by strategy, we would get no fight on the square. It was then that our [guide and interpreter] Jack came into play. The Indians had raised their war-flag on the mountain to our rear, and were gathering in that direction to cut off our retreat. Our Captain told Jack to ask them what they were going to do. They remarked that they had us in a place that we could not get out, and that they intended to kill us; [they] said that we came to fight, and that they would give us a chance. They said they knew from the fact of our following the tracks of the stolen horses that we came to punish them, and dared us, and they kicked dirt at us, suiting the action to the word with the toe of their moccasins.[20]

This turn of events was certainly disconcerting to the Indian hunters, who had now become the hunted. The Indians, estimated at between 300 and 500 in number, maintained a position only some 100 yards above Woolsey's camp—just out of rifle range. The men herded their animals into a place where they could not be stampeded and hunkered down to assess their situation.

Unless some strategy could be readily developed, they would be compelled to retreat for many miles back down the canyon while dodging bullets, arrows, and rocks from above as they passed through a gauntlet of Indians. After some meaningful discussion, it was decided that Jack would make an effort to reason with them. The Indian interpreter explained that they were merely a party of prospectors and invited a delegation into camp, where they would receive presents of tobacco and pinole.

The Apache initially scoffed at such an idea but eventually agreed to send six of their chiefs to meet with King Woolsey and five others halfway between the two forces. Woolsey advised his men to be alert, telling them that he would raise his hat with his left hand as a signal for them to start shooting if treachery was afoot. The men promised to watch for any signal but also were keenly aware that just one volley from the surrounding Indians would probably kill or wound everyone in their ranks. Their only hope, they believed, was that Woolsey could in some manner persuade the Apache to grant permission for them to safely leave the area.[21]

The parley was progressing in fine fashion, with King Woolsey acting as the gracious host, passing out lavish quantities of tobacco and pinole to his guests. When one chief demanded that Woolsey brush away the dirt so that he could sit down without soiling his buckskins, the captain instead spread out a new, blood-colored blanket for that Indian. One by one, other Indians drifted into the camp to share in Woolsey's generosity.

The Apache were quite amused by Woolsey's good-humored pleas to allow him and his "prospectors" to leave the country unharmed. The chiefs would repeat Woolsey's translated words to the hundreds of warriors perched on the rocky hillsides, who would howl with laughter at the absurd request.

Capt. King Woolsey, however, had never intended to place himself or his men at the mercy of the Indians. The Apache did have one disadvantage in that they had no interpreter of their own and could not understand what Woolsey was saying when he spoke English. While Woolsey pretended to negotiate for his release, he "selected each of his companions [an] Indian to kill" and laughingly warned them in English "not to let one chief escape to rally the privates and the battle would be thus already half won."[22]

The chiefs were unaware of this scheme and were enjoying themselves immensely, grinning and chatting amiably, pleased with this apparent hospitality shown by their enemy. Without warning, Woolsey reached to raise his hat with one hand and drew his pistol with the other.

The Indian hunters responded to the signal with a crashing volley of fire that, within an instant, killed every chief but one. The sixth chief, who had been shot twice in the body, raised his eight-foot-long lance and thrust it through the heart of Cyrus Lennan, before being dispatched by a bullet from the pistol of Joe Dye.

Woolsey's men rushed forward, with repeating rifles and six-shooters aflame, and managed to kill more of the nearby stunned Indians. The Apache on the hillside fired an aimless volley, then, fulfilling Woolsey's prediction, turned and ran as the white men chased after them up a draw for about half a mile before losing contact.[23]

Woolsey's outfit had suffered one man killed—Lennan—and several others wounded, including Jack the interpreter, who took an arrow in the neck. None of the wounds, however, were of a serious nature.

Woolsey estimated that they had killed twenty-four Indians, but the precise number was never determined—they never waited around to make an exact tally. His men, anxious to leave that "unholy place," quickly loaded the pack animals and rode until they had exited the canyon before stopping, perhaps somewhere near the junction of the Verde and Salt Rivers. They had, however, paused long enough before leaving to take a few scalps and appropriate some pairs of moccasins.

Cyrus Lennan's body had been lashed across a pack mule and taken along. He was subsequently buried under a cottonwood tree, upon which his name and the date were carved. A fire was built on top of the grave to conceal its location. The Indian hunters then retraced their route and returned home.[24]

There has been some question about the precise location of this engagement, which has yet to be settled. Artifacts and relics have been uncovered at Bloody Tanks, at the head of Bloody Tanks Wash, the west branch of Pinal Creek, near Miami. This, however, was documented as the site of a fight between 1st Lt. Howard B. Cushing and the Apache several years after the Woolsey affair, and it is presumed that the artifacts came from this conflict. Therefore, the site of Woolsey's battle in the Pinal Mountains remains a mystery. This fight with the Apache has been commonly referred to as the Bloody Tanks battle, or massacre, but occasionally it has been confused with the "Pinole Treaty," the poisoning episode that had occurred earlier in Woolsey's life.

Woolsey's fight at Bloody Tanks, or whatever the exact location, has been branded a massacre by some. Was Woolsey's scheme—taking the initiative and getting the jump on the Indians—an act of savagery that constitutes a massacre, or was it merely an act of desperation viewed as the only way to possibly save the lives of his men?

The definition of a massacre would be a case where the indiscriminate killing of human beings—especially noncombatants—occurred. The facts reveal that Woolsey and his men were surrounded by a well-armed enemy. The whites were outnumbered at least four or five to one and had been threatened with death. The Indians had good reason to harm the whites, not wanting to be made in any way to pay for stealing livestock, an act of which they were likely guilty.

Woolsey and his men had certainly realized that their lives were in grave danger, and the captain resorted to what he believed was his only chance to save their lives or at least go down fighting—outsmart them, which he did with what can only be termed a mighty gutsy move. He could have calculated wrong in his belief that the Indians would run away when their chiefs were gunned down, which would have resulted in the annihilation of the whites.

Some historians may have labeled the fight a massacre because they confused it with the poisoning incident. Otherwise, the evidence does not fit the crime.

Perhaps J. P. Dunn, Jr., put it best in his *Massacres in the Mountains: A History of the Indian Wars of the Far West, 1815–1875,* when he wrote about Bloody Tanks:

> These Indians would undoubtedly have murdered their new white friends if they had obtained the opportunity. They are entitled to no compassion on the ground of treachery used against them. The Apache makes war by treachery. His object is to harm his enemy but escape unharmed, and he thinks that a man who walks up to open danger is a fool. He will go into dangerous places himself, but he goes by stealth. He never attacks except by surprise. He is brave but has no ambition to die a soldier's death. Apache glory consists strictly in killing the enemy.[25]

Two months passed, and Woolsey's Indian-hunting expedition had had little effect with respect to subduing or diminishing the Indian menace around Prescott. In fact, as word of his deed spread throughout Indian country, the killings might have even served to incite more violence among the enraged Apache. Conditions had become so bad that it was as if the whites lived on reservations and the Indians occupied the free country. The army that garrisoned Fort Whipple had yet to mount an effective campaign; therefore, King S. Woolsey decided that a second venture into hostile Apache country would be in order.

On the night of March 29, 1864, Woolsey led a party of about eighty experienced Indian hunters—outfitted with ten days' rations—from his Agua Fria ranch. Twenty other men would follow the next day with a pack train loaded with additional provisions. The men rode in a southerly direction across the low range of Granite Hills, through dense oak brush, until about 2:00 A.M., covering perhaps three to four miles, when they decided to camp for the night.

At sunrise, the expedition resumed its march through a volcanic formation of black lava. It halted in the early afternoon to rest on the east branch of the Agua Fria. The men were roused at dusk and traveled until about 11:00 P.M. At that time, Woolsey determined that it would be prudent to scout the area in daylight and called a halt for the night. The following day, the horses grazed in the grassy pasture, and the men fished in a stream they called Ash Creek, while Woolsey scouted. He returned from his reconnaissance without having found any Indian sign, and moved the men out of the pleasant camp at about 10:00 P.M.

Scouts who had been dispatched earlier reported back to Woolsey on the march that fresh Indian sign had been found about a mile ahead along a stream. The men ventured forward with caution, passing several creeks that ran from the Agua Fria, but discovered only a group of deserted wigwams. They pushed ahead for about fifteen or sixteen more miles to the south, before arriving within proximity of a place where they had received earlier reports that Indians were camped.[26]

Woolsey intended to take these Indians by surprise. He set out at 10:00 P.M. with forty-five men, who traveled in single file for less than an hour before halting. The captain then divided his men into three companies: A, B, and C. He led Company A, in his personal command, on an easterly course, while Company C went to the southwest, and Company B held the center. By 9:00 A.M. on April 1, the companies approached an Apache encampment in a nearby canyon.

Company B, which was the closest detachment, advanced to within rifle range of the camp before being discovered by the Indians. Upon being noticed, the group of men charged, firing first with rifles, then closing in with pistols smoking. The Indians could not withstand the pressure of this furious rush and fell back up the canyon—right into the sights of Company C. The point-blank volleys from these rifles had a devastating effect on the oncoming Indians, and many hit the ground instantly dead, with the others, including the wounded, scampering away into the brush.

When it was over, fourteen bodies—presumedly male, although no gender was mentioned—were counted on the field, with an unknown number of those who managed to escape thought to be badly wounded. Woolsey's party emerged from the skirmish unscathed. The men were somewhat disappointed by the small size of the camp, however, and guessed that most of the Indians had been out raiding and had thereby escaped death for the time being.

In this place of eighteen wigwams, which the men dubbed "Squaw Canyon," they found about 1,000 recently made arrow points, a large amount of mescal—the tops of which contain a narcotic stimulating substance—and a collection of rawhides, several burned with brands that were recognized, including one piece from a large American bull that had been stolen from King Woolsey.[27]

On the morning of April 2, the expedition set out to rendezvous with the pack train. At about noon, while the men were eating lunch at Cane Creek, one of the party, Artemus Ingalls, who had been out on his own hunting deer and antelope, stumbled into camp with two arrows stuck in his body—one in the back, the other in his right shoulder. Ingalls had ventured into a war party of Indians and was able to escape before falling into their hands, although his hat had also been shot from his head and lost. Ingalls received prompt attention from Dr. John T. Alsap, who had also accompanied Woolsey's first expedition. The doctor determined that Ingalls would fully recover from his brush with death.

Woolsey's Indian hunters arrived at about sunset at Ash Creek, where they camped. The following day, April 3, thirty men were dispatched to scout the vicinity of a pine-covered mountain that bordered the upper valley of the Verde River. The remainder of the party made contact with their pack train that evening. They settled in to rest at the head of the east branch of the Agua Fria River. They were later visited by a detachment of Missouri volunteers under a Colonel Chavez, who were passing through while exploring a feasible route through the area toward the Little Colorado River, which was intended to shorten the trip to Wingate.

On April 5, Woolsey led his men through Diablo Canyon, where they noticed "a fair copper lode of that class called atacamite, which if in the vicinity of a navigable river, or a railroad, would undoubtedly be valuable." They were camped on the Verde River when the scouting party that had been out for three days began to straggle in, some arriving after dark. These men were exhausted and hungry, several suffering from foot ailments caused by walking on sharp lava rock, but their mission had been successful.

They had surprised two Indian camps located twenty miles north of Squaw Canyon—at a place they had named Quartz Canyon—and killed sixteen Indians. The fight had begun when damning evidence was revealed that branded these Indians positively hostile. John Dickson recognized one of the Indians as someone to whom he had given tobacco at Woolsey's Agua Fria ranch, and this particular warrior happened to be parading around wearing the hat that had belonged to Artemus Ingalls, the man who had been the recipient of two Apache arrows in his body. The party also destroyed a large amount of deerskins, mescal, and other vital supplies.[28]

On April 5, Woolsey headed up one of the branches of the Verde River, which they named Clear Fork, and went into camp about six miles from where they had left the main river. Smoke was soon observed at a place estimated at about twelve miles from their location, and the men, thinking that it may be an Apache camp, set out to determine its source. After a difficult ride, they reached their destination, only to find one male and two female Apache tending a mescal pit. They vented their frustration by firing round after round at the three surprised Indians, who ran off in panic, but could not ascertain whether any of the bullets had hit its mark. It was 2:00 A.M. before the weary Indian hunters made it back to camp.

On the following morning, Woolsey remained on course up the creek, crossed a ridge, and halted at noon. Scouts were dispatched to search for a road or trail and returned with the news that they had found an Apache camp that had only recently been abandoned. The men descended into a canyon, with plans to strike a well-worn trail that led up the mountain to a high plateau, but first decided to camp. To their dismay, they discovered after an ambitious search that the location was lacking in water. The party had found plenty of mescal, however, and satisfied themselves with that pleasant narcotic. Henry Clifton remarked that "most of us had by this time become very fond of [mescal]."[29]

Woolsey's camp was roused at daybreak the next morning, April 7, when a man named J. Donohugh was shot in the neck by an arrow. He had been on guard duty, heard a sound, and went into the brush to investigate, when he was struck. Woolsey and several others tore after the assailant, emptying their pistols at a clump of brush believed to be the place from which the arrow was shot, but returned to camp empty-handed. The arrow was stuck between Donohugh's windpipe and jugular vein, with the point pricking through the skin on the other side. Dr. Alsap dressed the wound and proclaimed that the injury was not life-threatening.

The Indian hunters commenced climbing the mountain trail, or road, which was found to be quite adequate for travel, and at sunset camped in the proximity of some water tanks near the head of Fossil Creek. It was noted that night that they were within twenty-five miles of a stronghold of the Apache known as Big Rump Valley, which had been named in honor of Chief Big Rump, or Wah-poo-eta, who made his headquarters there.

Captain Woolsey, who may have earlier chosen this valley as his primary destination without mentioning that fact to the men, decided that a visit to Big Rump's domain would be in order, which created much excitement among the party. They hastily packed four days' rations and their blankets, and started out two hours before dawn on April 9.[30]

It was sundown when the party, according to Daniel Conner, observed their objective, the several-mile-wide Big Rump Valley:

> Instead of a valley it was rather a low rolling and knobby desert country sparsely studded with low stunted mesquite trees. From amongst these trees all over the valley arose the smoke curling like incense away from the numerous kilns in which the Apaches roast mescal bulbs into a jelly. From the number of these arising smokes, it appeared indeed that we were really at the door of the Apache capitol and our party of one hundred was not too huge at all.[31]

The order was given to make camp, with plans for an attack at dawn. It was then that Captain Woolsey made an error in judgment by permitting the men to build fires. By morning, Indian smoke signals curled into the air from the tops of neighboring mountainsides, trumpeting the presence of the outsiders, and Woolsey's hunters had lost that all-important element of surprise.

One version of the expedition, written by Henry Clifton, states:

> It would have been folly to descend to the valley, expecting to surprise any of the Indians, for it was evident that they were aware of our whereabouts and would be prepared to receive us. . . . Therefore, it was best to return to camp, start anew from there.[32]

According to Clifton, the party then wandered around for a while and, upon realizing that they were low on rations, thought it best to return to

Woolsey's Agua Fria ranch, with an agreement between them to start anew after the Apache the following month.[33]

And that was that—the end of Clifton's story, which has been the primary source for researchers studying this particular expedition.

There exists, however, another account—albeit brief—that described events in Big Rump Valley that day. This version—buried in obscurity—does not mention King Woolsey, or specific dates, or the previous itinerary or exploits of the Indian hunters, and therefore its connection may have been overlooked, but it unmistakably referred to the March–April 1864 expedition at the time when it arrived at Big Rump Valley.

Daniel Conner, in *Joseph Reddeford Walker and the Arizona Adventure,* contended that the Indian hunters indeed descended into Big Rump Valley, prepared to fight the Apache who resided there. The Indians, however, had heeded the smoke signal warnings and deserted the camp. Some were overtaken, and a running battle ensued, resulting in the Apache eventually vanishing into the landscape. Woolsey's men then set about destroying everything in the camp, which must have been quite a task, considering the apparent size of Big Rump's valley village.

Conner then describes two incidents—atrocities—committed by one of the members of the party, which provoked great discord among the men. This individual who gained attention for his actions was none other than Sugarfoot Jack, the young man who had gained acclaim for killing the Indians who had ambushed George Goodhue—the first Indians ever killed in the Prescott area. While the party was gathering to leave after torching the village, Jack was observed throwing a papoose, an Indian child, into the flames of a burning *jacal,* or hut. The young man calmly stood there watching as the child burned, "then passed on as though in search of another living, human creature to cremate alive." Conner's description of this scene is quite graphic and therefore will not be quoted here. Several men attempted to pull this tiny body from the flames but, due to its rapidly deteriorating condition, were unsuccessful.

Conner described what happened next:

When the fact became generally known, there was much dissatisfaction expressed over the occurrence. But while these murmurs were boiling a little, Sugarfoot had discovered another papoose and had taken his seat upon a large stone and was engaged in playing with it. He would dance it upon his knee and tickle it under the chin and handle the babe in the manner of a playful mother, and seemed to be enjoying himself splendidly.[34]

When Sugarfoot Jack had finished playing, he pulled out his six-shooter and executed the child with a bullet through the head.

Conner related that the men reacted with disgust and indignation:

Sugarfoot thus defied the murmurs and complaints for the burning of one by blowing the brains out of another. But with all of his bold and recklessness he discovered in an instant that his time was at hand, without an accident, and for once in his life precipitately fled. He knew too well the character of the men who turned to pick up their guns, to believe that they were capable of making false motions. He escaped to the brush and remained away long enough for their foolish passions to subside a little.[35]

The actions by Sugarfoot Jack evoked a debate among the men pertaining to the propriety of killing any Indian regardless of age, size, or sex. Some thought that it was proper to exterminate the entire race; others protested that if this was to be the type of warfare carried on against the Indians, then they would no longer participate.

The latter faction separated themselves from the main body and headed home. Their crossing of the Agua Fria River was contested, and they killed two Indians and wounded an unknown number of others, the only fighting in which they engaged before reaching the settlements.

The remainder of the expedition, with Sugarfoot Jack in their ranks, returned home about four weeks later. It is not known in which group Capt. King Woolsey traveled, although at the beginning of the expedition, he had expressed his opinion when writing to General Carleton: "It sir is next thing to impossible to prevent killing squaws in grumping a rancheria even were we disposed to save them. For my part I am frank to say that I fight on the broad platform of extermination."[36]

Conner mentioned that Sugarfoot Jack was subsequently killed—stabbed to death at a Mexican fandango on the Rio Grande—and died "unwept, unhonored, and unsung."[37]

Apparently shame, or a pact made among the men, or a wary editor, or a combination of those factors was the basis for the exclusion of even the fact that the men had entered Big Rump Valley in Henry Clifton's version, which was published in the Prescott *Arizona Miner* newspaper on May 25, 1864. The manuscript of Daniel Conner's *Joseph Reddeford Walker and the Arizona Adventure*, written from notes he had taken in the 1860s, did not see the light of day until 1956, which made the information unavailable to most early researchers.

Meanwhile, other citizens and detachments of soldiers, often together, were also out hunting Indians in various parts of Arizona Territory. Hardly a week passed that miners, frontiersmen, or the army was not skirmishing with the Apache.

Gen. James Carleton enthusiastically approved of the efforts of people like King Woolsey and encouraged "every citizen of the Territory who has a rifle to take to the field. . . . In this way, where many parties are in pursuit of Indians at the same time, the Indians, in endeavoring to escape from one, run into others."

Carleton urged the governors of the Mexican states of Chihuahua and Sonora to establish militias that would also fight the Apache, who knew no borders. "Every effort must be made," Carleton wrote, "to have a general uprising of both citizens and soldiers, on both sides of the line, against the Apaches."[38]

In April, while King Woolsey was out scouring the countryside for Apache, Capt. James H. Whitlock and sixty-one California volunteers were in pursuit of a band of about 100 Chiricahua who had stolen a herd of horses and mules. On April 7, the trail led the soldiers to a camp inhabited by about 250 Indians, located near Grays' Peak in eastern Arizona Territory. Whitlock attacked and managed to kill twenty-one Apache, wound countless others, recover the livestock, and destroy the entire camp, which included more than a ton of dried mescal and mule meat.[39]

In early May, Capt. Thomas T. Tidball, with twenty-five California volunteers from Fort Bowie, where he was commander, and a handful of civilians, took to the field. They patiently tracked a war party of Apache for five days, traveling by night and hiding by day. Tidball caught up with his prey at the Apache camp in Aravaipa Canyon, southeastern Arizona Territory, and killed fifty, took sixteen prisoner, and confiscated sixty head of stock.[40]

On May 29, Captain Tidball, with eighty-six California infantrymen and a platoon of cavalry, surrounded an Apache camp located in the upper Gila River Valley in a canyon of the Mescal Mountains, just below present-day Coolidge Dam. Tidball's men killed fifty-one Indians, including two chiefs, wounded seventeen others, and captured sixteen women and children. Items were found in the village, such as a pistol, a diary, and a shotgun, that belonged to white men who had recently been massacred by Apache. The soldiers destroyed extensive wheat and corn fields, as well as large quantities of provisions vital to the Indians' sustenance.[41]

Three days after Tidball's smashing victory, Capt. King S. Woolsey once again took to the field, this time leading ninety-three civilians. The expedition left his Agua Fria ranch at about 6:00 P.M. on June 1 and traveled for several uneventful days before finally camping at Clear Creek, a branch of the Verde River. At this point, Woolsey decided to divide his command. He sent the pack train in the company of thirty-three men, led by M. Lewis, one of Joe Walker's original band of adventurers, southward with orders to seek out a pass through the mountains, while Woolsey and the remaining sixty men resumed their easterly course toward the Tonto Basin.

Woolsey's party trudged through the rugged terrain of the basin for five days without encountering any Indians, although fresh sign was plentiful. They rendezvoused with the pack train on a stream they called the East Fork of the Verde. Lewis and the pack train had followed the river, then struck across a mesa, and cut across Fossil Creek, much of the route in a lava bed covered with timber and excellent grass.[42]

On June 8, the combined party marched southerly, over the hills, to a waterway they called Tonto Creek, and continued along the creek across a mesa to Salt River. They passed many ruins of an ancient civilization of considerable size and prospected in several places for gold. Color was found, but not in paying quantities.

Provisions were running low, so Woolsey dispatched the pack train, escorted by twenty-three men, to the Pima villages, while the main force searched the area to the mouth of Tonto Creek. Woolsey came upon an abandoned Indian village of some fifty huts, which he believed had been the headquarters of Chief Big Rump—whether it was in the same location as on the previous expedition is not known. No Indians were found there, but from all indications, they were nearby, and Woolsey and his frustrated Indian hunters were determined to track them down.

Woolsey headed out with thirty-six men and six days' rations, and scouted the north side of the river. Finding themselves unable to ascend a high mountain, the men happened upon a well-worn trail. They followed it with great anticipation to an Indian camp that had been so recently deserted that the Indians had left behind their bows and arrows and their fires burning.

The party then scouted a waterway that they called Sycamore Creek to its mouth at the Salt River, where they were hailed by several Indians on nearby hills. A parley was arranged, but the Indians refused to venture close enough for any meaningful discussion.[43]

Woolsey picked up another trail and followed it over rough ground for about twelve miles, before camping for the night. In the darkness, the men could hear Indians all around them, but never caught a glimpse of one. In the morning, the party followed Pinal Creek to its mouth, then proceeded down the Salt River. Two days later, Woolsey dispatched fifteen men to meet the pack train and continued on with the remainder of his command to camp at his earlier location. While the men cut and thrashed wheat for the horses, a few Indians approached under a flag of truce and were cautiously received. Woolsey, who thought it prudent to be friendly toward his guests, speculated that the Indians were sizing up the outfit to determine whether they could overpower it with an attack. Apparently the visitors noticed that the men were well armed and prepared to fight, and thought it best to depart without provoking a confrontation.

At 6:00 A.M. on Independence Day, Woolsey and the reunited pack train set out toward the mouth of Pinal Creek in the Pinal Mountains. They located gold deposits at the head of the creek, but not enough with which to bother working. The expedition went into camp on the top of Pinal Mountain, where eighteen men decided to leave and return home. Woolsey and the rest picked around the area for minerals but found none.[44]

Woolsey then moved down the San Carlos River to the Gila River, and thence upriver to Fort Goodwin. He reported to the commander, Col. Edwin A. Rigg of the 1st California Infantry, and was issued rations. Rigg suggested that Woolsey rendezvous with Maj. Thomas J. Blakeney's command, which was operating in the vicinity of Pinal Creek and Signal Mountain on the north side of the Salt River. Woolsey agreed to meet Blakeney at that location on July 30.

On July 15, Woolsey left Fort Goodwin and traveled up the Gila River, before eventually reaching the Black River—a march of some fifty-five miles. While in camp, a Jaqui Indian girl, about ten years of age, approached. She claimed to have been a captive of the Apache and to have just escaped. The girl was subsequently taken to live at Woolsey's Agua Fria ranch.

The Indian hunters resumed their search for Apache through valleys, down streams, and along mountain passes, but without success. On July 25, while camped northwest of the Black River, one of the men, J. W. Beauchamp, climbed up a nearby mountain to view the surroundings. King Woolsey told of his fate:

> Upon arriving near the top of the mountain he was waylaid by six Indians, shot through the chest with a rifle, lanced, stripped and left for dead. He lived for some fifteen or twenty minutes, however, after we reached him, but died before we could get him to camp. We buried him at the foot of the Mountain, which we named Beauchamp Peak in memory of the unfortunate victim of Indian cruelty and cowardice.[45]

The expedition worked its way toward Pinal Creek, pausing at one point to hunt bears, and bagged one of a species they called a "Cinnamon" bear. Upon arrival at Pinal Creek, they were visited by nine Indians, who informed them of the presence of soldiers nearby.

The next morning, Woolsey and his men approached the army position and heard rifle fire. The soldiers under Major Blakeney were chasing several Indians, whom they failed to catch. The major did seize a few Indians to hold as hostages for the exchange of a boy that had been kidnapped. The boy was never returned, and Blakeney retaliated by later hanging two of his hostages.

Woolsey and Blakeney made plans to raid an Indian village at Signal Mountain, but before they could proceed, the major was ordered back to Fort Goodwin. Then, due to excessive rains that had flooded the streams, the expedition came to an inglorious end.[46]

King Woolsey wrote to Gov. John M. Goodwin:

> Notwithstanding the failure to find and kill Indians, I still think the expedition has been of great benefit. We have followed the trail of Apache to his home in the mountains, and have learned where it is located. We have dispelled the idea of vast numbers that has ever attached to that tribe. A few hundred of poor miserable wretches compose the formidable foe so much dreaded by many. They will be brought to terms speedily, or exterminated, I cannot doubt, when once the government shall know how small is the enemy by which so much annoyance has been caused.[47]

Woolsey returned to his Agua Fria ranch, received an appointment as a lieutenant colonel in the volunteer militia, and frequently served as a military aide to the governor. In time, he entered into speculative mining ventures with Governor Goodwin and Secretary of State Richard C. McCormick, but these businesses subsequently failed, and he was forced to sell his Agua Fria ranch to cover the losses. Woolsey remained a large landowner and leading citizen of the community, and in the early 1870s, he expanded his interests by developing a profitable trade in packaged salt and organized the Phoenix Flour Mills with two partners. He served five terms on the Territorial Council and was twice president of that body. In 1878, Woolsey ran for the office of delegate to Congress but was defeated.

King S. Woolsey was quite wealthy and at the height of his career when, on June 29, 1879, at the age of forty-seven, he died from a stroke. His funeral was the first conducted by the Masonic Order in the Valley and was attended by many of his friends from the Maricopa tribe. He left behind a wife and three children.[48]

General Carleton, meanwhile, had assured the citizens of Arizona that he was committed to an unrelenting war against the Apache, who remained a constant threat to towns and ranches. A major campaign of great destruction never materialized, however, in part because by autumn, enlistment terms of many of the California volunteers had come to an end. By necessity, Carleton's ambitious plans to exterminate the Apache were placed on hold, suspended in favor of a more defensive posture.

In the words of one Tucson resident, "The troops in their campaign have killed enough of the Apaches to enrage and irritate them without breaking their spirit, and we are still in such condition that every settlement must be a small military post of itself."[49]

Carleton, whose undermanned army was fighting a war on several fronts, would hand over responsibility of Arizona to the Department of the Pacific in January 1865. But first he was obliged to turn his attention to another threat—Comanche and Kiowa Indians whose raids were threatening to close the lifeline of New Mexico and the West, the Santa Fe Trail.

CHAPTER EIGHT

Northern and Southern Plains Vengeance

ARIZONA WAS NOT THE ONLY PLACE WHERE THE DISCOVERY OF GOLD HAD brought hordes of miners and adventurers into the less-traveled wilderness areas of the West.

By early 1864, thousands of prospectors were pouring into the northern Rockies, hoping to strike it rich in the burgeoning gold fields found there, such as those along the Clearwater and Salmon Rivers in Idaho and Grasshopper Creek and Alder Gulch in western Montana.

Many of the miners who ventured to the diggings from the East traveled by land across the plains and mountains to reach mining towns like Bannock, Lewiston, and Virginia City. Other adventurers journeyed up the Missouri River by steamboat from St. Louis or other port cities to the head of navigation at Fort Benton, Montana, then took one of the various short overland routes the remainder of the way.

This considerable river traffic along the Missouri—not just prospectors, but also those companies transporting machinery and freight to outfit and supply the mines—had become quite profitable for the riverboat business. And because those miners eventually returned east with gold that helped finance the Union cause, the government had an interest in maintaining safe travel on the Missouri.[1]

Officials in the state of Minnesota had noticed this influx of prospectors heading west and, being in relatively close proximity to the mines, sought a way to profit from these travelers. Several routes through that state had been established in 1862 and 1863—east and north of the vicinity of Sioux hostilities—and the state promoted its convenient location as a jumping-off place to the mining regions, as well as its appeal as an attractive area for new settlers. In time, these officials hoped, a northern railroad line would be constructed between St. Paul and the mines, which would without question guarantee prosperity for the state.[2]

In order to successfully entice people to travel to the West through Minnesota, now notorious as the site of bloody Sioux uprisings—not to mention to pacify their own residents, who feared further hostilities—the state demanded that the army act to assure the safety of the region. The 1863 campaigns had pushed the hostile Sioux—Mdewakanton from the late Little Crow's band and other Dakota, as well as the Lakota and Yanktonai—onto the plains of Dakota Territory, where they had resumed their nomadic lifestyle and remained a constant threat to white settlement and travel. Therefore, Minnesota's cry for action against the Indians was echoed by ambitious speculators in the southeastern frontier of Dakota Territory who sought to develop that fertile land for settlers.

These requests for assistance from the army were heartily embraced by Maj. Gen. John Pope, commander of the Military Department of the Northwest, who was nagged by the knowledge that his campaign the previous year had not accomplished its goal. With that in mind, the general went to work planning a new campaign that would ensure the security of the Missouri River and the northern overland route from the threat of Sioux attacks. Maj. Gen. Henry W. Halleck, commander of the Department of the Missouri, however, encouraged Pope to negotiate treaties with the Indians rather than fight them. "If you want war in the spring," Halleck caustically wrote, "a few traders can get one up on the shortest notice." But Pope was adamant about his desire to mount a campaign, and Halleck grudgingly relented.[3]

Inasmuch as Brigadier General Henry Sibley had received permission to remain at his headquarters in Minnesota, Pope's plan called for Brig. Gen. Alfred Sully to act as field commander of this new campaign. Sully's mission would be not only to engage any Sioux that he encountered, but also to establish two new forts—on Devil's Lake and on the James River—which would assist in effecting military control over the eastern half of Dakota Territory. The addition of two other forts—one on the Heart River and another on the Yellowstone River near the mouth of the Powder River—along with Fort Sully, which had been erected in 1863 on the Missouri near present-day Pierre, South Dakota, would form a line of defense running from Devil's Lake to the Yellowstone. These posts would go a long way in assuring the safety of travel on Missouri and along those emigrant routes on the upper Minnesota River that led to the mines.

Sully marched up the Missouri in June 1864 at the head of a column—1,800 men strong—that consisted of units from the 6th and 7th Iowa Cavalry, two companies of Dakota cavalry, four companies of Maj. Alfred Brackett's Minnesota Cavalry, four mountain howitzers under the command of Capt. Nathaniel Pope, the general's nephew, and a detachment of half-breed scouts and interpreters.

The presence of hostile Indians was evidenced on June 28 when three Sioux warriors ambushed and killed Capt. John Fielner, the outfit's topographical officer. Dakota cavalrymen swiftly hunted down the guilty parties and killed them. Sully then ordered that the heads of these dead warriors be chopped off and impaled on poles as a warning of what was in store for the hostiles should they dare to fight.

On June 29 at Swan Lake, near present-day Mobridge, South Dakota, Sully's brigade was joined by another brigade, 1,600 men of the 8th Minnesota Infantry, commanded by Col. Minor T. Thomas. Also accompanying this unit was the 3rd Minnesota Battery, under Capt. John Jones, the hero of the Fort Ridgely battle in 1862. Sully would assume overall command of both brigades.

There was one major drawback to this additional troop strength, however. The Minnesotans had brought along a train of 123 wagons drawn by lumbering oxen that carried some 200 men, women, and children headed for the Montana mines. To his dismay, Sully learned that he would be responsible for the protection of the cumbersome wagon train until it reached the Yellowstone River. This arrangement was further aggravated by the fact that Sully's troops regarded the emigrants as draft dodgers, or at the least Southern sympathizers, which resulted in bad blood between the two groups.[4]

The news that Sully's column was on the move spread quickly through Indian territory, especially word of the beheading of the three Sioux warriors, which was considered an outrage and reason to fight. Many tribes sought refuge in the wild country between the Missouri and Yellowstone Rivers, but various bands of young warriors vowed to engage the troops if opportunity presented itself.

On July 9, at the site of Fort Rice, General Sully encountered Father Pierre-Jean De Smet, the famous Jesuit missionary, who was on his way downriver to St. Louis after a trip to Fort Berthold, where he had met with several hundred Sioux warriors in an attempt to arrange a peace treaty.

De Smet informed Sully that the Indians "spoke favorably with regard to peace," but that he had been unable to persuade them to accept a treaty. De Smet later wrote of the meeting with Sully:

I gave the general an account of my mission and of my different interviews with the Sioux. He told me plainly that circumstances obliged him to punish by force of arms all the Sioux tribes that harbored in their camps the murderers of white men. "Unfortunately," he added, "all the Indian camps harbor some of these desperate ruffians, over whom the chiefs have little or no power." In consequence of the general's declaration and the circumstances of the case, my errand of peace, though sanctioned by the Government, became bootless.[5]

The missionary also informed Sully about the locations of several Lakota camps and the movement of a large force that was heading north from the Black Hills.

Sully was anxious to march against those Indians but had one obstacle with which to contend—the emigrant train. The general lamented: "I can't send them back. I can't leave them here, for I can't feed them. . . . Therefore I am forced to take them with me." He assembled the men of the train and told them: "Gentlemen, I am damn sorry you are here, but so long as you are, I will do the best I can to protect you. I expect to jump an Indian camp and give them hell. . . . Keep together for in union there is strength."[6]

On July 19, Sully and his force of nearly 3,000, including the emigrant wagon train, headed west up the northern fork of the Cannonball River. It was not long before his scouts picked up the fresh trail of the Sioux that Father De Smet had told him about, and the column veered to the northwest, reaching the Heart River on July 23. The march had been difficult—water had been scarce, and the daytime temperature hovered around 110 degrees—the troops and animals were exhausted. Sully decided to rest for a day but was determined to overtake the Indians, which he estimated were only a day or two ahead of him. To that end, he left the wagon trail behind, guarded by an adequate force, and on July 24 led 2,200 troops northward in an effort to locate and engage the Indians.

Two days later, the column approached the Killdeer Mountains, where enemy camps—at least 1,600 lodges that were home to several bands of Lakota Sioux, as well as a few Yanktonai and Dakota from Minnesota—could be observed hidden within the wooded slopes. Warriors from these camps steadily gathered to form a battle line to confront the troopers. Sully estimated that he faced more than 6,000 warriors, although the actual number was probably closer to 1,600. Within this mass of Indians were notables such as Sitting Bull, Gall, and other warriors who would for years to come fight to the bitter end against the army to protect what they considered their land.[7]

Sully dismissed the idea of employing a charge in the hilly terrain and instead formed his dismounted brigades in a huge square, enclosing the horses and artillery inside. With the 7th Iowa, commanded by Lt. Col. John Pattee, in a forward skirmisher line, this square of troopers advanced slowly but steadily over the five miles of barren, dusty terrain that separated them from the Indian villages.

At about noon, Sully's troopers and the long battle line of Sioux opened fire at each other. The Indians rode forward to harass the square of soldiers with volleys of arrows and bullets fired from every conceivable angle and mounted a series of determined charges at presumed weak points, but they failed to penetrate the tight formation. One group of warriors struck the rear of the square in an attempt to reach the supply train but was chased off with a barrage from Major Jones's howitzers. Sully's men held firm throughout the constant flurry of attacks and resolutely moved forward toward the Indian camps.

Late in the afternoon, the Sioux withdrew into the timbered ravines at the base of the mountains and assumed defensive positions behind rocks and trees in an effort to hold off the troops long enough for their women and children to escape the village.[8]

General Sully decided that the time had arrived to seize the initiative. He mounted a battalion under Maj. Alfred B. Brackett and sent the saber-wielding cavalrymen on a charge into a large group of warriors. The assault—in which two soldiers were killed and eight wounded—drove the Indians up the mountain, where the terrain made fighting difficult. Rather than send his men into the dense timber, Sully set up his artillery on nearby hills and shelled the enemy positions until nightfall.

This tactic caused the Indians to move even farther up the mountainside. Four companies of the 8th Minnesota Cavalry were then dispatched to comb the slopes, rooting out the final pockets of resistance and killing any stragglers. Finally, the Sioux warriors realized that they were greatly outgunned and prudently fled en masse, disappearing into the darkness.[9]

The army had lost only five killed and ten wounded during the day's fighting. Sully estimated that 100 to 150 Indians had been killed, but the Sioux later disputed that number, claiming that only thirty-one had died. A worse blow to the Sioux, however, was the loss of their village, which Sully's men ransacked and burned. This cost the Indians a great amount of personal possessions, including about 400,000 pounds of dried buffalo meat and berries used to make pemmican.[10]

Sully then retrieved the emigrant wagon train and turned his expedition westward toward the Yellowstone in pursuit of the Sioux. He marched for three days, August 6 to 9, across the badlands of the Little Missouri River—"Hell with the fires burned out," he called it—while scores of Sioux warriors harassed his front, rear, and flanks. On August 9, Sully deployed his howitzers and reportedly killed another 100 of the enemy with the bursting shells, which discouraged any further contact.[11]

On August 12, after a difficult march, with rations, forage, and water running out, Sully reached the Yellowstone River at a point about forty miles below present-day Glendive to happily discover that two supply steamers, the *Chippewa* and *Alone,* loaded with fifty tons of freight, were tied to the riverbank. The riverboats ferried the men across the Yellowstone, then escorted them downstream and once again ferried them across the Missouri, two miles below the mouth of the Yellowstone.[12]

The water level, however, was too low for the steamboats to travel any farther west than the mouth of the Powder River, the location where Sully intended to build his fort, which would make it difficult to lay in enough supplies to support the endeavor. This information, combined with the prospect of a sparsity of grass on the plains, compelled Sully not to pursue the Indians northeast of the Yellowstone or commence construction of a post. Instead, he decided to return to Fort Rice. The column forded the Yellowstone with the assistance of the steamboats, while floating the wagons and swimming the animals, then marched down the west bank of the Missouri.

Sully drew rations at Fort Union, the old fur-trading post, where a company of the 30th Wisconsin had been stationed to guard supplies. At this point, the emigrants hired a guide to take their wagon train to the gold mines and departed along with a quantity of government supplies that they had procured from the soldiers—a number of whom stowed away and accompanied the emigrants. Sully ordered the 30th Wisconsin to guard the fort through the winter. Then he marched down the east bank of the Missouri, arriving at Fort Berthold, another trading post, on August 28. At this home of the Arikara, Gros Ventre, and Mandan—traditional enemies of the Sioux—Sully assigned the 6th Iowa to winter at the post.

Sully departed three days later and marched across the barren prairies northeast of the Missouri to reach Fort Rice on September 8. Upon arrival, he was informed that another wagon train of emigrants had reportedly been attacked by 3,000 Sioux at a location some 200 miles to the west. A disgusted Sully dispatched 850 men in an effort to rescue the emigrants and bring them back to Fort Rice.

General Sully had completed his expedition without establishing the forts on Devil's Lake and the Yellowstone, although Fort Rice had been built, and he had not rid the area of hostile Sioux—although he had delivered a severe blow to some bands by destroying stores necessary for the upcoming winter. The two forts—Sully and Rice—afforded the army a foothold on the Missouri River.

After the Civil War, Alfred Sully remained in the West as a lieutenant colonel with the 3rd Infantry and, contrary to his previous accomplishments, gained a reputation as an "ambulance" general, one who was excessively slow and cautious. In September 1868, Sully served as commander of the District of the Upper Arkansas and led his 3rd Infantry and the 7th Cavalry—while George Armstrong Custer was serving a suspension—on an expedition into Indian Territory. During this campaign, however, he was quite timid and predictably cautious and was soon relegated to a desk at Fort Harker.

In 1869, Sully was appointed Superintendent of Indian Affairs for Montana, and the following year, he became embroiled in a controversy over the massacre of 170 Piegan of the Blackfoot Confederacy. He was promoted to colonel in 1873 and commanded the 21st Infantry in several Indian operations.

Over the years, Alfred Sully became an accomplished artist, like his father, and painted many Western landscapes, specializing in views of forts. He died on April 27, 1879, at Fort Vancouver, Washington.

Despite fears that this latest operation by Sully in Minnesota and Dakota Territory would incite other Plains tribes to go on the warpath against whites, the various chiefs had generally counseled against war, and the Indians in the region for the most part tended to their time-honored lifestyles.

Far south of Sully's responsibility, the Southern Sioux were occupied fighting their traditional enemy, the Pawnee, while the Arapaho and Cheyenne battled their ancient foe, the Ute. Cheyenne chiefs Black Kettle and White Antelope and Arapaho Little Raven had signed the Fort Wise Treaty of 1861 and were settled on reservations on the upper Arkansas. Those bands that had chosen not to sign the treaty continued to follow the buffalo herds between the Platte and the Arkansas. The infrequent Indian raids could be blamed on single bands, or small parties, without any responsibility of the tribes to which they belonged.[13]

That relatively placid behavior, however, was destined to be disturbed and would set the Plains aflame with further activity in 1864. Migration west had swollen the trails with wagon trains and travelers. Draft evaders, gold miners, settlers, and more than 20,000 Missourians escaping retribution for suspected ties to secessionist guerrillas, most not escorted by soldiers, were scattered across Indian country, making it inevitable that there would be occasional clashes of violence.

In Colorado, Gov. John Evans and his militia colonel John M. Chivington were crying wolf and rattling sabers. Inconsequential raids were blown out of proportion, and harsh retaliation by the Colorado militia only served to provoke the Indians. Angry Cheyenne war parties fought back against the heightened white aggression. Skirmishing within Colorado soon escalated into Kansas and threatened travel along the Platte, the Smoky Hill, and the Arkansas. Before long, marauding bands of young braves from various other tribes, usually without the sanction of their chiefs, joined the Cheyenne to ride through the Kansas frontier, burning, looting, and killing.[14]

Maj. Gen. Samuel R. Curtis, commander of the Department of Kansas, a West Pointer who had distinguished himself at the March 1862 battle of Pea Ridge, had no experience fighting Indians. Curtis, however, understood that he must react swiftly to this Indian revolt. In July, he assembled three columns—including Chivington's regiment—and marched down the Arkansas from Fort Lyon to comb the area south, west, and north of Fort Larned. The expedition returned to Fort Leavenworth on August 8 without making contact with any hostiles. The Indians, who had no interest in fighting such a large force, had fled to more secure territory. On the positive side, their flight for the time being restored travel to Denver and Santa Fe along the Arkansas.[15]

In the fall, General Curtis created the District of the Upper Arkansas and placed in command Maj. Gen. James G. Blunt, who had been a prominent doctor and antislavery leader in Kansas before the war. Blunt had been dismissed from his command of the District of the Frontier in October 1863, after guerrillas led by William C. Quantrill had attacked his wagon train and slaughtered ninety of his troops.[16]

On August 9, Blunt was directed to organize a 600-man strike force and mount an offensive against the Comanche and Kiowa. It was an ideal time of the year to hunt Indians. Bands that had an inclination toward raiding would be disregarding hostilities in favor of laying in provisions for winter. Curtis instituted a policy for Blunt that called for no mercy without reparation, and ordered that peace talks would not be entertained until double the amount of stolen stock had been returned.[17]

Meanwhile, Brig. Gen. Robert B. Mitchell, commander of the District of Nebraska, had his hands full along the Platte. A Cheyenne war party had killed fifteen settlers and captured several others along the Little Blue.

General Curtis quickly assembled a 628-man force at Fort Kearny and on September 3 marched to reinforce Mitchell. The operation scoured the upper Solomon and Republican Rivers, but two weeks later, it had not located any sign of Indians.[18]

On September 25, Maj. Scott J. Anthony, who led an advance party of General Blunt's column, happened upon a camp of Southern Cheyenne and Arapaho on the upper reaches of Walnut Creek. The warriors surrounded Anthony but fled when Curtis brought up the main body of troops. The general chased the Indians for two days, until his horses gave out and he was compelled to return to Fort Riley.[19]

Soon afterward, Curtis, Blunt, and a large number of the available troops in the area were hurried off to Missouri. Twelve thousand Confederate soldiers under Maj. Gen. Sterling Price had invaded that state, and the local militias were unable to contend with such a formidable force.

Prior to his departure for Missouri, General Blunt had been primarily searching for renegade Comanche and Kiowa bands, particularly one led by warrior Satanta, who would later become principal chief of the Kiowa.

It has been speculated that the Comanche at some point separated from other Shoshonean-speaking peoples in the Great Basin and western Wyoming, and migrated southeastward. By the late seventeenth century, the Comanche had reached the southern plains, assuming a range spanning northern Texas, eastern Oklahoma, southwestern Kansas, southeastern Colorado, and eastern New Mexico. With a reputation as skilled horsemen, the warring Comanche became the most dominant tribe on the plains, as they battled Indian enemies and mounted raids into Mexico to steal slaves, horses, and women.

In the late eighteenth century, the Comanche formed an alliance with another buffalo-hunting tribe, the Kiowa, and the two combined their strength and resources for mutual benefit, which gave rise to an adage known throughout the plains: "As the Comanche goes, so goes the Kiowa." Together the two tribes skirmished with the Spanish, effectively halting that country's expansion. The heart of their hunting ground was the Texas Panhandle, and they became bitter enemies of the Anglo-Americans residing there. The primary mission of the Texas Rangers from their formation during the Texas Revolution was to contain the Comanche-Kiowa tribes, and the two opponents over the years had engaged in many bloody battles.

When Federal forts in Texas had been abandoned during the early stages of the Civil War, and the services of the Texas Rangers were required elsewhere, the Comanche and Kiowa and their allies seized upon this

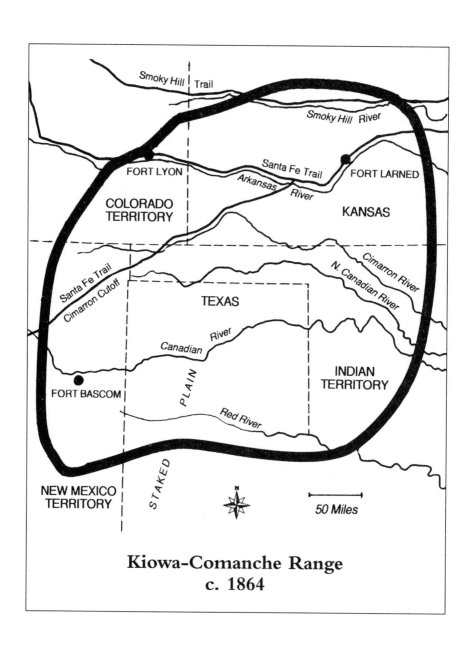

Kiowa-Comanche Range
c. 1864

opportunity to raid throughout the region. In an effort to curb the incessant violence, the Confederate army had signed a treaty with the Indians that provided for trade goods in return for their pledge that they would "live in peace and quietness."

That fragile arrangement had lasted less than a year, until the Indians became aware that the inexperienced and undermanned Texas militia units were incapable of protecting settlements. Comanche and Kiowa war parties swooped down on isolated Texas ranches and ran off herds of cattle, which they then sold to contractors who provided beef to Federal military posts in New Mexico and the Indian Territory. The threat of violence was so great that entire counties in Texas were evacuated.[20]

These marauding tribes, whether sincere or not, had indicated on several occasions that under certain conditions they would be interested in making peace with the Union army in New Mexico. In 1862, the Comanche helped in the capture of some Confederate sympathizers and were promised payment for any further information about Confederate movements. Throughout the next year, the Comanche and Kiowa were frequent visitors at Fort Bascom, which was located on the Canadian River near the Cerro Tucumcari in northeastern New Mexico Territory, and were given an assortment of provisions.

Raids in the vicinity of the fort subsided—until circumstances drastically changed. Post commander Capt. Edward H. Bergmann submitted a bill for $206.28 to the Indian Bureau for payment of the subsistence handed out to the Comanche and Kiowa tribes, but his request for reimbursement was denied. Provisions were promptly cut off at the fort, and the Indians responded by going back on the warpath.[21]

In 1863, Indian Agent S. G. Colley devised a plan designed to curtail the threat that the hostiles posed to travel across the plains. He invited a delegation of Comanche and Kiowa chiefs, along with a few Cheyenne, Arapaho, Apache, and Caddo, to visit Washington for an audience with President Lincoln. Each chief was treated like royalty and, upon departure, was presented a medal and a certificate proclaiming that he had "visited Washington, that he had behaved himself in a proper manner, and that he is a peaceful man," and "directed all white men not to give him cause to break his word."[22]

The awarding of compliments and souvenirs, however, was not the primary purpose for the excursion. The highlight of the visit occurred when the chiefs "touched the pen" to a treaty that would guarantee "peace, friendship, and unity." Each tribe agreed that it would not "resort to or encamp" upon the Santa Fe Trail, nor "molest, annoy or disturb the travel, the emigration or the United States mail." In return for this promise, the Indians would receive an annuity of $25,000 in "goods, merchandise, provisions or agricultural implements" for a period of five years, and for five additional years if approved by the president.

Congress, however, failed to ratify the treaty. The Indians, believing that the agreement was in effect, waited on the Arkansas River for the disbursement of goods that never arrived.[23]

Predictably, the furious tribes retaliated by going on a rampage throughout the spring and summer of 1864. Widespread depredations were committed in Colorado, New Mexico, and Texas. Ranches were burned, livestock was stolen, wagon trains were attacked, and travelers and settlers were taken captive or murdered.

These adventurous Comanche and Kiowa warriors needed no incentive for the raids other than revenge for the white man's betrayal, but part of the reason for their actions can be traced to the clandestine market that paid them well for their stolen goods. The warriors were encouraged to plunder by a shady group of traders called *Comancheros,* composed mainly of New Mexican Hispanos and Pueblo Indians. These outlaw merchants, who operated on the Staked Plain in the Texas Panhandle, had coveted guns and ammunition to trade. The stolen livestock provided by the Indians—as well as captive women and children, who would become slaves—would then be sold at a high profit by the *Comancheros,* mostly to New Mexico ranches.[24]

The Santa Fe Trail, the lifeline of New Mexico, had been hit particularly hard by these Indian raids. Safe travel was virtually impossible, a fact that caused great concern to army authorities. Not only did necessary items for settlers pass along this route, but it was also the sole connection with the East for moving military supplies to California and New Mexico volunteers. There was no way that resources available in New Mexico could sustain the army should the Confederates return. Therefore, the Santa Fe Trail became *the* vital supply link for the Union army on the Southern Plains.[25]

Brig. Gen. James H. Carleton, commander of the Military Department of New Mexico, understood that he must act without delay to protect the Santa Fe Trail. Michael Steck, New Mexico superintendent of Indian Affairs, notified Carleton that he had received word from *Comancheros* stating that Comanche had not been involved with any of the recent raids along the Santa Fe Trail. Carleton considered the source and, given the commercial relations between *Comancheros* and Comanche, discounted that information.

Carleton was convinced, correctly, that the Comanche and Kiowa were responsible for attacks at Walnut Creek on the Arkansas River, and on the upper and lower Cimarron crossings of the Santa Fe Trail; horse stealing between Forts Larned and Lyon; and an incident at Pawnee Fork, where five men were killed and scalped, and five small boys were taken captive from a wagon train. He was particularly upset that Comanche had on one occasion captured a group of Anglo-Americans and Mexicans, and chose to set free only the Mexicans while killing the Americans. "The discrimination which the Comanches have frequently made in favor of the people, natives to this Territory, and against Anglo-Americans," Carleton wrote, "cannot be regarded in any other light than as an insult to the Government and our people." Carleton declared that measures must be immediately taken to assure that the Santa Fe Trail would remain free for travel and, if possible, to punish the hostiles for these acts.[26]

Carleton, however, was placed in somewhat of a quandary, as enlistment terms for the Californians were running out, which would leave him short of troops. Given those circumstances, he decided that their first priority "should be the defensive—the preservation of our trains."

To this end, the general dispatched contingents of cavalry to strategic locations on both branches of the Santa Fe Trail, with orders to escort supply trains and travelers between Fort Larned and Fort Union near Santa Fe. He then set to work planning an offensive campaign.[27]

In September, *Comancheros,* who made it their business to learn such information, warned the Comanche and Kiowa that a military campaign was being planned against them. That knowledge caused the tribes enough concern that they dispatched representatives to visit Fort Bascom in an effort to arrange a truce.[28]

Carleton was in no mood for discussion. He advised the commanding officer at Fort Bascom to tell the Indians the following:

> Their people have attacked our trains, killed our people, and run off our stock. We believe their hearts are bad, and that they talk with a forked tongue. We put no confidence in what they say; they must go away, as we regard them not as friends; they need not come in with any more white flags until they are willing to give up the stock they have stolen this year from our people, and also the men among them who have killed our people without provocation or cause.[29]

The chastised Comanche and Kiowa returned to their encampments. In preparation for Carleton's fall campaign, word had been passed that "friendly Indians" should assemble at "places of safety," which for these tribes was Fort

Larned. Many straggled to the fort, but by fall, a large number of Comanche and Kiowa had settled in for the winter along the Canadian River in the Texas Panhandle.[30]

Carleton was determined to punish the renegades, which would perhaps discourage future raids. He had expected cooperation from the District of the Upper Arkansas, but now that General Blunt and most of his troops had gone to Missouri with General Curtis to fight the Confederates under Sterling Price, Carleton would have to make do with those available from his own thinly stretched command.

The general, however, was not worried that he would lack capable leadership for the campaign. He turned once again to his trusted subordinate, fifty-five-year-old Col. Christopher "Kit" Carson, the veteran Indian fighter who, in the past two years, had served admirably in operations against the Mescalero Apache and Navajo. Carson had been acting superintendent of the Mescalero-Navajo reservation at Bosque Redondo when he received orders to assemble his force for the march against the Comanche and Kiowa. Carleton ordered Carson

> not only to take the field promptly but to accomplish all that can be accomplished in punishing these treacherous savages before the winter fairly sets in. They have wantonly and brutally murdered our people without cause, and robbed them of their property; and it is not proposed that they shall talk, and smoke, and patch up a peace, until they have, if possible, been punished for the atrocities they have committed. To permit them to do this would be to invite further hostile acts from them as soon as the spring opens and our citizens once more embark on their long journey across the plains.[31]

Because of the shortage of troops, Carleton suggested that Carson use a force composed mainly of Ute and Jicarilla Apache Indians for the expedition. Colonel Carson was concerned that an Indian army would be unreliable but agreed to use them as auxiliaries. Carleton reluctantly acquiesced when Carson insisted that his main force, which he assembled in late October and early November at Fort Bascom, consist of troops from both California and New Mexico units drawn from other assignments.[32]

Carson's column was composed of 14 officers; 321 enlisted men—two and a half companies of the 1st New Mexico Cavalry, commanded by Maj. William McCleave, and one company of California infantry, commanded by Col. Francisco Abreau; 75 Ute and Jicarilla Apache scouts, commanded by Lt. Charles Haberkorn; twenty-seven wagons; an ambulance; two 12-pounder howitzers, under Lt. George Pettis; surgeon Gene S. Courtright; and a quartermaster.

With rations enough to last forty-five days, the column marched from Fort Bascom on November 12. The resolute troops headed east down the Canadian River toward Texas, across a wide open and seemingly endless, roadless plain inhabited by only those people that Carson intended to engage in battle and, as General Carleton had said, give "a sound drubbing." Their destination was Red Bluff, some 200 miles northeast of the fort, where a large group of Comanche and Kiowa were said to be camped near an abandoned trading post on the Canadian River.[33]

While Kit Carson followed this trail of blood and plunder on the frontier, half a continent away in the East, the war was progressing quite favorably for the Union. Four days earlier, Lincoln had been reelected president, receiving 212 electoral votes to George McClellan's 21. McClellan would resign his army commission as major general on November 14. Gen. William T. Sherman had destroyed Atlanta, leaving the city in ruins and its people with an emotional scar that would never heal, and was on the victory road toward Savannah. In the Shenandoah Valley, Phil Sheridan, who was promoted to major general on November 14 when McClellan resigned, had Jubal Early on the run, sparring with him at Middletown and Cedar Creek.[34]

And by this time, Maj. Gen. Sterling Price's raid into Missouri had been decisively repulsed. He had initially taken St. Louis and turned westward to march along the south bank of the Missouri River, destroying railroad tracks and skirmishing with hastily formed militias. In late October, near the Kansas-Missouri border, Price was threatened by enemy troops to his front and rear. Despite an open route of retreat, he chose to attack. In a battle at Westport on October 23, his army was repulsed by the Army of the Border, led by Department of Kansas commander Samuel Curtis, and forced to retreat. During the raid, Price had fought forty-three engagements and lost half his command.[35]

The fortunes of war and politics in the East, however, were of little consequence to those who faced an uncertain destiny against an enemy whose viciousness far surpassed that of the Union or Confederate troops who encountered each other on fields of battle.

On the fourth day of Kit Carson's march, the column passed the site of an earlier tragedy—one that assuredly reminded Carson of the extent of Indian brutality. In October 1849, the Jicarilla Apache had killed a prominent merchant, James W. White, and abducted his wife and daughter from

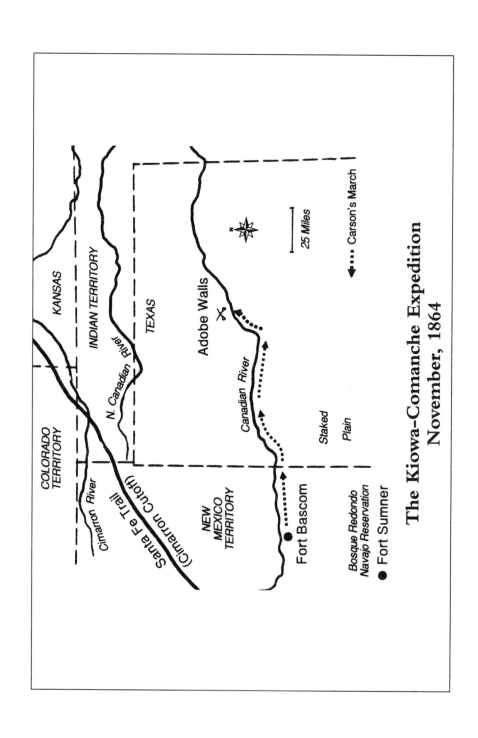

The Kiowa-Comanche Expedition
November, 1864

COLORADO TERRITORY

KANSAS

INDIAN TERRITORY

Cimarron River

Santa Fe Trail (Cimarron Cutoff)

N. Canadian River

TEXAS

NEW MEXICO TERRITORY

Canadian River

Adobe Walls

Staked Plain

Fort Bascom

Bosque Redondo Navajo Reservation

● Fort Sumner

25 Miles

····· Carson's March

a wagon train traveling along the Santa Fe Trail. A rescue party to search for the woman and girl was formed in Taos under the command of Maj. William Grier of the 1st U.S. Dragoons. Grier chose Kit Carson as guide, and for almost two weeks, Carson led the soldiers on the trail of the elusive Indians. Finally he located the Apache camp. Grier ordered his men to charge, which routed the Indians. But they left behind the warm body of Mrs. White, who had been shot through the heart by an arrow as she tried to run toward her rescuers. No trace of the child was ever found.[36]

Carson's column struggled on through a severe blizzard, which at one point forced a two-day delay. On November 24—the second nationally established Thanksgiving Day—Carson reached Mule Springs, commonly called *Arroya de la Mula,* about thirty miles west of Adobe Walls, and camped for the night. The march thus far had been executed without encountering any sign of Indians.

According to participant Lt. George H. Pettis of the California Cavalry, each evening's bivouac was enlivened by the Ute and Apache scouts:

> After making camp, being now on the war path, [they] indulged in their war dance, which, although new to most of us, became almost intolerable, it being kept up each night until nearly day-break, and until we became accustomed to their groans and howlings incident to the dance, it was impossible to sleep.[37]

At sundown, the troops were lazing around the camp, some gambling, others sleeping, most waiting for the soldiers' mess to prepare the evening meal, when the two Ute scouts who had been dispatched that morning returned to camp. The excited scouts reported that they had located the fresh trail of a large body of Indians with a sizable herd of horses and cattle that had passed that way that morning and were likely not too far ahead.[38]

Carson, with five companies of cavalry and a section of howitzers—all 13 officers and 246 men—moved out without delay. The infantry was ordered to remain with the supply train and follow the trail in the morning.

The detachment had covered fifteen miles by midnight when a "deep-worn, fresh trail of the hostile Indians" was struck, indicating that a large camp was somewhere nearby. Carson, who feared that a blunder now could cost him dearly, chose to wait until morning to resume his march. The men endured the freezing night standing by their horses, holding the bridle reins, with orders not to smoke, build fires, or talk.[39]

As the first gray streaks of dawn appeared in the eastern sky, the command—with Carson and the scouts wrapped in buffalo robes at the head—

cautiously followed the fresh trail down the Canadian River. Before long, a voice speaking Spanish was heard at a ford on the opposite side of the river: *"Bene-aca. Bene-aca."* ("Come here. Come here.")[40]

According to the Kiowa and Comanche, most of their younger men were away on the warpath at the time and had left their families behind. Some of the men had gone out early in the morning to bring up their horses and observed the presence of the cavalrymen. They hurried back to the village to sound the alarm and rally all available warriors to repel the soldiers.[41]

Carson ordered Maj. William McCleave and Company B, 1st California Cavalry, to cross the river. At the same time, the Indian scouts tossed off their robes, painted their faces, and donned feathers, then raced off in heated pursuit. The remainder of the troops moved down their side of the river. Carson tossed his overcoat on a bush, expecting to retrieve the garment later. Lieutenant Pettis denied permission for his men to abandon their coats, which was a prudent decision. Carson never saw his overcoat again.

There was no question that a village was within striking distance. As the sound of rifle shots echoed in the still air, Carson dispatched his remaining three companies of cavalry ahead with orders to attack, while he remained behind with an escort of cavalry to bring up the cumbersome howitzers. The cavalrymen in pursuit disappeared into the cottonwood groves, tall grass, and driftwood that covered the river bottoms. They pounded past a herd of stolen cattle and horses, where the Ute and Apache scouts stopped to appropriate new mounts before racing off toward the village.[42]

At about 9:00 A.M., the advance units arrived at a Kiowa village of about 150 to 170 bleached white buffalo skin lodges. The Indians—whose number included prominent old Chief Dohasan, or Little Mountain, an old Carson acquaintance, who apparently only had been visiting the village to care for those left behind by the war parties, and the dangerous Satanta, whose band had reunited with the tribe for the winter—were taken somewhat by surprise but offered stiff resistance to the presence of Major McCleave's troops. The warriors made "several severe" charges on the approaching vanguard, affording their women and children time to hurry to safety. The cavalrymen lay in the grass and fought as skirmishers.[43]

Carson arrived on the field and immediately deployed his howitzers on a small hill. The colonel ordered, "Pettis, throw a few shell into that crowd over thar." Several well-placed shots scattered the Indians, who withdrew out of range, with the command hot on their trail.[44]

By 10:00 A.M., Carson had pushed about four miles downriver to approach Adobe Walls, the eroded ruins of William Bent's trading post, which, when established by Bent about 1843, had been the first post in the Texas Panhandle. Bent had built the post with intentions of providing the Comanche and Kiowa a permanent alternative to trading with the nomadic *Comancheros*. The Indians, however, had been wary of the post, fearing that a settlement of whites would grow around it, and continued to patronize the *Comancheros*. Bent had eventually abandoned the site due to the lack of business and the high cost of transporting goods, and what remained had been reduced to little more than thick, weathering adobe walls.[45]

Carson arrived at Adobe Walls with his artillery to find that his cavalrymen had dismounted and were deployed in a wide arc behind the ruins of the trading post. Nearby, about 200 mounted warriors, covered with paint and feathers and whooping loudly, feinted charges while firing at the troops. Several cavalrymen had been wounded and were being treated as well as possible inside the walls.[46]

Beyond the fray appeared a most disturbing sight. Within plain view, about a mile away, loomed a second village of at least 500 lodges. Another 1,000 or more Comanche and Kiowa were pouring out of the lodges and gathering behind their brethren with obvious intentions of mounting an assault.

Carson quickly positioned his two 12-pounders on a small rise near the ruins and commenced firing. Pettis wrote:

> At the first discharge, every one of the enemy, those that were charging backwards and forwards on their horses but a moment before as well as those standing in line, rose high in their stirrups and gazed for a single moment, with astonishment, then guiding their horses' heads away from us, and giving one concerted, prolonged yell, they started in a dead run for the village. In fact when the fourth shot was fired there was not a single enemy within extreme range of the howitzers.[47]

Carson was inclined to believe that the Indians had lost their will to fight for the moment and allowed his men to eat breakfast—raw bacon and hardtack—and unsaddle, water, and graze the horses. Surgeon Courtright converted a corner of the fort into a hospital, where he tended to the half dozen or so wounded.[48]

The colonel doubted that the Indians would peacefully surrender or simply vanish into the snowy landscape and remained alert, scanning the area with his binoculars. He spotted several more villages within a distance of ten miles down the Canadian valley and noticed a frenzy of activity within each one.

His vigilance was eventually rewarded when suddenly he observed large groups of Indians approaching who "seemed to be anxious to renew the conflict." Before his command could resaddle and mount, at least 1,000 warriors had closed in on all sides of their position. The command found itself surrounded by an overwhelming number of Comanche and Kiowa, reinforced by small bands of Apache and Arapaho, mounted on what Carson described as "first-class horses." The warriors began firing in earnest at the cavalrymen huddled behind the walls.[49]

The Indians avoided gathering in large groups, which would have made easy targets for the howitzers. They instead charged back and forth from a distance of about 200 yards, firing under the necks of their horses. Chief Dohasan had joined the fray and had a horse shot out from under him. Another notable war chief, Stumbling Bear, who wore his daughter's shawl for good luck, killed a Ute scout and at least one soldier.

While the battle raged, war parties in size from five to fifty arrived on the field from the other villages, until an estimated total of 3,000 warriors were confronting Carson and his men. The Indians, Carson noticed, displayed more daring and bravery than he had ever previously witnessed. He also observed that their horses were fat and they appeared to have modern rifles and unlimited ammunition resources. Carson attributed this to the fact that tracks from *Comanchero* wagons were found downriver. General Carleton later complained to the adjutant general that passports were being issued by the Indian Department in New Mexico to these outlaw traders, a practice that was a great disservice to the army.[50]

Throughout the afternoon, the warriors maintained pressure on Adobe Walls, but few casualties were sustained on either side, and the presence of the howitzers prevented any threat of being overrun. Meanwhile, the Indians had been moving their stock, property, and families away in the event that Carson had intentions of attacking the large village to his front.[51]

Lieutenant Pettis mentioned one amusing detail concerning bugle calls. Each time Carson ordered his bugler to sound an order, someone among the Indians would respond by sounding the opposite call. Carson believed that the enemy bugler was a white man, although speculation pointed to Kiowa chief Satanta, but his identity remained a mystery. Regardless, the prankster's actions engendered much merriment and boosted morale among the troops, who shouted and laughed with every renegade bugle call.[52]

Although the fierce siege by the encircling Indians had them pinned down under intense fire and the situation was desperate, the officers and men encouraged Carson to advance and destroy the huge village down the river to their front. Carson weighed his options. The village was a great temptation, but the horses were worn out, supplies were running low, and the supply train, which was advancing from Mule Springs, could be threatened by warriors riding to his rear. He also understood that it was only the howitzers that had kept them from being overwhelmed, and if they were caught out in the open, the advantage would sway toward the Indians.

The colonel finally decided that the odds were too great against them but settled on a compromise. The column would retrace its original approach route and destroy that first village that they had encountered.

Lieutenant Pettis wrote:

> The most of our officers were anxious to press on and capture the village immediately to our front, and Carson was at one time about to give orders to that effect, when our Indians prevailed upon him to return and completely destroy the village that we had captured, and after finding our supply train . . . we could come back again and finish this village to our satisfaction. After some hesitation and against the wishes of most of his officers, Carson gave the orders to bring out the cavalry horses, and formed a column of fours.

After all, his orders had called for punishing the Indians, and an excellent opportunity to accomplish that task while extricating themselves from this entrapment waited to the rear, whereas that 500-lodge village to the front could place the command in peril.[53]

It was about 3:30 P.M. when Carson gave the order to prepare to march. The retreat from Adobe Walls was executed on foot, with horses assembled in fours and one horse handler assigned to each group of four. Skirmishers positioned themselves in the front, rear, and on both flanks of the formation, and the two howitzers brought up the rear.

The Indians quickly discerned the cavalrymen's destination and intensified their attack. Carson wrote in his official report:

> The Indians, seeing my object, again advanced, with the evident intention of saving their village and property if possible. The Indians charged so repeatedly, and with such desperation that for some time I had serious doubts for the safety of my rear, but the coolness with which they were received by Captain [Joseph] Berney's command, and the steady and constant fire poured into them, caused them to retire on every occasion with great slaughter.[54]

In an effort to prevent the cavalrymen from reaching their village, the warriors set fire to the tall, dry prairie grass in front of the column. The wind whipped the fire about with great fury, forcing the men to the bluffs and causing them to tighten up the formation as warriors used the smoke for cover and dashed up close. During this severe fighting, one California soldier was both shot and stuck with a lance, demonstrating the closeness of the Indians, but the trooper would survive. At one point, a New Mexican shot a warrior off his horse and rushed in to scalp the Indian—the only scalp taken by either side. Carson countered this move by setting a backfire, then retired to a piece of high ground on his right flank and ordered the 12-pounders into action to ward off his attackers.[55]

The column moved out slowly but steadily across the charred ground, with Indians harassing the troops at every step. Occasionally, when his enemy pressed too close, Carson would order a halt and turn the howitzers to cover his retreat. In this manner, he reached his objective by sunset. By then, a large number of Kiowa had reoccupied the village and were frantically trying to save their possessions from the inevitable.

Carson brought the howitzers into play and ordered a mounted charge, which drove the warriors to the far end of the village. One half of the command held back the Indians, while the other half systematically looted and destroyed this Kiowa winter headquarters. "The lodges were found to be full of plunder," Pettis reported, "including many hundreds of finely finished buffalo robes. Every man in the command took possession of one or more, while the balance were consumed in the lodges."[56]

In addition to hundreds of buffalo robes, the men put the torch to great quantities of dried meat, clothing, cooking utensils, gunpowder, and other provisions stored by the Kiowa for the winter. Two Ute Indian women had accompanied Carson's scouts and found "two old, decrepit, blind Kiowas and two cripples." The women killed the four "by cleaving their heads with axes."[57]

While the destruction was in progress, Carson found ample evidence to indicate that these Kiowa indeed had been responsible for raids along the Santa Fe Trail and Texas and Kansas settlements. The lodges held a number of women's and children's dresses, bonnets, and shoes, as well as several photographs. Also discovered were a cavalry sergeant's hat, saber, and belts, identified as those taken from a soldier who had been killed the previous summer, and a buggy and spring wagon allegedly belonging to Chief Little Mountain.[58]

Much to his regret, Carson later learned that five captive white women and two children had been in the village but had been concealed in the brakes north of the river when he had attacked.[59]

At dark, Carson was informed by his company commanders that ammunition was running dangerously low. At the same time, the men feared a nighttime attack in this position, 250 miles from their base, where they were surrounded by thousands of aroused enemy. They became greatly concerned about the safety of their wagon train, which was carrying food and spare ammunition.

The men loaded their wounded comrades onto ammunition carts and gun carriages, and set out upriver to rendezvous with the supply train. While Carson marched, the Indians entered the village to see what they could salvage of their precious winter provisions. Three hours later, fires appeared in the distance, and Carson was reunited after a thirty-hour absence with his train, which was safe and secure.[60]

The men were permitted to rest throughout the following day, with the Indians in view but remaining just out of cannon range. The majority of the officers still wanted to return to the battlefield and destroy the large village down the Canadian. Carson debated whether to wait for General Blunt to arrive with reinforcements or continue campaigning on his own. He chose a third option:

> I now decided that owing to the broken-down condition of my cavalry horses and transportation and the Indians having fled in all directions with their stock that it was impossible for me to chastise them further at present. Therefore, on the morning of the 27th, I broke camp and commenced my return march.[61]

Carson was privately aware that he had barely escaped a catastrophe at Adobe Walls and had not been about to tempt fate any further. The order to march was issued, according to Pettis, with

> much surprise and dissatisfaction of all the officers, who desired to go to the Comanche village that we had been in sight of on the day of the fight. It was learned afterwards that our Indians had advised Carson to return, and without consulting his officers the order was given and we commenced the return march.

On December 10, Col. Kit Carson and his command arrived at Fort Bascom "by easy marches" to save the horses and, despite destroying only one village, had accomplished its mission although faced with an almost impossible situation.

In the tradition of frontier army officers, he could not resist writing in his report a self-serving, if not presumptuous, compliment to himself: "I flatter myself that I have taught these Indians a severe lesson, and hereafter they will be more cautious about how they engage a force of civilized troops."[62]

Lt. George Pettis perhaps portrayed a truer picture of Carson's feelings when he wrote:

> The Indians claimed that if the whites had not had with them the two "guns that shot twice" referring to the shells of the mountain howitzers, they would never have allowed a single white man to escape out of the valley of the Canadian, and I may say, with becoming modesty, that this was also the often expressed opinion of Colonel Carson.[63]

Carson estimated Indian losses at not less than sixty, and his own at two killed and ten wounded, but more troops, perhaps as many as twenty-five, later reported injuries, and several would succumb from their wounds. The Indians scoffed at Carson's casualty figures and set their losses at five killed, two of them women.[64]

General Carleton, who was thrilled with the outcome of campaign, wrote in a letter that Carson's

> brilliant affair adds another green leaf to the laurel wreath which you have so nobly won in the service of your country. That you may long be spared to be of still further service, is the sincere wish of your obedient servant and friend, James H. Carleton.[65]

Carson perhaps deserved the accolades. If measured by sheer numbers, he had engaged a force of Indians larger than anyone else ever had or would on the Plains—including Custer at Little Bighorn, who faced fewer Indians with more troops and might have saved himself as well with Carson's howitzers, or the Gatling guns that he had refused to take with him due to problems transporting them over the rugged terrain. Had Custer been able to employ artillery, the battle of the Little Bighorn might have been reduced to the relative obscurity of Kit Carson's admirable achievement at Adobe Walls.

The campaign resulted in at least one Comanche chief visiting Fort Bascom to seek peace, but most of the Kiowa, Comanche, and their allies, aware that they could not escape army reprisals in that area, moved eastward into Indian Territory to find new locations for their winter camps. Their departure, at least for the time being, left the Santa Fe Trail relatively safe for travel.[66]

Carson, however, desired to return to Adobe Walls with four months' supplies and use the old trading post as a base for further operations. "Now is the time, in my opinion," he told General Carleton, "to keep after them." Carleton likely agreed that winter was an ideal time for campaigning against Indians, but unfortunately for Carson and his ambitions, the army at present lacked the resources for such an endeavor. Therefore, Kit Carson had fought his last battle with the Indians—thirty-five years after his first against the Apache on the Gila.

On March 13, 1865, Carson was breveted brigadier general of volunteers for his gallantry at Valverde in 1862, in addition to his conduct during his Indian campaigns—thus becoming the only general in the army who could not read or write. He continued on frontier duty until 1867, serving in his former rank as lieutenant colonel when his unit was downsized after the war. In 1868, Carson moved to Boggsville, Colorado (near present-day Las Animas), to resume life as a rancher. Along the way, he managed to dictate his autobiography (*Kit Carson's Autobiography,* edited by Milo Milton Quaife), which has been regularly embellished by others. Carson's own words tend to confirm his rather contradictory nature with respect to his treatment of Indians throughout his life. In his early years, Carson had gained a reputation as a man who was sympathetic and reasonable when dealing with his charges, then, perhaps due to Carleton's provocation, became a ruthless Indian fighter. He presently stands as the most hated white man in Navajo culture. Kit Carson, arguably the greatest frontier legend in U.S. history, died at Fort Lyon, Colorado, on May 23, 1868.

Brig. Gen. James H. Carleton remained in New Mexico until he was relieved of his command in 1867 and reassigned to Texas. Carleton, although sincere about his efforts to control the Indians of the Southwest, which he considered humanitarian, was nonetheless quite cruel and dictatorial. His Civil War legacy pertaining to the ruthless treatment of the Indians, the Navajo in particular, soon became a national scandal, often pointed to as the army's worst abuse in the handling of that race of man.

Kit Carson's minor victory at Adobe Walls against the Comanche and Kiowa may have engendered a temporary calm in New Mexico, but up in Colorado, Col. John M. Chivington had embarked on a campaign that would outrage the nation and stir up hostilities that would result in a reign of terror that would not subside for decades.

CHAPTER NINE

Blood along Sand Creek

THE MOST WIDELY KNOWN AND NOTORIOUS INCIDENT BETWEEN INDIANS and soldiers that occurred during the Civil War was without question the attack by Colorado militia under Col. John M. Chivington on an Indian village along the banks of Sand Creek, Colorado Territory, five days after Thanksgiving in 1864. This act of betrayal and barbarity, equally shared in responsibility by government and military authorities, as well as rank-and-file soldiers, would serve as combustible fuel dumped onto the smoldering coals of distrust and hatred and would ignite the plains in flames of violence for years to come.

The Indians involved in this engagement at Sand Creek were members of the Southern Cheyenne and Arapaho tribes, who had for generations roamed this territory that eventually became Colorado.

The Cheyenne, an Algonquin tribe, in their earliest days occupied villages in parts of Minnesota, where they farmed, hunted, gathered wild rice, and made pottery. At some point in the seventeenth century, they became tired of constant warfare with the Sioux and Ojibwa and began migrating to the Great Plains, where they acquired guns and horses and became nomadic hunters. In about 1832, the tribe split into two distinct bands: the Northern Cheyenne, who settled around the North Platte River in northern Nebraska and assumed a lifestyle similar to their allies, the Sioux; and the larger group, which became known as the Southern Cheyenne and established its domain between the Platte and Arkansas Rivers, from central Kansas to the Rocky Mountains.

The lifestyle and customs of the Southern Cheyenne were similar to those of other Plains tribes, although they did not consider their women to be chattels. Girls generally married young, and a celebration was held with the birth of each baby. Children were cherished, the elders patiently teaching the necessary skills that would enable them to grow into beneficial members of the tribe. Religion was part of every aspect of their daily life, expressed by many traditional ceremonies—the central element being the sacred pipe, which was believed to be the link between man, nature, and the supreme deity.[1]

The Arapaho, another Algonquin tribe, were thought to have migrated to the Great Plains from the headwaters of the Mississippi in the late seventeenth or early eighteenth century. At that time, the tribe gave up agriculture to become nomadic hunters. Around 1835, the Arapaho divided into two groups: the Northern Arapaho, which initially settled just east of the Rocky Mountains along the headwaters of the Platte River in Wyoming; and the Southern Arapaho, who moved to an area along the Arkansas River of Colorado.[2]

At about that time, the Southern Arapaho band aligned itself with the Southern Cheyenne. The two tribes camped, hunted, and held sacred ceremonies together, occasionally intermarried, and allied to wage war upon enemy tribes. By the early 1850s, the Cheyennes numbered nearly 4,000, and the Arapaho about 2,400.

Before the invasion of western Indian country by white trappers, settlers, and miners was of any consequence, this vast domain had been a battleground for warfare among various tribes. The Southern Cheyenne fought constantly with the Kiowa and the Pawnee, and to a lesser degree with the Apache and Comanche. The Cheyenne and Arapaho engaged in one monumental fight against the Kiowa and Comanche in 1838, called the battle of Wolf Creek. Two years later, in the summer of 1840, a lasting peace was negotiated among these tribes, as well as the Comanche and Apache.[3]

The first white men to visit Colorado were part of a 1541 expedition of Spanish explorers led by Francisco Vasquez de Coronado. These explorations by the Spaniards continued throughout the seventeenth and eighteenth centuries. Then along came the French, who claimed the land for France. In 1803, the Louisiana Purchase gave all the land within the Mississippi Basin, which included northern and eastern Colorado, to the United States. The first American exploration of the region was an 1806 trek by army captain Zebulon M. Pike, and subsequent expeditions were conducted by various military officers.

By that time, however, a steady stream of whites had been passing through the area, mainly trappers, mountain men, and other adventurers, such as Jim Bridger, Kit Carson, Thomas Fitzpatrick, and brothers Charles and William Bent. Trading posts—most notably Bent's New Fort on the Arkansas River (about six miles from present-day La Junta), which was established in 1831, the first in Colorado—had become operational, serving both whites and Indians.[4]

One main fort, which was located on the west bank of the Laramie River about one mile above its juncture with the North Platte River, had been established in 1834 as Fort William by fur trappers William Sublette and Robert Campbell. In March 1849, the fort was sold to the U.S. government and converted into a military post, renamed Fort Laramie after the river, which was named after French trapper Jacques Laramie, who had been killed by Arapaho in 1821. It had been garrisoned to protect travelers on the Oregon Trail and monitor the Plains Indians.[5]

Other than a few isolated incidents, relations between the whites and the Southern Cheyenne and Arapaho tribes, through whose traditional hunting grounds they traveled, could during this time of expansion be called accommodating, even friendly.

In 1851, in an effort to maintain peace between the Plains Indians and the whites, a treaty was negotiated on Horse Creek, thirty-five miles east of Fort Laramie between the U.S. government and the Southern Cheyenne and Arapaho, as well as various other southern Plains tribes. This treaty confirmed that the Southern Cheyenne and Arapaho controlled the vast territory between the trails to Oregon and Santa Fe—most of the Colorado plains, southeastern Wyoming, and parts of Kansas and Nebraska. In return, the Indians promised to refrain from waging war against the whites, and to permit the government to build roads and military posts within their territory.

The tribal chiefs, headed by Cheyennes Black Kettle and White Antelope and Arapaho Little Raven, were probably swayed by the pile of presents that were nearby waiting to be distributed when they "touched the pen"—not to mention the tempting promise of presents each year thereafter. They most likely did not understand this act, or perhaps did not even take it seriously. And unlike most other treaties, which recognized individual rights, this one stipulated that the chiefs spoke for all of their people. Nonetheless, the treaty was for the most part abided by on both sides, and relations remained cordial.[6]

By the mid-1850s, however, the Cheyenne chiefs were finding it quite difficult to restrain their hot-blooded young warriors from engaging in raiding parties, particularly against their traditional enemy, the Pawnee. New roads were being surveyed by the army in this territory, and Brig. Gen. William S. Harney, who in 1855 had severely punished the Sioux at Ash Hollow in retaliation for the massacre of Lt. John L. Grattan and his men the previous year, was worried that this conflict would threaten emigrant travel.

In the spring of 1856, he warned the Cheyenne and Arapaho to quit raiding the Pawnee or he would "sweep them from the face of the earth."

Several subsequent incidents occurred, one of which was the fault of an overanxious officer named Henry Heth (of Gettysburg fame), and the Indians became the subject of military action by the 1st Cavalry, who attacked a camp of eighty Cheyenne, killing ten and wounding a number of others. The Cheyenne struck back along the emigrant road by killing, wounding, or capturing at least a dozen whites.[7]

During May and June of 1857, Col. Edwin V. Sumner led six troops of cavalry and three of infantry, and along the way dispatched separate columns to hunt down the Cheyenne and punish them for their deeds. On July 29, the cavalry happened upon about 300 Cheyenne on Solomon's Fork of the Smoky Hill River in northwest Kansas. In the ensuing fierce skirmish, nine Indians were killed and many others wounded before the troops managed to rout their enemy and then destroy the village.

During the fight, two troopers were killed and nine wounded, including Lt. J. E. B. ("Jeb") Stuart, the future Civil War hero, who would—in a most admirable display of courage—lead a small group of soldiers over 120 miles of rugged terrain to reach Fort Kearny after Sumner moved on without the wounded. Sumner had intended to pursue his enemy, but changed directions when he received orders to join an expedition in Utah. The Cheyenne, however, had been appropriately chastised and promised to maintain friendly relations with whites from then on.[8]

In 1858, gold was discovered in Colorado where the Cherry Creek joins the Platte River, touching off a stampede of miners and fortune hunters from across the country to the Pikes Peak and South Platte region. This invasion of prospectors was similar to the 1849 California gold rush—with one exception. The Colorado miners, unlike those in the Far West, intended to remain in that region and began establishing permanent settlements around the mining districts.

But true to their word, the Cheyenne and Arapaho permitted these whites to pass unmolested through their territory. The Indians were astonished by this influx and regarded the whites as insane for the way they lusted after the yellow metal—the same soft substance from which the tribes had for years made bullets. There were occasions when the Cheyenne would encounter prospectors wandering around the foothills in a delirious condition from lack of food and water. They took these whites to the Indian camp and nursed them back to health.[9]

By 1859, an estimated 140,000 prospectors had ventured into Colorado, working big strikes in Central City, Idaho Springs, and Leadville. In Denver

City, the most rapidly growing population center, the presence of Indians on the streets was commonplace. In fact, one of the most frequent visitors was Arapaho chief Little Raven, who had "pledged his word for the preservation of peace and law and order by his people." He was said to have been "a very sensible and friendly disposed man" who "handles a knife and fork and smokes cigars like a white man."[10]

That was not to say that there were not incidences of abuses between the races. One example was the night when drunken "bummers," which was the name associated with those too lazy to work but not to steal, entered a camp of Cheyenne and Apache who were visiting Denver to trade buffalo robes. These white men raped and beat old and young women alike, and stole several mules that were later recovered. These Indians had been the guests of legendary mulatto mountain man Jim Beckwourth, who wrote in the *Rocky Mountain News:*

> The Indians are as keenly sensible to acts of injustice, as they are tenacious of revenge, and it is more humiliating to them to be recipients of such treatment upon their own lands, which they have been deprived of, their game driven off and they made to suffer by hunger, and when they pay us a visit, abused more than dogs. . . . All of our Indian troubles are produced by imprudent acts of unprincipled white men.[11]

In spite of these random acts of violence, or perhaps because of them, the Cheyenne and Arapaho, who remembered the lesson taught by General Sumner, were at this time quite anxious to negotiate a treaty with the U.S. government that would give them a permanent home and provide for them until, surprisingly, they could learn to become competent farmers. They understood that the white man was well on his way to occupying the whole country; the buffalo were already disappearing, their migration routes changed by the influx of ranches, farms, and settlements; and further warfare against the army would be fruitless, even suicidal. Many Indians had been reduced to begging food from miners, and the two tribes were quite destitute. Other Plains tribes, on the other hand, the Kiowa in particular, indicated that they would be unwilling to sign a treaty.

In September 1860, delegations from the Cheyenne, Arapaho, and Comanche tribes arrived to camp near Bent's Fort. The fort had recently been purchased by the War Department, and a new post, which would be called Fort Wise in honor of the Virginia governor, was under construction on a stone bluff about a mile upriver from Bent's location. Representing the government at this meeting was A. B. Greenwood, commissioner of Indian Affairs, and other dignitaries, including William Bent and A. G. Boone, son of Daniel Boone.[12]

The chiefs expressed their desire to live peaceably as farmers, if the government would teach them how, and were awarded medals bearing the likeness of President Buchanan. Skeptical frontiersmen at the fort scoffed at the idea that the rambunctious young men of the tribes would settle down and transform themselves into farmers, but cynically remarked that they were "fast becoming civilized. They get drunk as readily as white men and swear with great distinctiveness."[13]

An agreement between the parties proved difficult to reach, and Commissioner Greenwood eventually departed, leaving Boone with the responsibility to effect the signing.

It was February 1861 before the details had been ironed out and the Treaty of Fort Wise was finally consummated. The Cheyenne and Arapaho agreed to give up all the land that they had been awarded in the Fort Laramie Treaty of 1851, except for one gameless, arid scab of southeastern Colorado Territory on the upper Arkansas, which would serve as their reservation. The government would reward them with annuities of $30,000 ($15,000 for each tribe) for fifteen years, to be used for the purchase of implements and other items necessary to work the soil. The Indians would also receive a sawmill, various workshops, and assistance from millers, farmers, and mechanics for a period of five years.

On February 18, 1861, Cheyenne chiefs Black Kettle, White Antelope, Little Wolf, Left Hand, and two others signed for their tribe. Arapaho signees were Little Raven, Shave-Head, and Big Mouth.[14]

These tribal leaders would endure much abuse for their rash actions, especially by agreeing to such a radical change in their traditional lifestyle, much less relinquishing their homeland. The chiefs, however, had likely been misled and signed believing that they would live on their reservation but still could hunt buffalo in other areas of their choice. That, of course, was not the intention of the government. And the assigned reservation consisted of land so poor that whites would never consider settling on it. This desolate patch was nothing more than dry, sandy, barren, almost gameless land, so worthless that any lifelong farmer would have difficulty raising a crop on it. Due to the misunderstanding or perhaps resentment of the provisions when fully explained, a majority of the two tribes chose to ignore the treaty, refused to submit to the reservation, and continued to follow the buffalo between the Platte and Arkansas Rivers.

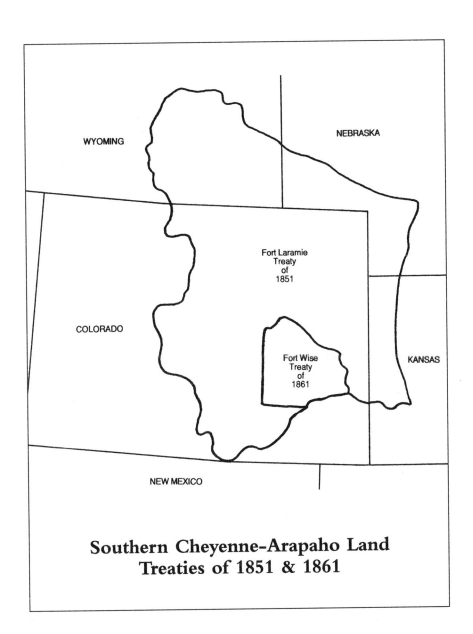

WYOMING

NEBRASKA

Fort Laramie
Treaty
of
1851

COLORADO

Fort Wise
Treaty
of
1861

KANSAS

NEW MEXICO

**Southern Cheyenne-Arapaho Land
Treaties of 1851 & 1861**

Colorado officially became a territory in February 1861, with the stroke of the pen by President Buchanan, but it was Abraham Lincoln who appointed the first officials. Local citizens had organized the region as the Provisional Territory of Jefferson in 1859, but Congress balked at naming a territory after a man and, after considering Idaho, Montana, and several other names, finally settled on Colorado.

Lincoln nominated William Gilpin as governor. Gilpin, who was born on the Brandywine Battlefield, had graduated from West Point and fought in the Seminole and Mexican Wars. He had also prevented the Cheyenne and Arapaho from joining an alliance against whites in 1847, when he had brazenly camped with his command of two cavalry companies in the middle of villages occupied by those two tribes. Gilpin was said to have been a romantic visionary, was an explorer, and had been a resident of Missouri at the time of his appointment.

Governor Gilpin assumed his office in May 1861—just after the outbreak of war between the North and South—with a promise to the president that he would keep his state loyal to the Union. On April 24, a Confederate flag had been unfurled over a store in downtown Denver City, but it had been quickly torn down by Union loyalists, who constituted the vast majority of citizens. The Union partisans then held a spirited rally—in conjunction with gatherings in other towns—and the territory of Colorado pledged its allegiance to Lincoln and the United States.[15]

Gilpin immediately set about the business of establishing a strong territorial government. He visited the various mining camps and settlements to assess the needs of his territory—a census showed a population of 25,331—and appointed district Federal judges, which in many cases replaced justice meted out by vigilante committees or people's courts. A twenty-two-member legislature, elected by the citizens, convened for the first time in Denver in September and, using law books from various states, wrote basic codes for both civil and criminal law.

The military defense of his territory became a major concern for Gilpin. The attraction of gold for the taking by Confederates could lead to an invasion, and he needed to be prepared to combat such a threat. Up to that point, Federal troops had garrisoned both Fort Garland in the San Luis Valley and the new Fort Wise, but most of these soldiers had been transferred back east to defend Washington. The governor issued $375,000 in drafts on the Federal Treasury—without Washington's approval—in order to obtain equipment and supplies necessary to organize and maintain an army. Although this controversial act was unpopular with some merchants, most went along with the governor's wishes, believing that the drafts would be honored by the government.

The 1st Regiment of Colorado Infantry, ten companies strong, commanded by Col. John Slough, came into existence, training at the newly constructed Camp Weld—named after Lewis L. Weld, the territorial secretary—near Denver.[16]

Meanwhile, that summer of 1861 was extremely hot and dry, and the Cheyenne and Arapaho land along the Arkansas was parched into dust by the interminable heat and lack of moisture. The tribes had been unable to farm under such conditions, and the people were hungry. In September, some 3,000 angry Indians assembled around Fort Wise demanding, even threatening, that they be paid their annuities. Capt. Elmer Otis, the post commander, distributed only a small amount of provisions, but it was sufficient to quiet the clamor for the time being.[17]

Also during that summer, a Confederate army of Texans under Brig. Gen. Henry Hopkins Sibley had invaded New Mexico Territory and captured Albuquerque and then Santa Fe. In March 1862, the 1st Colorado Volunteers were ordered to march south and reinforce the undermanned Union troops in New Mexico to repel Sibley's troops. On March 29, the combined Union units engaged the Confederates at La Glorieta Pass, east of Santa Fe. The two armies battled for most of the day, with the Confederates holding the field at the end. A flanking movement by Coloradans under the command of Maj. John Chivington, however, successfully destroyed eighty-five wagons that contained vital supplies and ammunition, as well as capturing 500 to 600 horses and mules. The action by Chivington compelled General Sibley, his ambitious plans to capture New Mexico for the Confederacy thwarted by the lack of provisions, to retreat back down the Rio Grande Valley to Texas.[18]

This victory would have apparently vindicated Gov. William Gilpin for his controversial decision to issue the Treasury drafts necessary to organize and outfit his troops. That, however, was not the case. Colorado Territory was in dire financial straits, and the Federal government refused to compensate merchants who had accepted the drafts. Gilpin was denounced by the citizenry, and a petition for his recall was circulated. The governor traveled to Washington to straighten out the matter. Although these drafts would eventually be paid by the Treasury, in April President Lincoln removed Gilpin from office for mismanagement, extravagance, and exceeding his authority.[19]

Lincoln's replacement for Gilpin was John Evans, a friend of the president. The forty-eight-year-old Ohio native had studied medicine at Clarmont Academy in Pennsylvania and, in addition to success in that profession, boasted profitable ventures in railroading—he was a director of the newly organized Union Pacific Railroad—and in real estate. He also had been involved in the founding of Northwestern University, as well as the city of Evanston, Illinois, which was named after him. Evans had turned down the position as governor of Washington Territory before accepting the Colorado appointment. He arrived in Denver in May 1862 with ambitious plans for the territory, one of which was making Denver the most important hub for the first transcontinental railroad, which would ensure the growth and prosperity of the region and likely put him in the U.S. Senate.

Evans was unconcerned about the possibility of a Confederate invasion of his territory, but he became greatly disturbed when the chilling news of the Sioux uprising in Minnesota reached him. This indiscriminate slaughter of hundreds of whites raised an immediate cry of alarm throughout the Plains. Colorado, with the largest population center in the region, was gripped with fear over rumors that this bloody trail of destruction and death would lead to its unprotected doorstep.

Although the nearby Cheyenne and Arapaho tribes remained at peace, it was noted that Colorado Territory was virtually defenseless against an Indian attack, inasmuch as the 1st Colorado Infantry was still in New Mexico. Governor Evans raised another regiment, the 2nd Colorado Volunteers, which was commanded by Col. Jesse H. Leavenworth, a fifty-six-year-old West Pointer and son of the man after whom Fort Leavenworth had been named. Leavenworth's men had initially garrisoned Fort Lyon—the former Fort Wise, whose name had been changed in June 1862 in honor of Gen. Nathaniel Lyon, the first Union general to die in the war—but subsequently had been transferred to Fort Larned, Kansas, leaving only a detachment behind.[20]

This force was bolstered when the soldiers from New Mexico were recalled, and Evans could report, "Now that the War Department has ordered the Colorado troops home, and mounted one regiment, giving us ample military protection, we have but little danger to apprehend from Indian hostilities."[21]

By this time, Colonel Slough had resigned as commander of the Colorado volunteers and had been replaced by John Milton Chivington, the hero of La Glorieta Pass, who had been appointed commanding colonel of the newly created Military District of Colorado.[22]

Chivington was a huge, imposing man—standing six feet, five inches tall and tipping the scales at about 250 pounds—and was said to be "strong as a bull elephant." He had been born into a farming family on January 27, 1821, in Lebanon, Ohio, and grew up working in the family lumber business, eventually taking over the marketing of their product. On one of his sales trips to Cincinnati, Chivington was introduced to Martha Rollason, a well-educated Virginian whose family owned a plantation. Martha had left home after the death of her mother and desired to become a teacher. After a whirlwind courtship, the two were married. They eventually would have three children.

Chivington's life changed in 1843, when he attended a series of revival meetings and became a born-again Christian. He voraciously studied everything he could find about the Methodist faith, a religion that stressed conversion, holiness, and social welfare. In September 1844, he was ordained in the 3 million-member Methodist-Episcopal Church. He subsequently moved his family around the Midwest, as he was sent on various circuit-riding preaching assignments in Ohio, Illinois, Missouri, Kansas, and Nebraska.

Chivington was quite conservative and essentially humorless, known for his gentlemanly behavior, and fervently opposed to slavery. One example of many that best portrayed his strong-willed character when demonstrating his beliefs happened in Ohio. The reverend had preached an antislavery message in a church whose congregation was for the most part proslavery. He was warned that if he ever again spoke against slavery, he would be tarred and feathered and run out of town. The following Sunday morning, Chivington stepped to the pulpit, placed two pearl-handled Colt revolvers on either side of his Bible, and railed about the evils of slavery. His message was greeted without protest, and there were no repercussions. This episode gained him recognition within the church and propelled him into a leadership role.

Chivington believed that the rush of miners to Colorado presented the perfect opportunity to spread the gospel in that region. He arrived in Denver with his family in May 1860 and assumed a position as presiding elder of the First Methodist Episcopal Church. Chivington immediately organized a Sunday school in his church and traveled as a circuit rider to the outlying mining towns to preach the gospel. It was said that he possessed such a powerful voice that his sermons could be heard within a radius of three blocks.

Chivington had initially been offered a commission as chaplain of the 1st Colorado Regiment, but he requested a "fighting" commission rather than a "praying" one and was appointed a major. His heroism at La Glorieta Pass had earned him regional and national attention as Colorado's "Fighting Parson," and he had set his sights on becoming a congressman when the territory was granted statehood.[23]

Governor Evans and his military commander were of like mind when it came to dealing with Indians. Both held the view that the red men were an obstacle in the pathway of Colorado's progress—as well as their ambitious plans for statehood. This realization, coupled with the bloody uprising in Minnesota, led Evans to decide that the Cheyenne and Arapaho bands, which had not abided by the provisions of the 1861 Fort Wise Treaty, must be made to comply.

The leaders of these tribes had been under the impression that the treaty had included their hunting grounds north and east of the headwaters of the Republican and Smoky Hill Rivers. Therefore, most of the Cheyenne and Arapaho had ignored the boundaries of their reservation and continued to follow the buffalo. A number of isolated incidents of conflict between whites and Indians had occurred—harassment of traffic on the overland trails and occasional livestock stealing—but the Southern Cheyenne and Arapaho tribes, although their condition was deteriorating due to hunger and disease, remained peaceful as 1863 arrived.

In March, at the urging of Cheyenne and Arapaho agent Samuel G. Colley, a delegation made up of chiefs from the Arapaho, Caddo, Cheyenne, Comanche, and Kiowa tribes went to visit Washington. It was hoped that this trip would strengthen bonds of friendship, as well as demonstrate the might of the white man's army, which would discourage any thought of an uprising.[24]

At about this time, however, conditions on the Plains were growing increasingly worse. Tension mounted as a severe drought dried up the grasslands that supported the huge buffalo herds. As a result, these herds migrated farther north, and the Indians were on the brink of starvation. To make matters worse, corruption was rampant, with agent Colley and his son allegedly making the Indians trade for their own annuities or selling the goods elsewhere for a profit.

Governor Evans learned in May that the Cheyenne and Arapaho were holding a conference with the Sioux, who were making entreaties about an alliance among the tribes for the purpose of fighting against the whites. Evans passed word to Arapaho who were camped nearby to relay to their brethren that "if they went to war with the whites it would be a war of extermination to them." Apparently, by the time word was passed, the Cheyenne and Arapaho had already declined the offer from the Sioux and had headed off for their summer buffalo hunt.[25]

Governor Evans remained adamant that the Southern Cheyenne and Arapaho, as well as other tribes, who were scattered in small bands around the territory, should be made to adhere to the Fort Wise Treaty and submit to their reservations. He decided that he would arrange a peace council to convince them that they must obey. The governor dispatched emissaries to the various locations to invite chiefs from the tribes to parley with him on September 1 on the Arikaree Fork of the Republican River, east of Denver.

Gov. John Evans arrived at the appointed place on time and cooled his heels for two weeks without any sign of Indians.

Emissaries scoured the area to find out why the Indians had snubbed Evans and were greeted with various excuses: The buffalo hunt was going too well to quit for a meeting; children were sick and needed attention. Finally the main reason for their absence emerged—dissatisfaction with the Fort Wise Treaty. The Indians considered the treaty a fraud, felt that the government had taken advantage of them, and now realized that they had not understood the provisions, all of which was true. There were not any buffalo on this new reservation, they argued, and the presence of that animal was a necessity for survival. Cheyenne chiefs White Antelope and Black Kettle both denied even having signed the treaty. They also denied that they had agreed to cede their land at the headwaters of the Republican and Smoky Hill Rivers and vowed never to relinquish it to the white man.[26]

Naturally, this response was quite disturbing to Evans and Chivington. Evans, who was accustomed to getting his own way, was bitter about being rebuffed by the Indians at his proposed council, but was for the time being unable to do anything about it. And in his estimation, there was no reason for immediate action. In October, he informed Washington that except for a few depredations by "single bands and small parties," his territory was relatively peaceful.[27]

In November, however, Evans received a report from a white man who lived with the Arapaho that all the Plains tribes had formed a secret alliance and had pledged to go to war against the whites "as soon as grass was up in the spring." Without questioning the credibility of this report, Evans—as well as Chivington—was convinced that Colorado was in imminent danger of a surprise attack, and that the only way to prevent it was to force the Indians onto their assigned reservations by the use of military might.[28]

The War Department, however, had been drawing Colorado volunteers for assignments in the East, and Evans was short on troop strength. The 1st Colorado Infantry had been converted into a cavalry regiment, and thus far Colonel Chivington had prevented that unit from being transferred away from Denver and the surrounding area.

Chivington demonstrated in one particular incident just how serious he was about keeping his troops close at hand—and under his strict control. Col. Jesse Leavenworth, who had initially commanded Fort Lyon, was presently at Fort Larned providing security for the Santa Fe Trail. Lt. Col. Samuel Tappan, a former correspondent for the *New York Tribune* and one of the original founders of Lawrence, Kansas, who had joined the gold rush to Colorado and had been second in command at the La Glorieta battle, had assumed command at Fort Lyon.

Both of these officers were annoyed that Chivington was keeping so many troops in Denver when they were greatly undermanned. Leavenworth, who found himself overwhelmed by more duties than he had men for, made a request for assistance from Tappan's garrison. Chivington turned down the request, but Tappan went ahead on his own and dispatched some troops to reinforce Leavenworth. Chivington then punished Tappan by removing him from command and exiling him to out-of-the-way Fort Garland. Ironically, Tappan, over Chivington's objections, would later serve on the commission investigating the colonel's actions at Sand Creek.[29]

Governor Evans made a trip to Washington in December 1863 to plead his case for the return of Colorado troops, as well as to request that other Federal soldiers be dispatched along the Platte and Arkansas supply routes. The War Department, however, did not share Evans's concern about the threat of the Plains Indians and was not about to transfer troops that were needed in the East. Evans returned home determined to prove in some manner that he was not simply crying wolf—perhaps even if it meant provoking a war.[30]

The winter of 1863–64 was extremely hard on the various Plains Indian tribes. The buffalo had wandered far away from traditional hunting grounds, and other wild game had become scarce. The Indians were starving, racked with smallpox, and compelled to visit trading posts to exchange anything of value that they possessed for food. Unscrupulous traders took advantage of their desperate clients, paying lower-than-normal prices for buffalo robes and other items—including women who were forced to prostitute themselves in order to feed their children. Many tribe members drowned their sorrows in watered-down rot-gut whiskey. Some traders went so far as to suggest to these alcoholic Indians that they steal livestock from ranches and farms to trade for whiskey. How many thefts can be blamed on this devious encouragement cannot be determined, but they were known to have occurred.[31]

In spite of their present poor condition, most of which could be blamed on the presence of white invaders, there was no indication that the Indians were anything but peaceful. There were a number of times when livestock had "wandered away" from ranches and were "found" by Indians, but those isolated incidents could not necessarily be classified as raiding—although there can be no doubt that some stealing took place in this tragic period that the Southern Cheyenne and Arapaho called "the year of hunger."[32]

Regardless of the pettiness of the crime, Evans and Chivington mentally filed away each minor infraction, as they continued to prepare their case for the war that they either advocated or merely assumed would flare up.

The plans being concocted by the governor and his military commander, however, suffered a severe blow on March 29, when Maj. Gen. Samuel R. Curtis, commanding officer of the Department of Kansas, notified them that he was obliged to draw every available trooper from the Plains to meet the threat of a Confederate invasion of Kansas. But to the relief of the two men, this setback proved to be only temporary. Within a week and a half, before their troops had been officially ordered away, evidence of the war that Evans and Chivington had predicted presented itself.[33]

On April 9, Chivington received a report—albeit of questionable credibility—that 175 cattle that were being wintered by a government contractor had been stolen by Cheyenne Indians. The following day, Lt. George S. Eayre, commanding a detachment of fifty-four troops and two 12-pounder mountain howitzers, set off to track down those thieves.[34]

While Eayre was on the march, another incident occurred some three miles from Fremont's Orchard on the north side of the South Platte River, in present-day Morgan County. Cheyenne chiefs Black Kettle and White Antelope later noted this as the spark that ignited all-out war.

On April 11, a rancher reported that Indians had appropriated some horses and mules from the Bijou Creek area. These marauders were also said to have been knocking down telegraph poles, as well as terrorizing local ranches.

Lt. Clark Dunn and forty men from the 1st Colorado Cavalry were dispatched with orders to recover these animals and disarm the perpetrators. Dunn arrived in the vicinity of the alleged theft and located a fresh Indian trail, but also spotted smoke up ahead. He decided to divide his command, sending half toward the smoke and leading the others along the trail. Dunn and about fifteen troopers had paused to water their horses when they observed a small party of Indians across the Platte River with a herd of animals. The Indians, said to be members of the Southern Cheyenne tribe, halted and waited as Dunn and his men crossed the river. The two lines approached within 100 feet of each other.

At this point, the actual sequence of events becomes somewhat foggy and open to interpretation.

Dunn reported that he dismounted, stepped forward, and made signs for the Indians to send someone out for a parley. Eventually all the Indians came forward to shake hands with the soldiers. Dunn, in accordance with his orders to disarm the Indians, reached out to take away a weapon held in the hands of one Indian. This affront apparently surprised and outraged the Indians, who responded by opening fire. The soldiers answered by discharging their own weapons, which resulted in a half-hour exchange between the two parties, until the Indians retreated. Dunn's command suffered four men wounded, two of whom later died. The lieutenant claimed to have killed eight or ten Indians and wounded as many as fifteen more.[35]

Another version of this episode was provided by Colonel Chivington. He claimed that when Dunn spoke with the leader of the Indians, the lieutenant was told that the Indians would rather fight than simply hand over the livestock. The Indian leader then gave the signal for his warriors to open fire, and the battle commenced.[36]

Indian accounts also varied. One related that the troops charged into them without warning or provocation and began firing. Black Kettle, in a statement to Lt. Joseph Cramer, contended that the Indians had happened upon some loose stock and were in the process of delivering the animals to their rightful owner when they were overtaken by the soldiers. The chief of the soldiers began taking arms from the Indians, until one of them resisted, and the fight was on.[37]

In any case, one point was clear to both sides: The Indians would not stand idly by and permit the army to disarm them under any circumstances. Word of this attempt by Dunn to take away their weapons reverberated throughout Indian country and predictably engendered ill feelings toward the government and the soldiers around every tribal fire. Any bond of trust between the two races had been shattered, and the Indians vowed to fight to the death before relinquishing their weapons to the soldiers.

While Dunn had been occupied with the Cheyenne horse thieves, Lt. George Eayre, who had been delayed by a snowstorm, was moving along a fresh trail made by at least 100 cattle down Sand Creek. He sent out scouts, who returned to report that they had located a village up ahead. Eayre divided his command into squads, ordering them to search the countryside for enemy warriors. The lieutenant himself, with three men, entered the now-deserted village. He found what he claimed to be "immense supplies of beef and buffalo," along with other personal possessions and supplies. The lieutenant destroyed everything he did not choose to take with him and burned the village.[38]

Eayre, who lost one man in an exchange with the retreating Indians, also recovered 20 stolen cattle. His report implied that he had scored quite a victory. One of his troopers, however, claimed that the village consisted of only five lodges. And Chivington, in a gross exaggeration, reported to General Curtis that Eayre had recovered 100 head of cattle.

The Indians in question were said to have earlier killed two herders and, what was not known at that time, were lurking nearby when Eayre destroyed the village and could have easily overwhelmed the soldiers. Black Kettle had allegedly warned them that to do so would only cause further retaliation.[39]

Several detachments of soldiers, including those commanded by Eayre and Dunn, remained in the saddle, with orders from Chivington to pursue the Indians. The colonel further ordered: "Be sure you have the right ones, and then kill them."[40]

Another fight of note occurred when Maj. Jacob Downing was dispatched from Denver after reports indicated that Cheyenne were raiding along the South Platte. At daylight on May 3, Downing, with about forty men, located a Cheyenne camp near Cedar Canyon and attacked. The inhabitants of this particular village—later said to have been mostly women and children—fled into a canyon that afforded a defensible position. In the ensuing three-hour battle, Downing claimed to have killed at least twenty-five warriors and wounded anywhere from forty to seventy-five—no prisoners were taken. One soldier was killed and another wounded. Downing's men ran out of ammunition and for that reason were unable to pursue the fleeing survivors. The village was destroyed, and about 100 horses were captured.[41]

About two weeks later, on May 16, Lieutenant Eayre and eighty-four men happened upon a large body of Cheyenne, perhaps as many as 400, near Smoky Hill while moving toward Fort Larned. Both sides claimed that the other attacked them. One version stated that Chief Lean Bear, who was known to be peaceful, had been lured over to the army column and killed, then the soldiers attacked. Whatever the circumstances, the result was a seven-and-a-half-hour battle. Eayre reported that at the end of the fight, twenty-eight Indians—including three chiefs—lay dead and an undetermined number wounded. Four soldiers were killed and three wounded. It was later revealed that the Indians were peaceful Cheyenne and Arapaho, with Chief Black Kettle in attendance, who had been camping nearby.[42]

After this alleged murder of Lean Bear and Eayre's unprovoked attack, peaceful chiefs such as Black Kettle and White Antelope could no longer restrain their hot-blooded young warriors, and raids on stage roads and ranches by the Cheyenne and Arapaho dramatically increased.

Evans wrote to General Curtis on May 28 with a plea that he allow the Colorado troops to stay put, and also requested authority to raise a militia and receive assistance from Federal troops:

> They [the Indians] are in strong force on the Plains . . . and if the U.S. troops are withdrawn I feel confident that they will wipe out our sparse settlements in spite of any home force we could muster against them. . . . Unless a force can be sent out to chastise this combination severely and at once the delay will cost us a long and bloody war and the loss of a great many lives, with untold amounts of property. . . . In the name of humanity, I ask that our troops now on the border of Kansas may not be taken away from us.[43]

Curtis responded by authorizing Evans to recruit a militia, which commenced immediately, and said he hoped that Federal troops would soon be available.[44]

Perhaps the Indians by now had been provoked to a higher level of violence than either Evans or Chivington had planned. The two men had likely envisioned a controllable conflict, with the two of them emerging as protectors. Now they faced an aroused Indian populace that threatened not only Colorado Territory, but surrounding states and territories as well. Chivington was nearly buried under an avalanche of reports of hostile Indian movements and ordered every available soldier into the field.

On June 11, an event occurred that struck fear into the hearts of every resident of Colorado Territory. Four Arapaho braves visited a ranch some thirty miles southeast of Denver, where Ward Hungate, his wife, and four-year-old and infant daughters lived. The Indians left behind a horrifying scene. The body of Ward Hungate was found on the road, riddled with arrows. His wife's nude body showed evidence of torture and multiple violations. The children had also been tortured—throats slashed, heads nearly severed, entrails torn out. They had all been scalped.[45]

The mutilated bodies of the Hungate family were carried by wagon into Denver.

> [They were] placed in a box, side by side, the two children between their parents, and shown to the people from a shed where the City Hall now stands. Everybody saw the four, and anger and revenge mounted all day long as the people filed past or remained to talk over Indian outrages and means of protection and reprisal.[46]

The citizens were not only outraged, but also panic-stricken. People from outlying ranches and settlements fled to Denver, and when the rumor spread that the Indians were preparing to attack that city, a general alarm was sounded. Women and children huddled in the Mint and other down-town buildings, while the men built fortifications on the outskirts of town. Governor Evans appealed directly to Secretary of War Edwin Stanton for assistance and called on every able-bodied man to enroll in the home guard. The immediate threat of an attack on Denver subsided, but prepara-tions continued for war.[47]

On June 27, Evans dispatched emissaries to inform the Indian tribes that those who were friendly should go to places of safety—the Cheyenne and Arapaho were told to report to Fort Lyon, Comanche and Kiowa to Fort Larned—where they would be protected and fed by the soldiers. "The object of this," wrote Evans, "is to prevent friendly Indians from being killed through mistake." At the same time, he vowed to wage a vigorous war against the hostile elements, "until they are all effectually subdued."[48]

This appeal by Evans, however, had come too late. The unprovoked attacks by the soldiers had undermined any faith in the white man's promises, and many Indians who once had been friendly chose to join their hostile comrades in a general uprising. Throughout July and into August, vicious attacks by Indians resulted in many incidents of bloodshed across the region, which, other than several reprisals, troops from Colorado, Kansas, and Nebraska were virtually helpless to prevent. Indian war parties had, for all intents and purposes, stopped movement on the Overland Trail along the South Platte River, and for a period of about six weeks, Denver was cut off from its main supply route.[49]

On August 11, Evans, who had been unable to gain assistance from higher authority and was becoming desperate, issued a proclamation:

All citizens of Colorado, either individually or in such parties as they may organize, [are authorized] to go in pursuit of all hostile Indians on the plains, scrupulously avoiding those who have responded to my said call to rendezvous at the points indicated; also, to kill and destroy, as enemies of the country, wherever they may be found, all such hostile Indians. And further, as the only reward I am authorized to offer such services, I hereby empower such citizens, or parties of citizens, to take captive, and hold to their own private use and benefit, all the property of said hostile Indians that they may capture, and to receive for all stolen property recovered from said Indians such reward as may be deemed proper and just therefore. . . . The conflict is upon us, and all good citizens are called upon to do their duty for the defence [sic] of their homes and families.[50]

How many citizen Indian-hunting expeditions were actually formed cannot be accurately calculated, but this effort by Evans to subdue his enemy had little effect—raids by large parties of Indians on whites intensified. In one instance, a general attack on a number of settlements by a force of 1,000 Apache, Comanche, Cheyenne, and Arapaho warriors was averted when friendly Indians informed trader Elbridge Gerry, who rushed to Denver to spread the alarm. The hostiles learned that their plans had been thwarted and, other than stealing some stock, chose not to attack.

On August 12, eighty covered wagons were attacked on the Wyoming-Nebraska border; nine whites were killed and about seventy-five horses and mules taken. Three days later, an Overland stage with five occupants vanished, and that same day, ranches within thirty miles of Denver were looted and burned. At least three more wagon trains were attacked that month, and two white trappers were captured, tortured, and killed near Fort Lyon. Marauding bands of hostile Indians were attacking at will on the trails up the Arkansas, the Platte, and the Smoky Hill—wagon trains, stagecoaches, ranches, stage stations—with dozens of people killed, women and children carried off, and hundreds of head of horses, mules, and cattle stolen.[51]

By this time, Black Kettle and other chiefs, who had failed to talk their young men out of participating in these raids, had heard from trader George Bent about the governor's entreaty to make peace. They held a council, decided to accept the offer, and wrote a letter to Maj. Edward Wynkoop, commanding officer at Fort Lyon, stating their intentions—and the fact that they held seven prisoners.[52]

The twenty-eight-year-old Wynkoop had been born in Philadelphia, emigrated to Kansas in the mid-1850s, and arrived in Colorado during the 1858 gold rush. He was one of the founding fathers of Denver and served as sheriff in 1859. In 1861, Wynkoop married Louise Wakely, an actress, with whom he would have eight children. He was commissioned a major in the 1st Colorado Volunteers in 1862 and fought as a company commander in the battles of Apache Canyon and La Glorieta Pass. Wynkoop was designated commander of Fort Lyon in early 1864.[53]

Wynkoop, who was eager to liberate the captives, mounted 130 men and rode toward the Indian camp, which was located at Hackberry Creek on the south branch of the Smoky Hill River. Along the way, he encountered a force of 800 hostiles who were prepared to fight, but Black Kettle and other chiefs interceded to prevent bloodshed. The council was held, and three prisoners—children—were released, with the promise that the others, who were being held elsewhere, would be delivered. Wynkoop then escorted Black Kettle, White Antelope, Bull Bear, and several Arapaho chiefs to Denver to meet with Governor Evans and Colonel Chivington.[54]

Evans and Chivington were not particularly pleased about the appearance of the Indians. Chivington, in particular, had become quite overbearing; was contemptuous of legal, ethical, or military authority; and behaved as if he could do whatever he pleased without being accountable to anyone. The two men—as well as General Curtis in a telegram—were unyielding in their opinion that the Indians had declared war, and no peace could be made until the guilty parties had been punished. They met with the Indians on September 28 at Camp Weld. In the end, they turned the matter over to Wynkoop for disposition—without informing the major that General Curtis had forbidden any peace until the Indians had suffered more.[55]

Wynkoop, who had not been told otherwise, was under the assumption that the proclamation Evans had issued on June 27, offering military protection to any tribe that chose to surrender, remained in effect and planned to settle the peaceful Indians at Fort Lyon. By mid-October, while Black Kettle gathered up his tribe, Chief Little Raven had assembled about 650 Arapaho and appeared at the fort, where Wynkoop received them and distributed rations. Black Kettle remained at a camp along Sand Creek, some forty miles northeast of Fort Lyon.

Chivington, however, was not in the mood to make peace, nor tolerate those who were, and Major Wynkoop became the target of his wrath. On October 17, Special Order No. 4 stated that Maj. Scott Anthony was relieved of his command at Fort Larned and would proceed to Fort Lyon, where he would assume command. Further, Anthony would "investigate and report on the rumor in regard to the treaty made at Fort Lyon" and "investigate and report upon unofficial rumors that reached headquarters that certain officers had issued stores, goods, or supplies to hostile Indians in direct violation of orders from the general commanding the department." Wynkoop, who had become quite friendly with Black Kettle and had been given the name Tall Chief, had been relieved of duty in favor of Anthony, who was a confirmed Indian hater. Chivington had placed his man in charge, replacing one who advocated peace. Wynkoop departed Fort Lyon on November 26, headed for Kansas with letters testifying to support for his actions—in an effort to clear his name and promote his peaceful Indian policy.[56]

Anthony faced a dilemma with the presence of the Arapaho. He fed them for ten days—in disobedience of orders—then told them to leave and go hunt buffalo. Little Raven, having no choice but to follow the major's orders, moved his band down the Arkansas, fifty-five miles below Fort Lyon. Chief Left Hand and a few Arapaho lodges decided to join Black Kettle's Cheyenne at the Smoky Hill Crossing of Sand Creek. Anthony was subsequently informed by Chief Black Kettle in person at the fort of the whereabouts of his peaceful tribe. The Southern Cheyenne chief was told to remain there with his people until further notice.[57]

Chivington's 3rd Colorado Cavalry, many of whom had been recruited after Evans's plea of August 11, had been called the "Bloodless Third" because it was assumed that the term of their enlistment would expire before they had engaged in a meaningful battle with hostile Indians. Chivington, however, did not intend to disappoint his men, who were anxious to fight.

Colonel Chivington, under a cloak of secrecy to conceal his movements from the Indians, assembled his troops and issued marching orders on November 15. He led his 3rd Cavalry, plus two companies of the 1st Colorado, toward the Arkansas River, where they rendezvoused with Col. George L. Shoup, who brought along four companies of the 3rd and 1st Colorado. The column was met there by Jim Beckwourth, who would serve as guide. Chivington then marched his men to Fort Lyon, his November 28 arrival surprising Major Anthony, and ringed the fort with troops to ensure that word of his presence would not reach the Indians.

Perhaps more of a surprise came when Chivington revealed that he planned to attack Black Kettle's Cheyenne who were presently camping on Sand Creek. Major Anthony was an enthusiastic supporter of the mission, but several other officers were quite disturbed. The officers held a meeting that night and attempted to dissuade Chivington from attacking what some considered friendly Indians. The colonel was furious that his intentions had been questioned, and he declared in no uncertain terms that any man who had sympathy for the Indians should get out of the army. End of discussion.

At 8:00 that night, Chivington formed his command for the march to Sand Creek. His column consisted of about 700 troops—including 125 men from the post garrison—divided into five battalions under Lt. Col. Leavitt L. Bowen, Maj. Scott J. Anthony, Maj. Hal Sayr, Capt. T. G. Cree, and Lt. Luther Wilson. Four pieces of artillery—12-pounder mountain howitzers—would be under the direction of Bowen and a Lieutenant Baldwin. Maj. Jacob Downing and Capt. A. J. Gill would serve as aides to Chivington.[58]

At daybreak, Chivington and Shoup, riding in advance of the column, topped a rise and observed the gently flowing waters of Sand Creek. Located to the west, less than a mile distant on the north bank, at a point known as Big South Bend, stood a village of more than 100 lodges that was home to about 500 Southern Cheyenne, under chiefs Black Kettle and White Antelope, and 50 of Chief Left Hand's Arapaho. Nearby, beyond a stand of cottonwood, grazed a sizable horse herd, in addition to another herd below the camp. Chivington and Shoup could hear the sound of barking dogs and view a flurry of activity within the camp, which indicated that their presence was known.

The colonel did not waste any time in deploying his troops. Lt. Luther Wilson, with Companies C, E, and F of the 1st Colorado, was sent across the creek to the north to strike between the village and the horse herd. Major Anthony, with three companies, thundered across the creek behind Wilson, halting just southeast of the camp and dismounting to wait for Chivington and his troops. The colonel arrived, positioned his artillery near the creek bank, ordered the men to remove their overcoats, and rallied them by shouting: "Remember the murdered women and children on the Platte! Take no prisoners!"[59]

American-educated half-breed trader George Bent, who was present in the village, described these initial moments:

> When I looked toward the chief's lodge I saw that Black Kettle had a large American flag in on a lodge-pole as a signal to the troop that the camp was friendly. Part of the warriors were running out toward the pony herds and the rest of the people were rushing about the camp in great fear. All the time Black Kettle kept calling out not to be frightened; that the camp was under protection and there was no danger. Then suddenly the troops opened fire on this mass of men, women, and children, and all began to scatter and run.[60]

Chief White Antelope rushed toward the soldiers, waving his arms and exhorting them not to fire. The chief finally stood at the creek bed, his arms folded across his chest to signify that the Indians did not want to fight, and was cut down by a hail of bullets. The soldiers scalped him and cut off his ears and nose—and scrotum, from which the violator planned to make a tobacco pouch.

The soldiers poured a murderous, indiscriminate fire into the panic-stricken Indians, and cannon shot rained down on the village. Anthony's

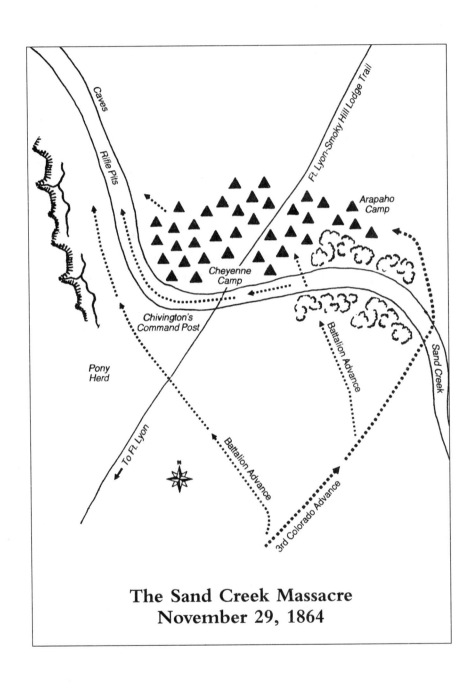

The Sand Creek Massacre
November 29, 1864

men headed to the south of the village toward another pony herd, while the three companies of the 1st Colorado under Wilson struck from the east and north. Shoup's men charged directly toward the lodges, shooting down the vulnerable, fleeing Indians.

Bent reported:

> All was confusion and noise. The Indians all began running, but they did not seem to know what to do or where to turn. The women and children were screaming and wailing, the men running to the lodges for their arms and shouting advice and directions to one another.[61]

At one point, a group of warriors, armed mostly with bows and arrows, attempted to hold off Shoup, but they were soon routed by devastating explosions of grape and canister shot. The determined soldiers then resumed their raid through the lodges, killing great numbers of men, women, and children, and riddling those who were already dead with bullets. Wounded Indians, many of them women and children, crawled toward the creek, marking their trail with blood and bodies, as one by one, the soldiers put them out of their misery. Other Indians—including Black Kettle—scattered in a frantic flight downstream or into the hills to escape the carnage.

The chief and about 100 Cheyenne—perhaps 30 men, the rest women and children—took refuge in the bank of the creek above the village, scooping out the loose sand to make pits for cover as they fought for their lives. They held off the inevitable for most of the morning, but in the end, this sole pocket of organized resistance was overrun and nearly wiped out.

In the meantime, the village and surrounding area had become the scene of the most heinous atrocities imaginable. The soldiers roamed through the village in a state of frenzied bloodlust, torturing and killing the wounded; scalping and mutilating the dead; and committing merciless acts on women and children, who screamed and pled for mercy, to the extent that many of these soldiers' comrades became physically ill at the sight of this barbarity.

Trooper John Smith recalled:

> All manner of depredations were inflicted . . . they were scalped, their brains knocked out; the men used their knives, ripped open women, clubbed little children, knocked them in the head with their guns, beat their brains out, mutilated their bodies in every sense of the word.[62]

Major Anthony estimated that the Indians battled the soldiers for perhaps four hours. "I never saw more bravery displayed by any set of people on the face of the earth than by these Indians," Anthony graciously complimented. "They would charge on the whole company singly, determined to kill someone before being killed themselves. . . . We, of course, took no prisoners."[63]

When the massacre had finally ended, as many as 200 Indians lay dead—two-thirds of them women and children. Chivington reported that he had killed between 400 and 500. Identification of the mangled corpses was difficult, but among the dead were Cheyenne chiefs White Antelope, Standing Water, One Eye, War Bonnet, Spotted Crow, Two Thighs, Bear Man, Yellow Shield, and Yellow Wolf. It was initially thought that Black Kettle's body had been found, but this proved incorrect. Those Indians who had managed to survive the carnage cautiously snuck out of their hiding places and headed north to seek refuge in the camps of Sioux and Cheyenne. The soldiers lost nine killed and thirty-eight wounded.[64]

Chivington's troops bivouacked on the battlefield that night, and in the morning, they were able to find and kill several more Indians. The soldiers set about looting the lodges and bodies—taking scalps, cutting off fingers and ears to collect jewelry, and slicing off pieces of flesh to save as keepsakes. A scalp alleged to have been taken from a white man was found in the village and has often been cited as proof to justify the attack, but a surgeon could only remark that "it looked like a fresh scalp." In the afternoon, Major Anthony led a detail to Fort Lyon to transport the dead, severely wounded, and captured property. What remained of the village was then burned into ashes, and the herd of perhaps 400 to 500 horses and mules confiscated.[65]

Chivington then marched his troops forty-two miles to the south, toward the mouth of Sand Creek, where he intended to strike the Arapaho village of Little Raven, whom Major Anthony had sent to camp at that location on the Arakansas River. Those Indians, however, had heard about the massacre of the Cheyenne and fled south. Chivington remained in that area until December 5, when he broke camp and marched up the Arkansas, finally arriving at Fort Lyon on December 10.

The 3rd Colorado, now hailed as the "Bloody Thirdsters," reached Denver on December 22 and triumphantly paraded through the streets—Chivington riding in front, with a live eagle tied to a pole—to the adoration of the local citizenry. The men proudly displayed their souvenirs, showing off earrings and rings—many attached to pieces of flesh—to those throngs along the way, on one occasion waving 100 scalps to cheering patrons in various theaters. Oddly enough, the alleged white man's scalp—or the scalps of several white men and women, as Chivington later claimed to have found—was never displayed. The *Rocky Mountain News* summed up this tremendous "victory" by writing:

> Among the brilliant feats of arms in Indian warfare, the recent campaign of our Colorado Volunteers will stand in history with few rivals, and none to exceed it in final results. . . . A thousand incidents of individual daring and the passing events of the day might be told, but space forbids. We leave the task for eye-witnesses to chronicle. All acquitted themselves well, and Colorado soldiers have again covered themselves with glory.[66]

Col. John Chivington at first was hailed as a national hero for his actions, but within days, the truth about the "battle" began trickling out. The *Rocky Mountain News,* in a dispatch from Washington, was one of the first to report that it was a questionable victory:

> The affair at Fort Lyon, Colorado, in which Colonel Chivington destroyed a large Indian village, and all its inhabitants, is to be made the subject of congressional investigation. Letters received from high officials in Colorado say that the Indians were killed after surrendering, and that a large proportion of them were women and children.[67]

Although that newspaper mounted a passionate defense of the "boys of the Third," it could do little to thwart the flood of testimony that pointed toward a massacre and punishment for the guilty.

Maj. Gen. Henry W. Halleck, chief of staff of the Army, ordered an investigation. General Curtis called for a court-martial of Chivington, but by that time the colonel's term of service had expired, and he was now a civilian—beyond the reach of army justice.

Regardless, Maj. Edward Wynkoop, now reinstated as commander of Fort Lyon, was ordered "to make a thorough investigation of recent operations against the Indians and make a detailed report." Wynkoop, who was personally outraged by the incident, set to work immediately and compiled a report that, without exception, condemned the actions of Chivington and his men.[68]

The House of Representatives' Committee on the Conduct of the War held an inquiry into the attack by the Colorado volunteers and heard testimony from March 13 to March 15, 1865. Chivington presented his case, stating that he was unaware that the Indians were under the protection of the government, and that he had found nineteen scalps of white people in the camp. The committee's report, titled "Massacre of Cheyenne Indians," denounced Gov. John Evans for "such prevarication and shuffling as has been shown by no witness [we have] examined during the four years [we have] been engaged in investigations." The harshest criticism, however, was reserved for Chivington:

> As to Colonel Chivington, your committee can hardly find fitting terms to describe his conduct. Wearing the uniform of the United States, which should be the emblem of justice and humanity; holding the important position of commander of a military district, and therefore having the honor of the government to that extent in his keeping, he deliberately planned and executed a foul and dastardly massacre which would have disgraced the veriest savage among those who were the victims of his cruelty.[69]

Two other investigations were held, one by a Joint Special Committee of the two houses of Congress, and another in Colorado under the direction of the army. Chivington made an effort in both investigations to defend himself, but he was faced with overwhelming evidence against his conduct.

No formal action or punishment, however, was taken against the former colonel in any of these probes. He was involved in a freighting business in Nebraska from 1865 to 1867, then went to Cincinnati. In 1883, he returned to Denver, where he died of cancer on October 4, 1894—professing until the day he died to anyone who would listen that Sand Creek had been an honorable victory rather than a massacre. And to this day, as then, Chivington has many supporters who embrace his statement: "I stand by Sand Creek."

Gov. John Evans was forced to resign in 1865 and became a prominent business leader. He helped organize the Denver Pacific Railroad, which connected Denver to the Union Pacific line at Cheyenne, Wyoming. He also had other railroad enterprises and was founder of Colorado Seminary, which later was renamed the University of Denver. He lived in Colorado until he died in 1897.

In 1865, Edward Wynkoop became commander of the Veteran Battalion of the Colorado Cavalry and chief of cavalry for the District of the Upper Arkansas. He did not share the same philosophy of genocide concerning Indians that was embraced by Chivington and most of his fellow Coloradans, believing instead that hostilities could and should be prevented. This opinion made him a most hated man in Colorado, where Chivington was considered a hero. In July 1866, he resigned his commission and became an Indian agent for the Cheyenne and Arapaho, vigorously defending his charges whenever they were accused of depredations. Wynkoop could not, however, prevent the army—whose officers and men had little respect for him—from waging war. He accompanied the Hancock expedition of 1867 and was outraged by General Hancock's aggressive actions, in particular the destruction of the Cheyenne village on Pawnee Fork. Finally, to protest the attack by George Armstrong Custer's 7th Cavalry at Washita, he resigned his post as Indian agent in November 1868.

Wynkoop moved back east to Pennsylvania, but failed in an iron-making business and returned west in 1874 to participate in the Black Hills gold rush—where he fought Indians with the local ranger unit under Capt. Jack Crawford, the so-called poet scout. He then served in various positions, including adjutant general of New Mexico Territory and warden of the territorial penitentiary. Wynkoop died in Santa Fe of Bright's disease on September 11, 1891.

Black Kettle's Cheyenne fled from Sand Creek battered and beaten, but the chief remained an advocate of peace with the white man. That sentiment, however, was not echoed by most Plains Indians, and repercussions from this massacre would be felt far and wide across the region.

CHAPTER TEN

Total War

WORD OF THE SAND CREEK MASSACRE SPREAD ACROSS INDIAN COUNTRY to the various winter camps like a Plains wildfire. Cheyenne messengers carried the news from their village at the head of the Smoky Hill River to the northern tribes—the Sioux, Northern Cheyenne, and Northern Arapaho—which were camped on the Solomon and Republican Rivers. And instead of striking fear into the heart of each Indian, this act of treachery served to stir up a cry for vengeance. By the end of December 1865, a huge village—900 lodges and about 1,500 warriors—had assembled on Cherry Creek for a council to plan a course of action in retaliation for this mass murder by Chivington and his Colorado volunteers.[1]

It was decided that the first attack would target Julesburg, a small settlement in the northeastern corner of Colorado that boasted a stage station, express and telegraph office, large store and warehouse, and stables and corrals. Fort Rankin (later Fort Sedgwick), which had been established in 1864, was located a mile to the west of town. This small post was surrounded by a stockade and guarded by a company of the 7th Iowa Cavalry, under the command of Capt. Nicholas J. O'Brien.

The Indian war party, which numbered about 1,000 Arapaho, Cheyenne, and Sioux, broke camp on January 5 or 6 and headed in a northwesterly direction toward Julesburg. The Indians had brought along some women with extra ponies on which to load the plunder they planned to capture by sacking the town.

Before daybreak on January 7, the Indians assumed concealed positions around the sand hills south of town. Seven warriors—five Cheyenne and two Sioux—were chosen to approach Fort Rankin and attempt to lure the soldiers out of the fort and into the hills. As the sky brightened into day, this Indian decoy party noticed a detail of soldiers outside the stockade. The seven warriors mounted their ponies and charged the troopers, who dashed inside the fort. Within moments, Captain O'Brien and between thirty-eight and sixty men—accounts differ and include an undetermined number of civilians—thundered out of the fort to chase these brazen Indians.

The hidden Indians could hear the firing as the Iowa troopers raced toward the sand hills in hot pursuit of the warriors. The trap, however, was sprung prematurely when a group of young warriors lost its patience and charged out from behind the hills when the troops were still at least a half mile from that position. Now that the element of surprise had been compromised, the signal was given for the entire war party to charge into the soldiers.

Captain O'Brien immediately pulled up and ordered a retreat. The troopers galloped for their lives toward the safety of the fort, with the Indians nipping at their heels. The Indians overtook the column, forcing some troopers to dismount and fight on foot, but those men were quickly overwhelmed. O'Brien and his men were surrounded by circling warriors as they struggled in a running battle to reach the fort. Fortunately for those troops, they managed to outrun the main body of Indians and burst through the gate to safety. O'Brien's detail lost fourteen soldiers and four civilians killed during their mad dash back to the security of the post.

By this time, the residents of Julesburg, along with recently arrived stagecoach passengers, had heard the firing and taken refuge inside the sturdy timber walls of Fort Rankin.

The Indians then turned their attention to a warehouse and store in Julesburg and commenced looting everything in sight—other than canned goods, which they had never before encountered and had no idea what was inside the containers. They also smashed open a metal box but were disappointed to discover that it held only "green paper," and simply dumped the contents on the ground. This strongbox had been abandoned by a stage passenger in his haste to reach the fort and contained the pay for Colorado troops. Bills were later found scattered across the valley, but less than half of the money was ever recovered.

The Indians plundered the town well into the evening hours, finally riding away leading their heavily laden pack ponies.[2]

The Julesburg attack was followed by raids on telegraph lines, ranches, stage stations, supply and mail trains, army patrols, and any travelers unlucky enough to be caught out in the open as the Indians swept along both branches of the Platte River to wreak havoc on the region. On February 7, Julesburg was struck again. This time, the Indians sacked a couple of supply trains and burned the town to the ground.

By mid-February, a total of about fifty whites had been killed, at least 1,500 head of cattle taken, tons of government hay burned, and a vast amount of food and supplies carted away. At that time, the Indians apparently believed that they had exacted sufficient revenge for the Sand Creek massacre, and about 6,000 strong headed northward toward the Black Hills, where the soldiers dared not pursue them.[3]

Meanwhile, Gen. Ulysses S. Grant had become concerned about the fact that soldiers needed in the East were engaged in a losing cause on the frontier and blamed the ineptitude of the officers in charge. To remedy this problem, Grant appointed Maj. Gen. John Pope to the post of commander of the new Division of the Missouri, which would be responsible for all operations in the Plains region.[4]

Pope immediately went to work planning an aggressive campaign that called for three columns to march under orders to rid the Plains of hostile Indians and secure the roads leading to the mines in Montana. Brig. Gen. Alfred Sully would lead one column into the Powder River area and strike the Sioux. At the same time, Brig. Gen. Patrick E. Connor, who now commanded the District of the Plains, would mount an offensive along the Oregon and Overland Trails, and then rendezvous with Sully. The third column, commanded by Brig. Gen. James H. Ford, who had led the 2nd Colorado Cavalry and presently commanded the District of the Upper Arkansas, would take on the Cheyenne, Comanche, and Kiowa south of the Arkansas River.[5]

The implementation of Pope's plan was delayed by supply and transportation problems, as well as the weather, and was finally complicated by a historic moment in time that the country had been looking forward to for four long and bloody years.

On the afternoon of April 9, 1865, Generals Ulysses S. Grant and Robert E. Lee met at the home of Wilmer McLean in Appomattox, Virginia, and signed a surrender that ended the Civil War.

This action was a welcome relief to a nation weary of war and desiring peace. This conclusion of hostilities in the East, however, provided only a brief respite from bloodshed for the postwar U.S. Army.

Pope's ambitious campaign, intended to strike on several fronts in Indian country, was now stalled by the mustering out of volunteer units, which included General Ford, and the wait for Regular troops to replace them. Another problem was also encountered—a peace movement that had been initiated after the Sand Creek massacre.

Government policy with respect to the "Indian problem" became the subject of fierce contention between two diverse factions. The Indian

Bureau combined with Eastern humanitarian groups to encourage a policy of tolerance, generosity, and fair treatment, which they believed would lead the Indians to respond in kind. Westerners were of like mind with the army and ridiculed this notion, which they deemed idealistic and impractical. They were of the opinion that the only way in which to deal with the Indians was by a show of military strength—first punishment for their actions, and then supervision on reservations.

Both sides, however, did finally agree that all Plains Indians should be removed from the pathway of westward expansion between the Platte and Arkansas Rivers and resettled onto reservations north of Nebraska and south of Kansas. To that end, a peace commission was created by Congress with intentions of negotiating workable treaties.[6]

The first successful act of peace commissioners came in October 1865, when a council was held on the Little Arkansas between a commission that included Brig. Gen. William S. Harney, Kit Carson, Jesse Chisholm, trader William Bent, and Brig. Gen. John B. Sandborn, who had replaced General Ford, and chiefs from the Kiowa, Kiowa-Apache, Comanche, Arapaho, and Southern Cheyenne. On October 4, a treaty was signed, and land was set aside south of the Arkansas River for these tribes. Some of the chiefs who signed were Little Raven for the Arapaho; Little Mountain and Lone Wolf for the Kiowa; and Black Kettle and Little Robe for the Southern Cheyenne.[7]

The signing of this treaty removed the need for General Sandborn's column to march, but both Sully and Connor took to the field under their original orders.

Sully, however, abandoned plans to march to the Powder River and instead headed for Devils Lake in a futile search for Sioux Indians. While Sully was on the march, a few bands of that tribe in the Missouri River area met with peace commissioners and signed treaties.[8]

Connor's portion of the campaign led him through the plains of present-day Wyoming and southeastern Montana. The land was poorly mapped, and even guide Jim Bridger could not prevent the column from staggering through the difficult terrain while suffering from lack of water and food and encountering vicious weather. Connor's men clashed with the Indians on several occasions, without resolution, until the column was plagued by broken-down horses and threatened with mutiny. Pope finally was compelled to order the column out of the field and sent Connor back to his old command in Utah.[9]

At this time, the Southern Plains were relatively quiet, other than an occasional minor raid or incident of stealing. Pope's campaign in the north, however, had concluded in a miserable failure and only served to intensify the anger of the Sioux, who vowed to fight to the death against the invasion of whites in their domain.

These Lakota Sioux and Northern Cheyenne—along with some bands of Minnesota Santee or Dakota Sioux, perhaps led by the outlaw Inkpaduta—had been aroused by the Civil War expeditions conducted by Generals Sibley, Sully, and Connor, but their rage exploded into violence in 1866 with the establishment of the Bozeman Trail, a shortcut to the Montana gold fields that passed through traditional Sioux hunting ground. Worse yet, the army commenced building three forts—Phil Kearny, C. F. Smith, and later Reno—with which to guard this strategic trail. The Sioux, led by Red Cloud and Spotted Tail, and their allies, which now included groups of Arapaho, frequently attacked miners, wagon trains, and army patrols on the Bozeman Trail.

The Indians refused to negotiate a treaty until the army agreed to remove its forts, a demand deemed unacceptable to the government. Fort Phil Kearny was kept under a constant stage of siege by Red Cloud's warriors, which included Crazy Horse, Gall, and Rain-in-the-Face. In December 1866, the Sioux killed Capt. William J. Fetterman and eighty troopers in an ambush. Other bloody raids kept the soldiers virtual prisoners in the fort, and safe travel along the Bozeman Trail was impossible.[10]

At the same time, Southern Cheyenne, Arapaho, Kiowa, and Comanche warriors, in violation of the 1865 treaty, continued attacking white travelers and settlers along the Smoky Hill, Arkansas, and Platte Roads, as well as work crews from the Kansas Pacific Railway. In 1867, the army formed an expedition under the leadership of Gen. Winfield Scott Hancock for the purpose of punishing these hostiles. Field commander Lt. Col. George Armstrong Custer and his 7th Cavalry pursued the Indians throughout Kansas, Nebraska, and Colorado, and engaged in several minor skirmishes but failed to deter the raids. Perhaps the most inflammatory act of the expedition occurred when General Hancock, against the advice of Indian agent Edward Wynkoop and others, decided to burn down a 300-lodge Sioux-Cheyenne village on Pawnee Fork.[11]

The fact that the army was pursuing them, however, did in fact persuade the tribes to discuss terms of peace. In late October 1867, more than 5,000 members of the Kiowa, Kiowa-Apache, and Comanche tribes gathered at Medicine Lodge Creek, Kansas, a traditional Sun Dance location about seventy miles from Fort Larned, to meet with representatives of the United States. After several days of negotiation, feasting, and receiving presents, the Kiowa, Kiowa-Apache, and Comanche chiefs "touched the pen" to the treaty.

The Cheyenne and Arapaho had been wary about attending the meeting due to animosity over Hancock's destruction of the village on Pawnee Fork. The dissident tribes, however, eventually wandered in—perhaps tempted by the promise of gifts—and their chiefs, including Black Kettle, also signed the treaty.

The Medicine Lodge Treaties provided for two large reservations in western Indian Territory—present-day Oklahoma. The Kiowa, Kiowa-Apache, and Comanche would share one; the Cheyenne and Arapaho the other. The Indians agreed to relinquish all territory beyond these specified reservations—except in the case of buffalo hunting south of the Arkansas. They also promised to cease attacks on the railroad, military posts, and white settlements and travelers outside of reservation boundaries. In return, the government would furnish every adult with agricultural equipment and seed, and teach them the rudiments of farming. Other essential supplies would be issued each year for the next thirty years. No whites, other than authorized personnel, would be permitted on these reservations.

The provisions of the Medicine Lodge Treaties were designed to be the example of how kindness and assistance, rather than force, would be the guidelines for the future of interracial relations. In other words, the Indians would be removed from the pathway of Western expansion and, by eliminating their own culture, taught how to live like whites.

These Indians, whose traditional lifestyle had never been anything other than that of nomadic hunters, would find it difficult to abandon their inherent nature in favor of settling down as common farmers. Added to that was the fact that Congress did not readily enact the provisions of the treaty, which delayed sufficient rations from reaching the reservations. Therefore, in order to hunt for food, most Indians once again ignored the treaty and roamed their customary territories, which resulted in a resumption of raids against the populace and bloody encounters with the U.S. Army.[12]

On the Northern Plains, "Red Cloud's War" finally compelled the United States to cry uncle. The constant harassment by the Lakota Sioux and their allies was successful, and Red Cloud became the only Indian in history ever to force the U.S. government to grant treaty demands due to acts of violence. The Fort Laramie Treaty of 1868 provided that the army would abandon the three forts and establish a reservation—the Great Sioux Reservation—which was composed of most of present-day South Dakota west of the Missouri River. Hunting rights for the Sioux and Cheyenne were also granted to a wide area of the Republican River and in Wyoming and Nebraska north of the Platte River. In addition, other concessions were guaranteed, including the construction of buildings, medical care, education, agricultural equipment, and money. Red Cloud and many of his people obediently retired to this reservation. The younger warriors, led by Sitting Bull, however, refused to sign the treaty and continued to resist Western settlement by whites.[13]

While the Sioux and Northern Cheyenne moved onto their reservation, peace was elusive on the Southern Plains. The Kiowa and their allies were raiding across Kansas, attacking settlements as well as detachments of the army that had been dispatched to subdue the hostiles.

In the fall of 1868, the army under Generals William T. Sherman and Philip Sheridan was called upon to initiate a major winter campaign designed to restore peace in this region. The two men had decided that a new, ruthless measure was required to punish the Indians, and they implemented the concept of "total war," which both officers had employed in the Civil War—Sherman on his March to the Sea across Georgia, and Sheridan in the Shenandoah Valley.

Total war meant subjecting the civilian populace, not just the enemy fighting force, to a reign of terror. By invading the enemy's homeland and mercilessly destroying property—lodges, food stores, and ponies—the will of the Indians to fight would be broken. Rarely could these nomadic Indians be caught in the summer, but a winter campaign would find them vulnerable—camped along some accessible waterway, ponies weakened from lack of forage, caches of food barely sufficient to last until spring. Sherman and Sheridan held the view that the torch would be as effective a weapon as the sword, that poverty would bring about peace more quickly than the loss of human life. And if the lives of noncombatants happened to be lost in the execution of this strategy, that would be merely a regrettable but excusable tragedy—presently known as collateral damage.[14]

This strategy, however, was hardly new and innovative when it came to fighting Indians. Actually, total war had been practiced for more than a decade.

In 1854, a Sioux warrior killed an ox from a wagon train, which resulted in the brutal murder of arresting officer Lt. John L. Grattan and twenty-nine soldiers. The officer selected to punish the Indians for their treachery was Brig. Gen. William S. Harney, who could be called the "godfather" of total war.

Runners were dispatched to the various Indian camps to advise the chiefs that all friendly Indians were to report to Fort Laramie, where they would be protected. Otherwise they would be considered hostile and could expect the army to pay them a visit. By early September 1855, hundreds of lodges had gathered on the Laramie Fork, thirty-five miles above the fort.

One Lakota band, under chief Little Thunder, which was composed of forty lodges—about 250 people—remained camped on Bluewater River, a tributary of the Platte, about six miles northwest of Ash Hollow and 100 miles east of Fort Laramie. Little Thunder had always been considered friendly and had dismissed any notion that he would be attacked.

On September 3, 1855, General Harney arrived on Little Thunder's doorstep with 600 troops and, after a brief parley, proceeded to assault the village. In the ensuing massacre, eighty-six Lakota were killed and another seventy women and children taken prisoner. The village and its valuable contents were destroyed and the pony herd captured. Revenge for Lieutenant Grattan had been exacted, and total war against Indians had been born.

The destruction of Little Thunder's camp was a catastrophe of proportions previously unheard of in the annals of Plains Indian warfare. Never before had an enemy killed so many of them, or captured their wives and children in such great numbers, or so thoroughly ravaged a village.

The gauntlet had been thrown down in challenge. Many Sioux chiefs appealed for conciliation, but the army in its infinite wisdom was convinced that Harney's action confirmed that the only way to deal with Indians was through brute force. Those Indians who refused to submit to the reservation would be marked for death and compelled to defeat the mighty United States of America if they were to preserve their culture and territorial rights.[15]

In an effort to force the Kiowa and their allies onto the reservation, Gen. Phil Sheridan launched his campaign of total war in the fall of 1868. In September, a force of 900 Cheyenne and Sioux warriors, under Roman Nose and Pawnee Killer, attacked Maj. George Forsyth and fifty seasoned scouts at a place known as Beecher Island. This resulted in a nine-day siege by the Indians against the trapped soldiers, which ended only when the 10th Cavalry's African-American "Buffalo Soldiers" arrived to rescue the troops. By that time, five soldiers had been killed and nineteen wounded. Perhaps as many as thirty-two, but more likely about nine, Indians lost their lives.[16]

The most famous and controversial engagement of the campaign occurred in late November, when Lt. Col. George Armstrong Custer and his 7th Cavalry, along with the 19th Kansas Volunteer Cavalry, were dispatched to attack a Cheyenne-Arapaho village on the Washita River in present-day Oklahoma. Custer had been assigned the command when Brig. Gen. Alfred Sully, who had enjoyed some success in Minnesota, was relieved of duty for being too timid in his approach to hostilities.

The head chief of this village on the Washita was none other than Black Kettle, who had continued to advocate peace in spite of the betrayal that led to the Sand Creek massacre. At the request of his friend, Indian agent Edward Wynkoop, he had attended the council at Medicine Lodge and signed the treaty. Violations of this treaty became commonplace; therefore, Black Kettle moved his tribe to a location on the Washita River that he believed would allow them to avoid any conflict with the army.

In early November 1868, Black Kettle met with Col. William B. Hazen, who had the unenviable task of determining which Indian tribes were friendly and which were hostile. Hazen was convinced that Black Kettle was peaceful, but he advised the Cheyenne chief to make peace with General Sheridan, who had initiated an offensive against hostiles.

But before Black Kettle could locate Sheridan, Custer's scouts had tracked some renegade hostiles to Black Kettle's village and attacked at dawn on November 27, 1868. When the smoke had cleared, 103 Indians were reportedly killed, and another 53 women and children were captured. Two of the casualties were Black Kettle and his wife, who were shot down while trying to escape. The entire village, as well as a pony herd that numbered about 875, was destroyed. The army lost twenty-one killed and fourteen wounded. Other hostiles' villages, occupied by thousands of Cheyenne, Arapaho, Comanche, and Kiowa warriors, were located downstream from Black Kettle, but Custer withdrew rather than face this overwhelming force.[17]

All evidence indicates that Black Kettle was a peaceful Indian. He could not, however, control the activities of the hot-tempered young men of his tribe, and he always offered refuge to those warriors. The Cheyenne chief paid for his loyalty to his tribe members with his life.

Black Kettle's death sparked outrage among both Indians and whites, and initiated a debate about whether the attack by Custer was a battle or a massacre similar to Sand Creek. The affair at Washita, however, had none of the characteristics of that massacre and should without question be classified as a battle in which Custer employed the element of surprise.

Sheridan's campaign continued with a sweep of the Southern Plains, which encouraged many bands to submit to their reservation. Southern Cheyenne under Tall Bull were defeated by Maj. Eugene Carr at the July 11, 1869, battle of Summit Springs, an action that effectively ended hostilities in that region when most of the Cheyenne and their allies, the Comanche and Kiowa, submitted to the reservation at Fort Cobb.[18]

The hostile elements of those tribes aligned themselves with Kiowa chief Satanta and moved farther south into Texas. During the Red River War of 1874–75, the Comanche and Kiowa fought under Chief Quanah

Parker, whose mother had been a white captive. In September 1874, Col. Ranald Mackensie defeated these Indians at Palo Duro Canyon and destroyed their pony herd and village. The following year, Parker led his destitute refugees into Fort Reno and Fort Sill, which ended Comanche and Kiowa hostilities.[19]

The Sioux had harassed Custer and his 7th Cavalry on the Yellowstone expedition of 1873, when the army served as an escort for surveyors plotting the line for the Northern Pacific Railroad. But it was Custer's Black Hills expedition of 1874, which was an intrusion and perhaps a treaty violation into their territory, that most threatened the Sioux and their allies.

Gold deposits were discovered in the Black Hills on that expedition, and a horde of prospectors poured onto Sioux land. The government made entreaties toward the Indians to sell their sacred land. Most reservation tribe members were willing to sell, but dissidents led by Sitting Bull and Crazy Horse refused and initiated attacks on miners, wagon trains, and white settlements.[20]

In late 1875, the government dispatched runners to the Sioux and their Cheyenne allies camped in the area of the Yellowstone, informing them that they must submit to the reservation by January 31, 1876, or the army would march against them. This edict led to the Great Sioux War of 1876-77, a series of skirmishes and battles, including the battle of the Little Bighorn, that resulted in the eventual submission of most members of those tribes to their assigned reservations. Sitting Bull and a small band of followers fled to Canada, where they remained until 1881. The Northern Arapaho were eventually settled on the Wind River Reservation in Wyoming with their former enemy, the Shoshone.[21]

Following the November 1876 Dull Knife fight, in which Col. Ranald Mackensie defeated Northern Cheyenne under Dull Knife and Little Wolf, that tribe was settled on a reservation with their Southern Cheyenne brethren in Indian Territory—present-day Oklahoma—far removed from their traditional homeland in Montana. In September 1878, some members of the tribe, led by Dull Knife and Little Wolf, fled the reservation, heading north toward their former Tongue River homeland. More than 10,000 soldiers and civilians pursued and eventually apprehended the escaping Cheyenne. In the early 1880s, the Northern Cheyenne were finally granted their wish and received an agency on Tongue River.[22]

The last tribe to be beaten into submission by the army was the Apache, who had waged war ever since the Bascom incident. In postwar Arizona, the army had its hands full contending with small bands of Apache who regularly raided ranches and settlements in order to survive. Efforts by

Lt. Col. George Crook and his troops were unsuccessful at containing the violence.[23]

In 1873, Cochise was finally persuaded by his friend, Indian agent Thomas Jefferies, to submit with his band to the reservation. He remained there until his death the following year. At that time, however, the Chiricahua lost their reservation and were sent to the San Carlos reservation, where they were forced to reside with other Apache groups. Chief Victorio fled that unworkable situation and led his warriors in a series of engagements against army troops, until he was killed by the Mexican militia in October 1880.

Geronimo then assumed the mantle of leadership and bolted from the reservation. This fierce chief terrorized the territory—including a brazen raid on San Carlos reservation in 1882—which led to the return of George Crook, now a brigadier general, in an effort to quell this uprising. Crook embarked on an operation in 1883 and convinced Geronimo and many of his band to return to San Carlos. Two years later, however, Geronimo broke out again and eluded army troops for fifteen months. In March 1886, Crook nearly persuaded Geronimo to surrender, but he was thwarted by a bootlegger who got the chief and his warriors drunk and warned them against submitting.

Crook requested to be relieved of command and was replaced by Brig. Gen. Nelson A. Miles. Finally, in September 1886, Miles enticed Geronimo to surrender. The great Apache chief and his band were then imprisoned in various places—Florida, Alabama, and Oklahoma—for the next twenty-seven years, until 1913, when the surviving members were given the choice of remaining in Oklahoma or returning west to New Mexico. Geronimo did not live to return to his beloved homeland—he died of pneumonia in 1909 at Fort Sill, Oklahoma.[24]

And thus ended any action of consequence between Indians and the army, other than the December 29, 1890, conflict at Wounded Knee, when the 7th Cavalry subdued a band of Sioux Indians, which resulted in as many as 150 Indians and 19 soldiers losing their lives.[25]

It could be argued that had the treaties negotiated between the government and the various Indian tribes prior to and during the Civil War been strictly adhered to, violence could have been altogether avoided or never would have escalated into the spilling of as much blood as now stains the pages of history. That premise *could* be argued.

The truth of that matter is that, when taking into consideration the cry of "manifest destiny" that encouraged thousands of white settlers to head west after the war to join those already there, perhaps nothing could have prevented warfare between the two races. Add to the equation the inept and often ruthless character of many of the army officers assigned to Western commands, and a middle ground gradually became beyond reach. Also, neither race would endeavor to learn enough about the other to understand beliefs, traditions, or inherent behavior patterns, which could have engendered respect. Therefore, it was inevitable that the two races would eventually clash, and the stronger—in this case, the white man—will always prevail.

The Indians, in an effort to maintain their culture, had little choice but to resort to violence as they sought to reverse the radically changing face of the land, a transformation that prevented them from partaking in nature's abundance, a lifestyle that they had enjoyed for generations. The homeland that had provided such a prosperous existence gradually became a place rife with disease, hunger, despair, and uncertainty as a result of this white invasion. And when asked to change from a nomadic to a more structured and permanent lifestyle—from hunters to farmers—tribes were torn apart by the loss of their identity and unity.

Treaties did succeed in effecting some measure of peace, but they produced a troubling legacy for the Indians involved. As more and more of them were enticed to dwell on reservations, where their daily survival depended on government rations, they experienced further indignities and turmoil. Those who bowed to the wishes of missionaries, Indian agents, the army, and any other appointed authority were often compelled to betray their own people. Those who followed traditional values and religious practices were dangerous to the government and thus victimized in any manner possible.

Had the Civil War not occurred, perhaps relations between whites and Indians might not have been quite as violent. But inasmuch as no one to this day has provided a solution to the so-called "Indian problem" in the frontier West, speculation accomplishes little more than to fuel the age-old debate about blame that continues to rage between the races to this day.

NOTES

Only primary sources have been noted.
Other relevant sources can be found in the Bibliography.

CHAPTER ONE: THE FLIGHT OF OPOTHLEYAHOLA

1. Stan Hoig, *Tribal Wars on the Southern Plains* (Norman: University of Oklahoma Press, 1993), 185–87.
2. Angie Debo, *The Road to Disappearance: A History of the Creek Indians* (Norman: University of Oklahoma Press, 1941), 142–44.
3. U.S. War Department, *The War of the Rebellion: A Compilation of the Official Records of the Union and Confederate Armies,* hereafter referred to as *O.R.* (Washington, DC: Government Printing Office, 1880–1901), ser. 1, vol. 1, 648.
4. Wilfred Knight, *Red Fox: Stand Watie's Civil War Years in Indian Territory* (Glendale, CA: Arthur H. Clark, 1988), 62–63; Gary S. Moulton, ed., *The Papers of Chief John Ross* (Norman: University of Oklahoma Press, 1985), 465; *O.R.,* ser. 1, vol. 1, 590–92; 683–84.
5. Edwin C. Bearss, "The Civil War Comes to Indian Territory, 1861: The Flight of Opothleyahola," *Journal of the West* 11, no. 1 (January 1972): 9–10; Debo, *Road to Disappearance,* 98.
6. Ibid., 145–46.
7. Knight, *Red Fox,* 63–64.
8. Ibid., 64–65; Moulton, *Papers of John Ross,* 481.
9. Debo, *Road to Disappearance,* 144; Bearss, "Civil War Comes to Indian Territory," 9; "Report of Albert Pike on Mission to the Indian Nations," December 12, 1861, Western Americana Microfilm Series, reel 1330.
10. John Bartlett Meserve, "Chief Opothleyahola," *Chronicles of Oklahoma* 9 (December 1931): 445–53.
11. Debo, *Road to Disappearance,* 147–48.
12. *O.R.,* ser. 1, vol. 8, 5; Bearss, "Civil War Comes to Indian Territory," 10.

13. Pike to Opothleyahola, October 7, 1861, in Cherokee Papers, University of Oklahoma, Western History Collections, Norman, OK; Chief Ross to Opothleyahola, October 8, 1861, in Ross Papers, 61 ser., 41, Thomas Gilcrease Institute of American History and Art, Tulsa, OK.
14. Debo, *Road to Disappearance,* 151.
15. Ibid., 149–52; *Commissioner of Indian Affairs, Annual Report, 1862,* 157.
16. *O.R.,* ser. 1, vol. 8, 5.
17. Ibid., 5–6.
18. Ibid., 5–6, 14–15; Wiley Britton, *The Civil War on the Border, 1861–62,* 2 vols. (New York: G. P. Putnam's Sons, 1890–94), vol. 1, 166–67; Knight, *Red Fox,* 73–76.
19. Debo, *Road to Disappearance,* 151–52.
20. *O.R.,* ser. 1, vol. 8, 6, 14–15.
21. Ibid., 7.
22. Ibid., 8; W. Craig Gaines, *The Confederate Cherokees: John Drew's Regiment of Mounted Rifles* (Baton Rouge: Louisiana State University Press, 1989), 40–42.
23. Gaines, *Confederate Cherokees,* 45–47; *O.R.,* ser. 1, vol. 8, 8, 17.
24. *O.R.,* ser. 1, vol. 8, 17; Gaines, *Confederate Cherokees,* 45.
25. Gaines, *Confederate Cherokees,* 48–49; Britton, *Civil War on the Border,* vol. 1, 169; *O.R.,* ser. 1, vol. 8, 8.
26. *O.R.,* ser. 1, vol. 8, 8.
27. Ibid., 8–9.
28. Ibid., 9, 16; Britton, *Civil War on the Border,* vol. 1, 170–71.
29. *O.R.,* ser. 1, vol. 8, 9, 15, 19–21.
30. Ibid., 15, 19–21.
31. Ibid., 9–10, 15, 19–21; Britton, *Civil War on the Border,* vol. 1, 171.
32. Gaines, *Confederate Cherokees,* 52; *O.R.,* ser. 1, vol. 8, 10.
33. *O.R.,* ser. 1, vol. 8, 10, 11.
34. Ibid., 11; Bearss, "Civil War Comes to Indian Territory," 28–29.
35. *O.R.,* ser. 1, vol. 8, 22, 715.
36. Ibid., 22.
37. Ibid., 11–12, 22.
38. Ibid., 22; Victor M. Rose, *Ross' Texas Brigade: Being a Narrative of Events Connected with Its Service in the Late War Between the States* (Kennesaw, GA: Continental Book Co., 1960), 46–47.
39. Rose, *Ross' Texas Brigade,* 47.
40. *O.R.,* ser. 1, vol. 8, 22.
41. Ibid., 23, 26, 30.
42. Ibid., 23.

43. Rose, *Ross' Texas Brigade,* 43.

44. *O.R.,* ser. 1, vol. 8, 23.

45. Ibid., 23, 29; Rose, *Ross' Texas Brigade,* 48.

46. *O.R.,* ser. 1, vol. 8, 29, 30.

47. Rose, *Ross' Texas Brigade,* 44.

48. *O.R.,* ser. 1, vol. 8, 24.

49. Ibid., 24–25.

50. Ibid., 24–25, 32–33.

51. Ibid., 12–13.

52. Debo, *Road to Disappearance,* 151.

53. *O.R.,* ser. 1, vol. 8, 12–13.

54. Debo, *Road to Disappearance,* 152.

55. Ibid., 153.

56. Gaines, *Confederate Cherokees,* 81–91; Kenny A. Franks, *Stand Watie and the Agony of the Cherokee Nation* (Memphis: Memphis State University Press, 1979), 124–26.

57. Annie Heloise Abel, *The American Indian as a Participant in the Civil War* (Cleveland: Arthur H. Clark Co., 1919), 102.

CHAPTER TWO: BEAR RIVER MASSACRE

1. The best volume pertaining to the war of 1857–58 is Norman F. Furniss, *The Mormon Conflict* (New Haven, CT: Yale University Press, 1960). Excellent information about the Mormon settlement of Utah is found in Brigham D. Madsen, *The Shoshoni Frontier and the Bear River Massacre* (Salt Lake City: University of Utah Press, 1985), 25–39.

2. Scott R. Christensen, *Sagwitch: Shoshone Chieftain, Mormon Elder* (Logan: Utah State University Press, 1999), 1–6.

3. Madsen, *Shoshoni Frontier,* 95–113.

4. Raymond W. Settle and Mary L. Settle, *Saddles and Spurs* (Harrisburg, PA: Stackpole Books, 1955), 136–43.

5. Madsen, *Shoshoni Frontier,* 143, 145.

6. Ibid., 124, 133–36.

7. Christensen, *Sagwitch,* 33.

8. Ibid., 34.

9. Madsen, *Shoshoni Frontier,* 152.

10. Virginia Cole Trenholm and Maurine Carley, *The Shoshonis: Sentinels of the Rockies* (Norman: University of Oklahoma Press, 1964), 190–91.

11. Edward W. Tullidge, *History of Salt Lake City and Its Founders* (Salt Lake City, UT: Edward W. Tullidge, Publisher and Proprietor, 1886), 252; Madsen, *Shoshoni Frontier,* 150.

12. Madsen, *Shoshoni Frontier*, 150; Tullidge, *History of Salt Lake City*, 252–53.

13. Madsen, *Shoshoni Frontier*, 150–51.

14. Orson F. Whitney, *History of Utah* (Salt Lake City: George Q. Cannon and Company, 1893), 45.

15. Madsen, *Shoshoni Frontier*, 151–52; Ray C. Colton, *The Civil War in the Western Territories* (Norman: University of Oklahoma Press, 1959), 162–63.

16. Madsen, *Shoshoni Frontier*, 164.

17. Trenholm and Carley, *Shoshonis*, 192.

18. *Deseret News*, August 27 and October 8, 1862; Salt Lake City correspondent to the *Sacramento Union*, April 28, 1862.

19. Biographical information about Connor can be found in Fred B. Rogers, *Soldiers of the Overland: Being Some Account of the Services of Gen. Patrick Edward Connor and His Volunteers in the Old West* (San Francisco, Grabhorn Press, 1938); and Leo P. Kibby, "Patrick Edward Connor: First Gentile of Utah," *Journal of the West* 2, no. 4 (October 1963).

20. *O.R.,* ser. 1, vol. 50, pt. 2, 55; Richard H. Orton, comp., *Records of California Men in the War of the Rebellion, 1861 to 1867* (Sacramento: State Printing Office, 1890), 507.

21. *O.R.,* ser. 1, vol. 50, pt. 2, 119–20.

22. Ibid., 133.

23. Ibid., 144.

24. Ibid., 178–79.

25. Ibid., 119–20, 195; E. B. Long, *The Saints and the Union* (Urbana: University of Illinois Press, 1981), 106–12.

26. *O.R.,* ser. 1, vol. 50, pt. 1, 181–83; Newell Hart, "Rescue of a Frontier Boy," *Utah Historical Quarterly* 33 (Winter 1965): 51–54.

27. *Sacramento Union*, December 26, 1862; James H. Martineau, "The Military History of Cache Valley," *Tullidge's Quarterly Magazine* 2, no. 1 (April 1882): 125.

28. *Deseret News*, December 10 and 17, 1862.

29. Ibid., December 31, 1862.

30. Ibid., January 14, 17, 21, 1863; Madsen, *Shoshoni Frontier*, 178.

31. *O.R.,* ser. 1, vol. 50, pt. 1, 187.

32. Ibid., 185.

33. Ibid., 182; Rogers, *Soldiers of the Overland*, 69–70.

34. Rogers, *Soldiers of the Overland*, 70.

35. Madsen, *Shoshoni Frontier*, 183–84.

36. Christensen, *Sagwitch*, 47–48.

37. Ibid., 48; Rogers, *Soldiers of the Overland,* 71.
38. Madsen, *Shoshoni Frontier,* 186; *San Francisco Bulletin,* February 20, 1863.
39. *San Francisco Bulletin,* February 20, 1863; Rogers, *Soldiers of the Overland,* 71–72; Madsen, *Shoshoni Frontier,* 186–87.
40. Madsen, *Shoshoni Frontier,* 187–88; Rogers, *Soldiers of the Overland,* 72.
41. Rogers, *Soldiers of the Overland,* 73; Madsen, *Shoshoni Frontier,* 188–93, 234; Christensen, *Sagwitch,* 52–54.
42. Connor's official report: *O.R.,* vol. 50, pt. 2, 184–87.
43. Madsen, *Shoshoni Frontier,* 194.
44. *O.R.,* vol. 50, pt. 2, 368–69.
45. Madsen, *Shoshoni Frontier,* 211.
46. Madsen, *Shoshoni Frontier,* 212; Robert M. Utley, *Frontiersmen in Blue: The United States Army and the Indians, 1848–1865* (New York: Macmillan Co., 1967), 225.

CHAPTER THREE: SIOUX UPRISING

1. William W. Folwell, *A History of Minnesota,* 2 vols. (St Paul: Minnesota Historical Society, 1924), vol. 1, 10–210.
2. Thom Hatch, *The Custer Companion: A Comprehensive Guide to the Life of George Armstrong Custer and the Plains Indian Wars* (Mechanicsburg, PA: Stackpole Books, 2002), 47.
3. Edward D. Neill, "Dakota Land and Dakota Life," *Minnesota Historical Collections* 1 (1850–56): 205–40.
4. Charles J. Kappler, *Indian Affairs, Laws and Treaties,* 2 vols. (Washington, DC: Government Printing Office, 1904), vol. 2, 493–94; Roy W. Meyer, *History of the Santee Sioux: United States Indian Policy on Trial* (Lincoln: University of Nebraska Press, 1967), 56–71.
5. Meyer, *History of the Santee Sioux,* 75–77.
6. Ibid., 78–81, 84, 88; Kappler, *Indian Affairs,* vol. 2, 781–89.
7. Doane Robinson, *A History of the Dakota or Sioux Indians* (Minneapolis: Ross and Haines, 1956), 257; Thomas Hughes, *Old Traverse des Sioux* (St. Peter, MN: Herald Publishing Co., 1929), 3–5.
8. Meyer, *History of the Santee Sioux,* 880–89; Secretary of the Interior Robert McClelland to Commissioner George Manypenny, April 13, 1854, NARS, RG 75, LR.
9. Gary Clayton Anderson and Alan R. Woolworth, *Dakota Eyes: Narrative Accounts of the Minnesota Indian War of 1862* (St. Paul: Minnesota Historical Society Press, 1988), 23.

10. Thomas Hughes, "Causes and Results of the Inkpaduta Massacre," *Minnesota Historical Collections* 12 (1905–08): 264–69; Folwell, *History of Minnesota,* vol. 2, 400–415.

11. An excellent biography of Little Crow is Gary Clayton Anderson's *Little Crow: Spokesman for the Sioux* (St. Paul: Minnesota Historical Society Press, 1986). Other interesting biographical information, including the quotations, can be found in C. M. Oehler, *The Great Sioux Uprising* (New York: Oxford University Press, 1959), 17–20.

12. Kappler, *Indian Affairs,* vol. 2, 781–89.

13. Anderson and Woolworth, *Through Dakota Eyes,* 23.

14. Meyer, *History of the Santee Sioux,* 104; Barbara T. Newcombe, "'A Portion of the American People': The Sioux Sign a Treaty in Washington in 1858," *Minnesota History* 45, no. 3 (Fall 1976): 82–96; St. Paul *Pioneer and Democrat,* June 29, 1858.

15. Folwell, *History of Minnesota,* vol. 2, 393–400.

16. Kenneth Carley, *The Sioux Uprising of 1862* (St. Paul: Minnesota Historical Society, 1961), 13–14; Stephen Longstreet, *War Cries on Horseback: The Story of the Indian Wars of the Great Plains* (Garden City, NY: Doubleday & Co., 1970), 110.

17. Board of Commissioners, *Minnesota in the Civil and Indian Wars, 1861–1865,* 2 vols. (St. Paul, MN: Pioneer Press, 1890, 1893), vol. 2, 162–63.

18. Ibid., 163; Folwell, *History of Minnesota,* vol. 2, 228–29.

19. Ibid., 231–32.

20. Ibid., 232–33.

21. Ibid., 233.

22. Oehler, *Great Sioux Uprising,* 3–4.

23. Ibid., 4–5.

24. Ibid., 5.

25. Ibid. 6–8.

26. Carley, *Sioux Uprising of 1862,* 18–19; "Taoyateduta Is Not a Coward," *Minnesota History* 38 (September 1962): 115; Meyer, *History of the Santee Sioux,* 115–17.

27. Utley, *Frontiersmen in Blue,* 264–65.

28. For details of many specific atrocities, see Oehler, *Great Sioux Uprising,* chaps. 4–6, 28–61.

29. Anderson, *Little Crow,* 135–36, 222 n3.

30. Ibid., 75–95; *Minnesota in the Civil and Indian Wars,* 166–82; Folwell, *History of Minnesota,* vol. 2, 30.

31. Utley, *Frontiersmen in Blue,* 265.

32. Oehler, *Great Sioux Uprising,* 92–95.
33. Ibid., 96–97.
34. Ibid., 98.
35. Ibid., 98–99.
36. Ibid., 99–100; Folwell, *History of Minnesota,* 129–33.
37. Oehler, *Great Sioux Uprising,* 121–22; *Minnesota in the Civil and Indian Wars,* vol. 2, 184–85.
38. Oehler, *Great Sioux Uprising,* 122–23.
39. Ibid., 123–24.
40. Ibid., 126–130.
41. Ibid., 130–31.
42. Ibid., 132.
43. Ibid., 133–38.
44. Carley, *Sioux Uprising of 1862,* 48–49; *Minnesota in the Civil and Indian Wars,* vol. 2, 211–20.
45. *Minnesota in the Civil and Indian Wars,* 220–21; Oehler, *Great Sioux Uprising,* 167–172.
46. Oehler, *Great Sioux Uprising,* 173–75.
47. Ibid., 177–79.
48. Ibid., 180–82.
49. *Minnesota in the Civil and Indian Wars,* vol. 2, 224–25, 231.
50. Carley, *Sioux Uprising of 1862,* 56–57.
51. Oehler, *Great Sioux Uprising,* 185–91.
52. Ibid., 192–93.
53. *O.R.,* ser. 1, vol. 13, 278–81; Oehler, *Great Sioux Uprising,* 193–96; Carley, *Sioux Uprising of 1862,* 58–59; *Minnesota in the Civil and Indian Wars,* vol. 2, 249–50.
54. Oehler, *Great Sioux Uprising,* 199.
55. Ibid., 196–97.

CHAPTER FOUR: CARLETON, CARSON, AND THE APACHE

1. Martin Hardwick Hall, *The Confederate Army of New Mexico* (Austin, TX: Presidial Press, 1978), 18.
2. The best information about Sibley's invasion of New Mexico and the two major battles can be found in Thomas Edington and John Taylor, *The Battle of Glorieta Pass: A Gettysburg in the West, March 26–28, 1862* (Albuquerque: University of New Mexico Press, 1998); Don E. Alberts, *The Battle of Glorieta: Union Victory in the West* (College Station: Texas A & M Press, 1998); Martin H. Hall, *Sibley's New Mexico Cam-*

paign (Austin: University of Texas Press, 1960); and David P. Perrine, "The Battle of Valverde, New Mexico Territory, February 21, 1862," *Journal of the West* 19, no. 4 (October 1980): 26–38.

3. *O.R.,* ser. 1, vol. 50, pt. 1, 88–145; Utley, *Frontiersmen in Blue,* 219, 233.

4. The best source about the early life of Carleton is Aurora Hunt's somewhat generous biography, *Major General James Henry Carleton, 1814–1873* (Glendale, CA: Arthur H. Clark Co., 1958).

5. Utley, *Frontiersmen in Blue,* 233; C. L. Sonnichsen, *The Mescalero Apaches* (Norman: University of Oklahoma Press, 1958), 97.

6. Utley, *Frontiersmen in Blue,* 234.

7. Boyd Finch, "Sherrod Hunter and the Confederates in Arizona," *Journal of Arizona History* 10, no. 3 (Autumn 1969): 178.

8. Ibid., 219.

9. Robert M. Utley, "The Bascom Affair: A Reconstruction," *Arizona and the West* 3 (1961): 59–68.

10. *O.R.,* ser. 1, vol. 50, pt. 1, 120.

11. Ibid., 120–22.

12. Ibid., 128–31.

13. Edwin R. Sweeney, *Mangas Coloradas: Chief of the Chiricahua Apaches* (Norman: University of Oklahoma Press, 1998), 431–32.

14. *Rio Grande Republican,* January 2, 1891.

15. *O.R.,* ser. 1, vol. 50, pt. 1, 131.

16. Ibid., 132.

17. Sweeney, *Mangas Coloradas,* 438–39.

18. *O.R.,* ser. 1, vol. 50, pt. 1, 131–32.

19. Ibid., 128.

20. *O.R.,* ser. 1, vol. 50, pt. 2, 40–41; vol. 9, pt. 1, 565.

21. Hunt, *Carleton,* 236.

22. *O.R.,* ser. 1, vol. 9, 557–59.

23. Utley, *Frontiersmen in Blue,* 232.

24. Sonnichsen, *Mescalero Apaches,* 57–95; Superintendent James Collins, *Annual Report of the Commissioner of Indian Affairs, 1861,* 122.

25. Perhaps the best biography of Carson is Tom Dunlay, *Kit Carson and the Indians* (Lincoln: University of Nebraska Press, 2000).

26. *O.R.,* ser. 1, vol. 15, 579–80.

27. Jerry D. Thompson, *Desert Tiger: Captain Paddy Graydon and the Civil War in the Far Southwest* (El Paso: Texas Western Press, 1992), 52–54; Sonnichsen, *Mescalero Apaches,* 99–101.

28. James L. Haley, *Apaches: A History and Culture Portrait* (Norman: University of Oklahoma Press, 1981), 236–37.

29. Sonnichsen, *Mescalero Apaches,* 101.
30. Dunlay, *Kit Carson and the Indians,* 245.
31. R. S. Allen, "Pinos Altos, New Mexico," *New Mexico Historical Review* 23 (1948): 302–32.
32. *O.R.,* ser. 1, vol. 50, pt. 1, 105–6.
33. Perhaps the best biography of Mangas is Sweeney, *Mangas Coloradas;* see also Ray Brandes, "Mangas Coloradas: Apache Warrior and Diplomat," *Mankind: The Magazine of Popular History* 3, no. 9 (October 1972): 54–58.
34. Alvin M. Josephy, Jr., *The Civil War in the American West* (New York: Alfred A. Knopf, 1991), 274.
35. Sweeney, *Mangas Coloradas,* 444.
36. *O.R.,* ser. 1, vol. 50, pt. 2, 147–48.
37. Sweeney, *Mangas Coloradas,* 446–47.
38. Utley, *Frontiersmen in Blue,* 251.
39. Daniel Ellis Conner, *Joseph Reddeford Walker and the Arizona Adventure* (Norman: University of Oklahoma Press, 1956), 34.
40. Ibid., 36.
41. Sweeney, *Mangas Coloradas,* 448.
42. James H. McClintock, *Arizona: Prehistoric, Aboriginal, Pioneer, Modern* (Chicago: S. J. Clarke Publishing Co., 1916), 176–77; Sweeney, *Mangas Coloradas,* 449–50.
43. Sweeney, *Mangas Coloradas,* 453.
44. Conner, *Walker,* 37.
45. Sweeney, *Mangas Coloradas,* 454.
46. McClintock, *Arizona,* 176–78.
47. Conner, *Walker,* 38–39.
48. U.S. Smithsonian Institution, National Museum of Natural History, report, "The Skull of Mangas Coloradas."
49. Sweeney, *Mangas Coloradas,* 457–58.
50. Ibid, 460; Conner, *Walker,* 41; *O.R.,* ser. 1, vol. 50, pt. 2, 296–97.
51. Sweeney, *Mangas Coloradas,* 460.
52. *O.R.,* ser. 1, vol. 50, pt. 2, 296–97.
53. Ibid., 462.
54. Lawrence Kelly, *Navajo Roundup: Selected Correspondence of Kit Carson's Expedition against the Navajo, 1863–1865* (Boulder, CO: Pruett Publishing Co., 1970), 15–16.
55. Frank McNitt, "Fort Sumner: A Study in Origins," *New Mexico Historical Review* 45 (April 1970): 101–17.

CHAPTER FIVE: SIBLEY, SULLY, AND THE SIOUX

1. Anderson and Woolworth, *Through Dakota Eyes*, 224.
2. Carley, *Sioux Uprising of 1862*, 62.
3. Kenneth Carley, "The Sioux Campaign of 1862: Sibley's Letters to His Wife," *Minnesota History* 38, no. 3 (September 1962): 109.
4. Carley, *Sioux Uprising of 1862*, 61–62.
5. Anderson and Woolworth, *Through Dakota Eyes*, 223.
6. Meyer, *History of the Santee Sioux*, 126.
7. *Goodhue County [Minnesota] Republican*, August 22, 1862; Mankato, Minnesota, *Semi-Weekly Record*, August 30, 1862; Faribault, Minnesota, *Central Republican*, February 18, 1863.
8. Oehler, *Great Sioux Uprising*, 202–3.
9. Ibid., 203–5; Meyer, *History of the Santee Sioux*, 126–27.
10. Stephen R. Riggs, *Mary and I: Forty Years with the Sioux* (Boston: Congregational Sunday-School and Publishing Society, 1880), 206–7; Meyer, *History of the Santee Sioux*, 126.
11. Oehler, *Great Sioux Uprising*, 206.
12. Carley, *Sioux Uprising of 1862*, 63; Anderson and Woolworth, *Through Dakota Eyes*, 221.
13. Anderson and Woolworth, *Through Dakota Eyes*, 233; Oehler, *Great Sioux Uprising*, 212.
14. Oehler, *Great Sioux Uprising*, 221; Meyer, *History of the Santee Sioux*, 127–28; Carley, *Sioux Uprising of 1862*, 64; Anderson and Woolworth, *Through Dakota Eyes*, 264.
15. David A. Nichols, *Lincoln and the Indians* (Columbia: University of Missouri Press, 1978), 141.
16. Ibid.; Oehler, *Great Sioux Uprising*, 208.
17. Oehler, *Great Sioux Uprising*, 213.
18. Ibid., 208–9, 214; Carley, *Sioux Uprising of 1862*, 66.
19. Oehler, *Great Sioux Uprising*, 213–14.
20. Ibid., 214; Meyer, *History of the Santee Sioux*, 128–29.
21. Meyer, *History of the Santee Sioux*, 129.
22. Oehler, *Great Sioux Uprising*, 215–220.
23. Ibid., 220.
24. Ibid., 221–22; Carley, *Sioux Uprising of 1862*, 66–67.
25. Carley, *Sioux Uprising of 1862*, 68; Oehler, *Great Sioux Uprising*, 225–26; Anderson, *Little Crow*, 162.
26. Anderson, *Little Crow*, 162.
27. Ibid., 168.
28. Oehler, *Great Sioux Uprising*, 225.

29. Ibid., 226–227; Carley, *Sioux Uprising of 1862,* 68.

30. Oehler, *Great Sioux Uprising,* 226–27.

31. Carley, *Sioux Uprising of 1862,* 67.

32. Richard N. Ellis, *General Pope and U.S. Indian Policy* (Albuquerque: University of New Mexico Press, 1970), 16–17.

33. Carley, *Sioux Uprising of 1862,* 69; Oehler, *Great Sioux Uprising,* 227–29.

34. Anderson, *Little Crow,* 178; Carley, *Sioux Uprising of 1862,* 69–70; Oehler, *Great Sioux Uprising,* 229–31.

35. Anderson, *Little Crow,* 181.

36. Utley, *Frontiersmen in Blue,* 270–71.

37. Carley, *Sioux Uprising of 1862,* 72.

38. Ibid.; Utley, *Frontiersmen in Blue,* 272.

39. Utley, *Frontiersmen in Blue,* 272; Carley, *Sioux Uprising of 1862,* 72.

40. Utley, *Frontiersmen in Blue,* 272.

41. Anderson and Woolworth, *Through Dakota Eyes,* 284.

42. Carley, *Sioux Uprising of 1862,* 73.

43. Utley, *Frontiersmen in Blue,* 273.

44. Anderson and Woolworth, *Through Dakota Eyes,* 270.

45. Utley, *Frontiersmen in Blue,* 273.

46. J. H. Dripps, *Three Years among the Indians in Dakota* (New York: Sol Lewis, 1974), 54.

47. Utley, *Frontiersmen in Blue,* 274; Robinson, *History of the Dakota,* 329.

48. Robinson, *History of the Dakota,* 326–29; Dripps, *Three Years among the Indians,* 45–46; Sully's report can be found in *O.R.,* ser. 1, vol. 22, pt. 1, 555–68.

49. Anderson and Woolworth, *Through Dakota Eyes,* 21.

50. Oehler, *Great Sioux Uprising,* 233–35.

CHAPTER SIX: THE NAVAJO LONG WALK

1. Utley, *Frontiersmen in Blue,* 155, 165–68; Frank McNitt, ed., *Navaho Expedition: Journal of a Military Reconnaissance from Santa Fe, New Mexico, to the Navaho Country Made in 1849 by Lieutenant James H. Simpson* (Norman: University of Oklahoma Press, 1964), 194–200; Clifford E. Trafzer, *The Kit Carson Campaign: The Last Great Navajo War* (Norman: University of Oklahoma Press, 1982), 39–42; Lynn R. Bailey, *The Long Walk: A History of the Navajo Wars* (Los Angeles: Westernlore Press, 1964), 15–17, 51–57, 71–78.

2. Trafzer, *Kit Carson Campaign,* 41–42.

3. Bailey, *Long Walk,* chap. 5.

4. *Santa Fe New Mexican,* December 21, 1858.
5. William Dickinson, "Reminiscences of Fort Defiance, 1860," *Journal of the Military Service Institution of the United States* 4 (1883): 90–92; Bailey, *Long Walk,* 16–22.
6. Trafzer, *Kit Carson Campaign,* 44.
7. Bailey, *Long Walk,* 16–22; Utley, *Frontiersmen in Blue,* 170.
8. Utley, *Frontiersmen in Blue,* 170–71.
9. The best biography of Canby is Max L. Heyman, Jr., *Prudent Soldier: A Biography of Major General E. R. S. Canby, 1817–1873* (Glendale, CA: Arthur H. Clark, 1959).
10. Bailey, *Long Walk,* 59–69; Max L. Heyman, Jr., "On the Navaho Trail: The Campaign of 1860," *New Mexico Historical Review* 26 (1951): 44–63; Utley, *Frontiersmen in Blue,* 170–71.
11. Utley, *Frontiersmen in Blue,* 172; for specifics about "Total War," see chapter 10 in Utley's book.
12. McNitt, *Navajo Wars,* 391–409; Bailey, *Long Walk,* 127–39.
13. Bailey, *Long Walk,* 138–39; Trafzer, *Kit Carson Campaign,* 48–49.
14. McNitt, *Navajo Wars,* 415–16; Heyman, "On the Navaho Trail," 54–63; Utley, *Frontiersmen in Blue,* 172–73.
15. McNitt, *Navajo Wars,* 421–28.
16. *O.R.,* ser. 1, vol. 4, 77–78.
17. Ibid., ser. 1, vol. 15, 670.
18. An excellent view of Navajo religious beliefs can be found in Gladys A. Reichard, *Navajo Religion* (New York: Bollingen Foundation, 1950); and Paul G. Zolbrod, *Dine Bahana: The Navajo Creation Story* (Albuquerque: University of New Mexico Press, 1984).
19. Utley, *Frontiersmen in Blue,* 239; Dunlay, *Kit Carson and the Indians,* 274.
20. Kelly, *Navajo Roundup,* 21–22.
21. Utley, *Frontiersmen in Blue,* 239–40.
22. Trafzer, *Kit Carson Campaign,* 83–84.
23. Kelly, *Navajo Roundup,* 26–29.
24. Ibid., 28–33; Lawrence C. Kelly, "Where Was Fort Canby?" *New Mexico Historical Review* 42 (January 1967): 49–62.
25. Trafzer, *Kit Carson Campaign,* 85; Kelly, *Navajo Roundup,* 35; Colton, *Civil War,* 139.
26. Raymond E. Lindgren, ed., "A Diary of Kit Carson's Navajo Campaign," *New Mexico Historical Review* 21 (July 1946): 228–31.
27. Kelly, *Navajo Roundup,* 30.
28. Ibid., 31.
29. Trafzer, *Kit Carson Campaign,* 86–87.

30. Ibid., 87.

31. Ibid., 89.

32. Kelly, *Navajo Roundup*, 43.

33. *O.R.*, ser. 1, vol. 26, 233–335; Colton, *Civil War*, 138, 139–40.

34. Kelley, *Navajo Roundup*, 44–50.

35. Ibid., 52.

36. *O.R.*, ser. 1, vol. 26, 252–54.

37. Trafzer, *Kit Carson Campaign*, 103–4.

38. Kelly, *Navajo Roundup*, 61, 65, 66; Colton, *Civil War*, 142.

39. *O.R.*, ser. 1, vol. 26, 33–34.

40. Kelly, *Navajo Roundup*, 69–70.

41. McNitt, *Navajo Wars*, 149, 196, 341; Lynn R. Bailey, ed., *The Navajo Reconnaissance: A Military Exploration of the Navajo Country in 1859* (Los Angeles: Westernlore Press, 1964), 37–55.

42. *O.R.*, ser. 1, vol. 34, 72.

43. Ibid., 73; Kelly, *Navajo Roundup*, 98.

44. Kelly, *Navajo Roundup*, 98–99, Pfeiffer's report, 102–5; *O.R.*, ser. 1, vol. 34, 73; Trafzer, *Kit Carson Campaign*, 144–53.

45. *O.R.*, ser. 1, vol. 34, 74; Kelly, *Navajo Roundup*, 99.

46. Kelly, *Navajo Roundup*, Carey's report, 105–7.

47. Ibid., 100; *O.R.*, ser. 1, vol. 34, 75.

48. Trafzer, *Navajo Roundup*, 110–14.

49. Gerald Thompson, *The Army and the Navajo: The Bosque Redondo Reservation Experiment, 1863–1868* (Tucson: University of Arizona Press, 1976), 42–45; Charles Amsden, "The Navajo Exile at Bosque Redondo," *New Mexico Historical Review* 8 (1933): 31–50.

CHAPTER SEVEN: THE WOOLSEY EXPEDITIONS

1. Conner, *Walker*, 43–83.

2. Ibid., 64.

3. Ibid., 84–101.

4. Ibid., 102–3.

5. Ibid., 104; Frank C. Lockwood, *Pioneer Days in Arizona: From the Spanish Occupation to Statehood* (New York: McMillan, 1932), 124–27.

6. Conner, *Walker*, 103–5.

7. Ibid., 109–10, 113.

8. Utley, *Frontiersmen in Blue*, 255; for a brief history of the founding of Prescott, see Pauline Henson, *Founding a Wilderness Capital: Prescott, A.T., 1864* (Flagstaff, AZ: Northland Press, 1965).

9. Utley, *Frontiersmen in Blue*, 255; Haley, *Apaches*, 9.

10. Conner, *Walker*, 148–50; Thomas Edwin Farish. *History of Arizona*, 8 vols. (San Francisco: Filmer Brothers Electrotype Co., 1915–18), vol. 2, 32.

11. Dan L. Thrapp, *The Conquest of Apacheria* (Norman: University of Oklahoma Press, 1967), 26.

12. Utley, *Frontiersmen in Blue*, 255–56.

13. Clara T. Woody, ed., "The Woolsey Expeditions of 1864," *Arizona and the West* 4, no. 2 (Summer 1962): 157–58; Farish, *History of Arizona*, vol. 2, 215–26; Thrapp, *Conquest of Apacheria*, 27.

14. Woody, "Woolsey Expeditions of 1864," 158–59.

15. Ibid., 159.

16. Ibid., 160–61; *Sacramento Union*, February 10, 1864.

17. Woody, "Woolsey Expeditions of 1864," 161.

18. Ibid., 161–62.

19. Ibid., 162.

20. Ibid.; *Sacramento Union*, March 9, 1864; Conner, *Walker*, 171–72.

21. Connor, *Walker*, 172–73; Woody, "Woolsey Expeditions of 1864," 162–63.

22. Woody, "Woolsey Expeditions of 1864," 163; Conner, *Walker*, 173.

23. Conner, *Walker*, 173–75.

24. Ibid., 175; Woody, "Woolsey Expeditions of 1864," 163–64; J. Ross Browne, *A Tour through Arizona* (Tucson: Arizona Silhouettes, 1951), 123–24.

25. J. P. Dunn, Jr., *Massacres in the Mountains: A History of the Indian Wars of the Far West, 1815–1875* (New York: Archer House, 1958), 337–38.

26. Woody, "Woolsey Expeditions of 1864," 164–65.

27. Ibid., 166.

28. Ibid., 166–67.

29. Ibid., 167; Prescott *Arizona Miner*, May 25, 1864.

30. Woody, "Woolsey Expeditions of 1864," 168; Conner, *Walker*, 264, 265n.

31. Conner, *Walker*, 265.

32. Woody, "Woolsey Expeditions of 1864," 168.

33. Ibid., 169.

34. Conner, *Walker*, 265–66.

35. Ibid., 267.

36. Ibid., 268; Utley, *Frontiersmen in Blue*, 256.

37. Conner, *Walker*, 150, 268.

38. Utley, *Frontiersmen in Blue*, 257.

39. *O.R.*, ser. 1, vol. 50, pt. 2, 827–28.

40. Utley, *Frontiersmen in Blue*, 256.

41. Ibid., 258.
42. Woody, "Woolsey Expeditions of 1864," 170.
43. Ibid., 171.
44. Ibid., 172.
45. Ibid., 174.
46. Ibid., 175.
47. Ibid., 176.
48. Ibid., 158.
49. Utley, *Frontiersmen in Blue,* 259.

CHAPTER EIGHT: NORTHERN AND SOUTHERN PLAINS VENGEANCE

1. For information about prospectors traveling the Missouri River to the gold fields, see Hirum M. Chittenden, *History of Early Steamboat Navigation on the Missouri River* (Minneapolis: Ross & Haines, 1962).
2. For information about prospectors traveling these overland routes, see Helen McCann White, ed., *Ho! For the Gold Fields* (St. Paul: Minnesota Historical Society, 1966).
3. *O.R.,* ser. 1, vol. 22, pt. 2, 633.
4. Ibid., 109–11, 152–56, 256–59, 540–41, 608–9, 622–24; Louis Pfaller, "Sully's Expedition of 1864 Featuring the Killdeer Mountain and Badlands Battles," *North Dakota History* 31, no. 1 (January 1964): 20–26; Utley, *Frontiersmen in Blue,* 275–76.
5. Hirum Martin Chittenden and Alfred Talbot Richardson, *Life, Letters and Travel of Father Pierre-Jean De Smet, S. J., 1801–1873,* 4 vols. (New York: Francis P. Harper, 1905), vol. 3, 833–34.
6. Pfaller, "Sully's Expedition," 36; *O.R.,* ser. 1, vol. 41, pt. 2, 228.
7. Utley, *Frontiersmen in Blue,* 277; Pfaller, "Sully's Expedition," 38–40.
8. Pfaller, "Sully's Expedition," 40–43.
9. Ibid., 43–50; Utley, *Frontiersmen in Blue,* 277–78.
10. Utley, *Frontiersmen in Blue,* 278.
11. Pfaller, "Sully's Expedition," 55–58.
12. *O.R.,* ser. 1, vol. 41, pt. 1, 147–48, 158.
13. George E. Hyde, *Spotted Tail's Folk: A History of the Brule Sioux* (Norman: University of Oklahoma Press, 1961), 83–88; Donald J. Berthong, *The Southern Cheyennes* (Norman: University of Oklahoma Press, 1963), chap. 7; George B. Grinnell, *The Fighting Cheyennes* (New Haven, CT: Yale University Press, 1923), chap. 11.
14. William E. Unrau, "A Prelude to War," *Colorado Magazine* 41 (1964): 299–313.
15. Utley, *Frontiersman in Blue,* 285, 287.

16. Patricia L. Faust, ed., *Historical Times Illustrated Encyclopedia of the Civil War* (New York: Harper & Row, 1986), 69.

17. *O.R.*, ser. 1, vol. 41, pt. 2, 610, 629–30.

18. Ibid., pt. 3, 36, 37, 98, 179–80, 218, 231.

19. Ibid., pt. 1, 818; Grinnell, *Fighting Cheyennes*, 161–64.

20. T. R. Fehrenbach, *Comanches: A History, 1706–1875* (New York: Alfred A. Knopf, 1974), 450.

21. Charles L. Kenner, *A History of New Mexico-Plains Indian Relations* (Norman: University of Oklahoma Press, 1969), 142.

22. Nathaniel G. Taylor, et al., *Papers Relating to Talks and Councils Held with the Indians in Dakota and Montana* (Washington, DC: Government Printing Office, 1910), 58.

23. Documents relating to this unratified treaty can be found in the National Archives and Record Service Microfilm Pub., T494, 930–38.

24. Carl C. Rister, *Border Captives: The Traffic in Prisoners by Southern Plains Indians, 1835–75* (Norman: University of Oklahoma Press, 1940), 193–211.

25. Robert M. Utley, "Kit Carson and the Adobe Walls Campaign," *American West* 2, no. 1 (Winter 1965): 7.

26. *O.R.*, ser. 1, vol. 41, pt. 4, 319–23.

27. Utley, "Kit Carson and Adobe Walls," 8.

28. Kenner, *New Mexico-Plains Indian Relations*, 146.

29. *O.R.*, ser. 1, vol. 41, pt. 3, 429–30.

30. S. G. Colley, Agent, Upper Arkansas Agency, *Annual Report of the Commissioner of Indian Affairs, 1864,* doc. 94 1/2.

31. Edwin L. Sabin, *Kit Carson Days, 1809–1868: Adventures in the Path of Empire,* 2 vols. (New York: Press of the Pioneers, 1935), vol. 2, 728; M. Morgan Estergreen, *Kit Carson: A Portrait in Courage* (Norman: University of Oklahoma Press, 1962), 253.

32. *O.R.*, ser. 1, vol. 41, pt. 3, 243–44.

33. Ibid., 295–96.

34. Robert E. Denney, *The Civil War Years: A Day-by-Day Chronicle* (New York: Gramercy Books, 1998), 486–88.

35. Stephen B. Oates, *Confederate Cavalry West of the River* (Austin: University of Texas Press, 1961), 140–54.

36. Estergreen, *Kit Carson,* 199–201.

37. George H. Pettis, "Kit Carson's Fight with the Comanche and Kiowa Indians," *Publications of the Historical Society of New Mexico* 12 (1908): 34. Pettis was a lieutenant serving with Company K, 1st Infantry California Volunteers, who accompanied Carson's campaign.

38. Pettis, "Kit Carson's Fight," 34; Carson's official report: *O.R.*, ser. 1, vol. 41, pt. 1, 940; Utley, "Kit Carson and Adobe Walls," 10.

39. Pettis, "Kit Carson's Fight," 34; Estergreen, *Kit Carson,* 255.

40. Pettis, "Kit Carson's Fight," 34.

41. Mildred P. Mayhall, *The Kiowas* (Norman: University of Oklahoma Press, 1962), 188.

42. *O.R.*, ser. 1, vol. 41, pt. 1, 941.

43. Ibid.; Mayhall, *The Kiowas,* 188.

44. *O.R.*, ser. 1, vol. 41, pt. 1, 941; Pettis, "Kit Carson's Fight," 34.

45. Pettis, "Kit Carson's Fight"; Wilbur S. Nye, *Carbine and Lance: The Story of Old Fort Sill* (Norman: University of Oklahoma Press, 1943), 33–35.

46. Utley, "Kit Carson and Adobe Walls," 11; Pettis, "Kit Carson's Fight," 34.

47. Pettis, "Kit Carson's Fight," 34.

48. Ibid.; *O.R.*, ser. 1, vol. 41, pt. 1, 941.

49. *O.R.*, ser. 1, vol. 41, pt. 1, 941; Harvey Lewis Carter, *"Dear Old Kit": The Historical Christopher Carson* (Norman: University of Oklahoma Press, 1968), 164–65.

50. *O.R.*, ser. 1, vol. 41, pt. 1, 942.

51. Ibid.; Sabin, *Kit Carson Days,* vol. 2, 743.

52. Pettis, "Kit Carson's Fight," 34.

53. *O.R.*, ser. 1, vol. 41, pt. 1, 942; Pettis, "Kit Carson's Fight," 35.

54. *O.R.*, ser. 1, vol. 41, pt. 1, 942.

55. Pettis, "Kit Carson's Fight," 35; Utley, "Kit Carson and Adobe Walls," 74.

56. Pettis, "Kit Carson's Fight," 35.

57. *O.R.*, ser. 1, vol. 41, pt. 1, 943; Pettis, "Kit Carson's Fight," 35; Utley, "Kit Carson and Adobe Walls," 75.

58. *O.R.*, ser. 1, vol. 41, pt. 1, 943; Pettis, "Kit Carson's Fight," 35; Sabin, *Kit Carson Days,* 745.

59. Rupert N. Richardson, *The Comanche Barrier to South Plains Settlement* (Glendale, CA: Arthur H. Clark, 1933), 285.

60. *O.R.*, ser. 1, vol. 41, pt. 1, 943; Pettis, "Kit Carson's Fight," 35; Utley, "Kit Carson and Adobe Walls," 75.

61. *O.R.*, ser. 1, vol. 41, pt. 1, 943.

62. Ibid.

63. Pettis, "Kit Carson's Fight," 35.

64. *O.R.*, ser. 1, vol. 41, pt. 1, 943; Mayhall, *The Kiowas,* 188–89.

65. Estergreen, *Kit Carson,* 261; Sabin, *Kit Carson Days,* vol. 2, 748.

66. *O.R.*, ser. 1, vol. 48, pt. 1, 611–12.

CHAPTER NINE: BLOOD ALONG SAND CREEK

1. The best information about the history and customs of this tribe can be found in Berthrong's *Southern Cheyennes* and Grinnell's *Fighting Cheyennes.*
2. The best source for the history of this tribe is Virginia Cole Trenholm's *The Arapahoes, Our People* (Norman: University of Oklahoma Press, 1973).
3. Grinnell, *Fighting Cheyennes,* 32–60.
4. For more about early Colorado, see Frank Hall, *History of the State of Colorado* (Chicago: Blakely Printing Company, 1889); Abbott, Leonard and McComb, *Colorado: A History of the Centennial State* (Boulder: Colorado Associated University Press, 1982). For information about Bent's New Fort, see George E. Hyde, *The Life of George Bent, Written from His Letters* (Norman: University of Oklahoma Press, 1968); and David Lavender, *Bent's Fort* (Lincoln: University of Nebraska Press, 1954).
5. Hatch, *Custer Companion,* 71.
6. Kappler, *Indian Affairs,* vol. 2, 594–96.
7. Berthrong, *Southern Cheyennes,* 127–36; Grinnell, *Fighting Cheyennes,* 107–111.
8. Grinnell, *Fighting Cheyennes,* 111–17; Thom Hatch, *Clashes of Cavalry: The Civil War Careers of George Armstrong Custer and Jeb Stuart* (Mechanicsburg, PA: Stackpole Books, 2001), 10–11.
9. Grinnell, *Fighting Cheyennes,* 119.
10. LeRoy R. Hafen, ed. *Colorado Gold Rush: Contemporary Letters and Reports, 1858–59,* Southwest Historical ser., vol. 10 (Glendale, CA: Arthur H. Clark Company, 1941), 349, 357, 363–64.
11. *Rocky Mountain News,* April 18, 1860.
12. Grinnell, *Fighting Cheyennes,* 120; Stan Hoig, *The Sand Creek Massacre* (Norman: University of Oklahoma Press, 1961), 8–11.
13. *Western Mountaineer,* October 4, 1860, 6.
14. Kappler, *Indian Affairs,* vol. 2, 807–11; Grinnell, *Fighting Cheyennes,* 120; Hoig, *Sand Creek Massacre,* 11–14.
15. Hall, *History of the State of Colorado,* 265, 275–76.
16. Carl Ubbelohde, Maxine Benson, and Duane A. Smith, eds., *A Colorado History* (Boulder, CO: Pruett Publishing Company, 1972, 1976, 1982), 104–6.
17. *Rocky Mountain News,* September 9, 1861.
18. See chapter 4 for details about this battle.
19. Ubbelohde, et al., *Colorado History,* 107.
20. Hoig, *Sand Creek Massacre,* 25–29.

21. *Annual Report of the Commissioner of Indian Affairs,* 1862, 373–76.
22. Hoig, *Sand Creek Massacre,* 20.
23. Accounts of Chivington's early life can be found in nearly every volume pertaining to Sand Creek. Also see Reyinald S. Craig's *The Fighting Parson* (Tucson, AZ: Westernlore Press, 1959).
24. Hoig, *Sand Creek Massacre,* 20–25; Grinnell, *Fighting Cheyennes,* 123–24.
25. *O.R.,* ser. 1, vol. 22, pt. 2, 294; *Annual Report of the Commissioner of Indian Affairs,* 1863, 239–46.
26. Grinnell, *Fighting Cheyennes,* 125–128; Hoig, *Sand Creek Massacre,* 31–33; Berthrong, *Southern Cheyennes,* 167–68.
27. *Annual Report of the Commissioner of Indian Affairs,* 1863, 121.
28. Hyde, *Life of George Bent,* 121.
29. *O.R.,* ser. 1, vol. 22, pt. 2, 172–73, 333–34, 400–402; Hoig, *Sand Creek Massacre,* 25–29.
30. Josephy, *Civil War in the American West,* 299.
31. Berthrong, *Southern Cheyennes,* 174; Grinnell, *Fighting Cheyennes,* 129; Hoig, *Sand Creek Massacre,* 35; *Annual Report of the Commissioner of Indian Affairs,* 1864, 393.
32. *Arapahoes, Our People,* 170.
33. Grinnell, *Fighting Cheyennes,* 131.
34. *O.R.,* ser. 1, vol. 34, pt. 1, 880.
35. Ibid., 884–85, 887–88.
36. Grinnell, *Fighting Cheyennes,* 135.
37. Ibid., 136; Hoig, *Sand Creek Massacre,* 41–42.
38. *O.R.,* ser. 1, vol. 34, pt. 1, 881–82.
39. Ibid.; Bob Scott, *Blood at Sand Creek: The Massacre Revisited* (Caldwell, ID: Caxton Printers, 1994), 52.
40. Grinnell, *Fighting Cheyennes,* 133; Hoig, *Sand Creek Massacre,* 43.
41. *O.R.,* ser. 1, vol. 34, pt. 1, 907–8; Grinnell, *Fighting Cheyennes,* 137–38.
42. Grinnell, *Fighting Cheyennes,* 139–40; *O.R.,* ser. 1, vol. 34, pt. 1, 935; Hoig, *Sand Creek Massacre,* 51–52.
43. *O.R.,* ser. 1, vol. 34, pt. 4, 97–99.
44. Ibid., 353.
45. Ibid., 353–54.
46. Robert Claiborne Pitzer, *Three Frontiers, Memories and a Portrait of Henry Littleton Pitzer as Recorded by His Son Robert Claiborne Pitzer* (Muscatine, IA: Prairie Press, 1938), 162–63; Hoig, *Sand Creek Massacre,* 59.
47. *O.R.,* ser. 1, vol. 34, pt. 4, 330, 449.

48. Ibid., vol. 41, 964.

49. Grinnell, *Fighting Cheyennes,* 145–49; Scott, *Blood at Sand Creek,* 84–104; Hoig, *Sand Creek Massacre,* 64–67; Berthrong, *Southern Cheyennes,* chaps. 8–9.

50. *Report of the Joint Committee on the Conduct of the War,* U.S. Senate Report 142, 38th Congress, 2nd Session, Washington, DC, 1865, pt. 3, 47; Hoig, *Sand Creek Massacre,* 69; Berthrong, *Southern Cheyennes,* 192–93.

51. Grinnell, *Fighting Cheyennes,* 148–52; Scott, *Blood at Sand Creek,* 105–11; O.R., ser. 1, vol. 41, pt. 2, 276, 368–69, 378–79, 413, 428–29, 445–47, 483–85, 491, 545, 610, 629–30, 722, 752, 765.

52. Grinnell, *Fighting Cheyennes,* 152–53; Hoig, *Sand Creek Massacre,* 97–98.

53. Hatch, *Custer Companion,* 71.

54. Grinnell, *Fighting Cheyennes,* 153; Hoig, *Sand Creek Massacre,* 99–107.

55. Hoig, *Sand Creek Massacre,* 111–21; Grinnell, *Fighting Cheyennes,* 153–54; *Annual Report of the Commissioner of Indian Affairs,* 1864, 221.

56. Grinnell, *Fighting Cheyennes,* 159–60; Hoig, *Sand Creek Massacre,* 122–28.

57. Hoig, *Sand Creek Massacre,* 160–61.

58. The following account of events is based on sources and official reports too numerous to specifically cite item by item. Only direct quotes are referenced. Sources include O.R., ser. 1, vol. 34, pts. 1, 3, and 4, and vol. 41, pts. 1–4; *Report of the Joint Committee on Conduct of the War,* U.S. Senate Report 142, 38th Congress, 2nd Session, Washington, DC, 1865; *Report of the Secretary of War,* Senate Executive Document 26, 39th Congress, 2nd Session, Washington, DC, 1867; *Annual Report of the Commissioner of Indian Affairs, 1864; Report of the Joint Special Committees on the Condition of the Indian Tribes,* Senate Report 156, 39th Congress, 2nd Session, Washington, DC, 1867; as well as those sources cited throughout this chapter.

59. Hoig, *Sand Creek Massacre,* 147.

60. Hyde, *Life of George Bent,* 151.

61. Ibid., 152.

62. Senate Reports, 39th Congress, 2nd Session, no. 156, 42.

63. Grinnell, *Fighting Cheyennes,* 166.

64. O.R., ser. 1, vol. 46, pt. 1, 948; Grinnell, *Fighting Cheyennes,* 167.

65. Grinnell, *Fighting Cheyennes,* 168; Hoig, *Sand Creek Massacre,* 153.

66. Hoig, *Sand Creek Massacre,* 161–62; Grinnell, *Fighting Cheyennes,* 168–69; *Rocky Mountain News,* December 17, 1864.

67. *Rocky Mountain News,* December 29, 1864.
68. *O.R.,* ser. 1, vol. 41, pt. 1, 959–62.
69. *Report of the Joint Committee on Conduct of the War,* summary.

CHAPTER TEN: TOTAL WAR

1. Grinnell, *Fighting Cheyennnes,* 174–75; Berthrong, *Southern Cheyennes,* 224–25.
2. Grinnell, *Fighting Cheyennes,* 177–79; Utley, *Frontiersmen in Blue,* 301; George E. Hyde, *Red Cloud's Folk: A History of the Oglala Indians* (Norman: University of Oklahoma Press, 1957), 110–11; Hyde, *Spotted Tail's Folk,* 94–95.
3. Utley, *Frontiersmen in Blue,* 301–3; *O.R.,* ser. 1, vol. 48, pt. 1, 88–92.
4. *O.R.,* ser. 1, vol. 41, pt. 4, 709.
5. Ibid., 923; vol. 48, pt. 1, 1212, 1295–96; pt. 2, 162–63, 237–38.
6. Hatch, *Custer Companion,* 150–52.
7. *O.R.,* ser. 1, vol. 48, pt. 1, 361–63, pt. 2. 1171–72; Grinnell, *Fighting Cheyennes,* 236; Berthrong, *Southern Cheyennes,* 239–40.
8. Utley, *Frontiersmen in Blue,* 322–33.
9. Ibid., 323–330.
10. Hatch, *Custer Companion,* 68–69.
11. Ibid., 35–42.
12. Ibid., 65–67.
13. Ibid., 68–69.
14. Ibid., 83–84.
15. Ibid., 49–52.
16. Ibid., 98–99.
17. Ibid., 75–78.
18. Ibid., 101–102.
19. Ibid., 46.
20. Ibid., 141–48.
21. Ibid., 257–62.
22. Ibid., 262–63.
23. Thrapp, *Conquest of Apacheria,* chapter 4.
24. The best source for this period of time is Thrapp's *Conquest of Apacheria.*
25. Hatch, *Custer Companion,* 263–64.

BIBLIOGRAPHY

NEWSPAPERS
Faribault, Minnesota, *Central Republican*
Golden, Colorado, *Western Mountaineer*
Goodhue County [Minnesota] Republican
Mankato, Minnesota, *Semi-Weekly Record*
Prescott *Arizona Miner*
Rio Grande Republican
Rocky Mountain News
Sacramento Union
St. Paul *Pioneer and Democrat*
Salt Lake City *Deseret News*
San Francisco Bulletin
Santa Fe New Mexican

COLLECTIONS
Cherokee Papers, University of Oklahoma, Western History Collections, Norman
Colorado College Special Collections
Colorado State Historical Society, Denver
Heritage Collection, Nebraska Public Library, Lincoln
National Archives and Record Service Microfilm Pub.
Ross Papers, Thomas Gilcrease Institute of American History and Art, Tulsa
U.S. Smithsonian Institution, National Museum of Natural History
Western Americana Microfilm Series

GOVERNMENT DOCUMENTS

U.S. Congress, House of Representatives. *Report of the Joint Committee on Conduct of the War,* U.S. Senate Report 142, 38th Congress, 2nd Session, Washington, DC, 1865.

———, Senate. *Report of the Joint Special Committees on the Condition of the Indian Tribes,* Senate Report 156, 39th Congress, 2nd Session, Washington, DC, 1867.

———, Senate. *Report of the Secretary of War,* Senate Executive Document 26, 39th Congress, 2nd Session, Washington, DC, 1867.

U.S. Interior Department, Bureau of Indian Affairs. *Reports of the Commissioner of Indian Affairs for the Years 1851 through 1865,* Washington, DC: Government Printing Office, 1852–66.

U.S. War Department. *The War of the Rebellion: A Compilation of the Official Records of the Union and Confederate Armies.* 128 volumes. Washington, DC: Government Printing Office, 1880–1901.

ARTICLES

Allen, James B., and Ted J. Warner. "The Gosiute Indians in Pioneer Utah." *Utah Historical Quarterly* 39, no. 2 (Spring 1971).

Allen, R. S. "Pinos Altos, New Mexico." *New Mexico Historical Review* 23 (1948): 302–32.

Amsden, Charles. "The Navajo Exile at Bosque Redondo." *New Mexico Historical Review* 8 (1933): 31–50.

Athearn, Robert G. "The Civil War and Montana Gold." *Montana, the Magazine of Western History* 12, no. 2 (April 1962).

Babcock, Willoughby M. "Minnesota's Indian War." *Minnesota History* 38, no. 3 (September 1962).

Bahos, Charles. "On Opothleyahola's Trail." *Chronicles of Oklahoma* 63, no. 1 (Spring 1985).

Bass, Henry. "Civil War in Indian Territory." *American Scene Magazine* (Gilcrease Institute, Tulsa) 4, no. 4 (1962).

Bean, Geraldine. "General Alfred Sully and the Northwest Indian Expedition." *North Dakota History* 33, no. 3 (Summer 1966).

Bearss, Edwin C. "The Civil War Comes to Indian Territory, 1861: The Flight of Opothleyahola." *Journal of the West* 11, no. 1 (January 1972): 9–42.

Brandes, Ray. "Mangas Coloradas: Apache Warrior and Diplomat." *Mankind: The Magazine of Popular History* 3, no. 9 (October 1972): 54–58.

Britton, Wiley. "Union and Confederate Indians in the Civil War." In *Battles and Leaders of the Civil War,* edited by Robert Underwood Johnson and Clarence Buell Clough, vol. 1. New York: Thomas Yoseloff, 1956.

Carey, Raymond G. "The Puzzle of Sand Creek." *Colorado Magazine* 41, no. 4 (Fall 1964).

Carley, Kenneth. "As Red Men Viewed It: Three Indians Accounts of the Uprising." *Minnesota History* 38, no. 3 (September 1962).

———. "The Sioux Campaign of 1862: Sibley's Letters to His Wife." *Minnesota History* 38, no. 3 (September 1962): 109.

Chandler, Robert J. "The Velvet Glove." *Journal of the West* 20, no. 4 (October 1981).

Clifford, Roy A. "The Indian Regiments in the Battle of Pea Ridge." *Chronicles of Oklahoma* 25, no. 4 (Winter 1947–48).

Dickinson, William ("Dick"). "Reminiscences of Fort Defiance, 1860." *Journal of the Military Service Institution of the United States* 4 (1883): 90–92.

Ellis, Richard N. "Civilians, the Army and the Indian Problem on the Northern Plains, 1862–1866." *North Dakota History* 37, no. 1 (Winter 1970).

English, Abner M. "Dakota's First Soldiers: History of the First Dakota Cavalry, 1862–1865." *South Dakota Historical Collections* 9 (1918).

Finch, Boyd. "Sherrod Hunter and the Confederates in Arizona," *Journal of Arizona History* 10, no. 3 (Autumn 1969): 178.

Gibson, Arrell M. "Native Americans in the Civil War." *American Indian Quarterly* 9 (Autumn 1985).

Goldman, Henry H. "General James H. Carleton and the New Mexico Indian Campaigns, 1862–1866." *Journal of the West* 2, no. 2 (April 1963).

Hart, Newell. "Rescue of a Frontier Boy," *Utah Historical Quarterly* 33 (Winter 1965): 51–54.

Henig, Gerald T. "A Neglected Cause of the Sioux Uprising." *Minnesota History* 45, no. 3 (Fall 1976).

Heyman, Max L., Jr. "On the Navaho Trail: The Campaign of 1860." *New Mexico Historical Review* 26 (1951): 44–63.

Hilger, Nicolas. "General Alfred Sully's Expedition of 1864." *Contributions to the Historical Society of Montana* 2 (1896).

Hughes, Thomas. "Causes and Results of the Inkpaduta Massacre." *Minnesota Historical Collections* 12 (1905–08): 264–69.

Jett, Stephen C., ed. "The Destruction of Navajo Peach Orchards in 1864." *Arizona and the West* 16 (Winter 1974): 365–78.

Johnson, Roy P. "The Siege at Ft. Abercrombie." *North Dakota History* 24, no. 1 (January 1957): 1–77.

Kelly, Lawrence C. "Where Was Fort Canby?" *New Mexico Historical Review* 42 (January 1967): 49–62.

Kibby, Leo P. "Patrick Edward Connor: First Gentile of Utah." *Journal of the West* 2, no. 4 (October 1963).

Kingsbury, David L. "Sully's Expedition against the Sioux in 1864." *Minnesota Historical Collections* 8 (1898).

Larson, Gustave O. "Utah and the Civil War." *Utah Historical Quarterly* 33, no. 1 (Winter 1965).

Lindgren, Raymond E., ed. "A Diary of Kit Carson's Navajo Campaign." *New Mexico Historical Review* 21 (July 1946): 226–46.

Martineau, James H. "The Military History of Cache Valley." *Tullidge's Quarterly Magazine* 2, no. 1 (April 1882): 125.

McNitt, Frank. "Fort Sumner: A Study in Origins." *New Mexico Historical Review* 45 (April 1970): 101–17.

Meserve, John Bartlett. "Chief Opothleyahola." *Chronicles of Oklahoma* 9 (December 1931): 445–53.

Moody, Marshall D. "Kit Carson, Agent to the Indians in New Mexico, 1853–1861." *New Mexico Historical Review* 28 (January 1953).

Myers, Lee. "The Enigma of Mangas Coloradas' Death." *New Mexico Historical Review* 41, no. 4 (October 1966).

Neet, J. Frederick, Jr. "Stand Watie, Confederate General in the Cherokee Nation." *Great Plains Journal* 6, no. 1 (Fall 1966).

Neill, Edward D. "Dakota Land and Dakota Life." *Minnesota Historical Collections* 1 (1850–56): 205–40.

Newcombe, Barbara T. "'A Portion of the American People': The Sioux Sign a Treaty in Washington in 1858." *Minnesota History* 45, no. 3 (Fall 1976): 82–96.

Perrine, David P. "The Battle of Valverde, New Mexico Territory, February 21, 1862." *Journal of the West* 19, no. 4 (October 1980): 26–38.

Pettis, George H. "The California Column." *Historical Society of New Mexico* 11 (1908).

———. "Kit Carson's Fight with the Comanche and Kiowa Indians." *Publications of the Historical Society of New Mexico* 12 (1908): 34–35.

Pfaller, Louis. "Sully's Expedition of 1864 Featuring the Killdeer Mountain and Badlands Battles." *North Dakota History,* 31, no. 1 (January 1964): 1–54.

Russo, Prisilla Ann. "The Time to Speak Is Over: The Onset of the Sioux Uprising," *Minnesota History* 45, no. 3 (Fall 1976).

"Taoyateduta Is Not a Coward." *Minnesota History* 38 (September 1962): 115.

Trenerry, Walter N. "The Shooting of Little Crow: Heroism or Murder?" *Minnesota History* 38, no. 3 (September 1962).

Unrau, William E. "A Prelude to War." *Colorado Magazine* 41 (1964): 299–313.

Utley, Robert M. "The Bascom Affair: A Reconstruction." *Arizona and the West* 3 (1961): 59–68.

———. "Kit Carson and the Adobe Walls Campaign." *American West* 2, no. 1 (Winter 1965): 4–11, 73–75.

Woody, Clara T., ed. "The Woolsey Expeditions of 1864." *Arizona and the West* 4, no. 2 (Summer 1962): 157–76.

BOOKS

Abbott, Leonard and McComb. *Colorado: A History of the Centennial State.* Boulder: Colorado Associated University Press, 1982.

Abel, Annie Heloise. *The American Indian as a Participant in the Civil War.* Cleveland: Arthur H. Clark Co., 1919.

———. *The American Indian as Slaveholder and Secessionist.* Cleveland: Scholarly Press, 1915.

Alberts, Don E. *The Battle of Glorietta: Union Victory in the West.* College Station: Texas A & M Press, 1998.

Alexander, Thomas G., and James B. Allen. *Mormons and Gentiles: A History of Salt Lake City.* Boulder, CO: Pruett Publishing Co., 1984.

Altshuler, Constance Wynn. *Cavalry Yellow and Infantry Blue: Army Officers in Arizona between 1851 and 1886.* Tucson: Arizona Historical Society, 1991.

Anderson, Gary Clayton. *Little Crow: Spokesman for the Sioux.* St. Paul: Minnesota Historical Society Press, 1986.

Anderson, Gary Clayton, and Alan R. Woolworth. *Dakota Eyes: Narrative Accounts of the Minnesota Indian War of 1862.* St. Paul: Minnesota Historical Society Press, 1988.

Bailey, Lynn R. *Bosque Redondo: An American Concentration Camp.* Pasadena, CA: Socio-Technical Books, 1970.

———. *The Long Walk: A History of the Navajo Wars.* Los Angeles: Westernlore Press, 1964.

———, ed. *The Navajo Reconnaissance: A Military Exploration of the Navajo Country in 1859.* Los Angeles: Westernlore Press, 1964.

Baird, W. David. *A Creek Warrior for the Confederacy.* Norman: University of Oklahoma Press, 1988.

Bancroft, H. H. *History of Arizona and New Mexico, 1530–1888.* San Francisco: History Company Publishers, 1889.

Berthong, Donald J. *The Southern Cheyennes.* Norman: University of Oklahoma Press, 1963.

Blackwater, Bernice. *Great Westerner: The Story of Kit Carson.* Caldwell, ID: Caxton Printers, 1962.

Board of Commissioners. *Minnesota in the Civil and Indian Wars, 1861–1865.* 2 vols. St. Paul, MN: Pioneer Press, 1890, 1893.

Britton, Wiley. *The Civil War on the Border, 1861–62.* 2 vols. New York: G.P. Putnam's Sons, 1890–94.

Browne, J. Ross. *A Tour through Arizona.* Tucson: Arizona Silhouettes, 1951.

Carley, Kenneth. *The Sioux Uprising of 1862.* St. Paul: Minnesota Historical Society, 1961.

Carson, Christopher. *Kit Carson's Autobiography.* Edited by Milo Milton Quaife. Lincoln: University of Nebraska Press, 1966.

Carter, Harvey Lewis. *"Dear Old Kit": The Historical Christopher Carson.* Norman: University of Oklahoma Press, 1968.

Chittenden, Hirum M. *History of Early Steamboat Navigation on the Missouri River.* Minneapolis: Ross & Haines, 1962.

Chittenden, Hirum Martin, and Alfred Talbot Richardson. *Life, Letters and Travel of Father Pierre-Jean De Smet, S. J., 1801–1873.* 4 vols. New York: Francis P. Harper, 1905.

Christensen, Scott R. *Sagwitch: Shoshone Chieftain, Mormon Elder.* Logan: Utah State University Press, 1999.

Colton, Ray C. *The Civil War in the Western Territories.* Norman: University of Oklahoma Press, 1959.

Conkling, Roscoe P., and Margaret B. Conkling. *The Butterfield Overland Mail, 1858–1869,* 3 vols. Glendale, CA: Arthur H. Clark Co., 1947.

Conner, Daniel Ellis. *A Confederate in the Colorado Gold Fields.* Edited by Donald J. Berthrong and Odessa Davenport. Norman: University of Oklahoma Press, 1970.

———. *Joseph Reddeford Walker and the Arizona Adventure.* Norman: University of Oklahoma Press, 1956.

Connor, Seymour V., and Jimmy M. Skaggs. *Broadcloth and Britches: The Santa Fe Trade.* College Station: Texas A & M University Press, 1977.

Courwright, George S. *An Expedition against the Indians in 1864.* Lithopolis, OH: Canal Winchester Times Press, 1911.

Craig, Reyinald S. *The Fighting Parson.* Tucson, AZ: Westernlore Press, 1959.

Cremony, John C. *Life among the Apaches, 1850–1868.* Lincoln: University of Nebraska Press, 1983.

Cunningham, Frank. *General Stand Watie's Confederate Indians.* San Antonio, TX: Naylor Co., 1959.

Danzinger, Edmund J., Jr. *Indians and Bureaucrats.* Urbana: University of Illinois Press, 1974.

Debo, Angie. *The Road to Disappearance: A History of the Creek Indians.* Norman: University of Oklahoma Press, 1941.

Denney, Robert E. *The Civil War Years: A Day-by-Day Chronicle.* New York: Gramercy Books, 1998.

Drinnon, Richard. *Facing West: The Metaphysics of Indian-Hunting and Empire-Building.* Minneapolis: University of Minnesota Press, 1980.

Dripps, J. H. *Three Years among the Indians in Dakota.* New York: Sol Lewis, 1974.

Dunlay, Tom. *Kit Carson and the Indians.* Lincoln: University of Nebraska Press, 2000.

Dunn, J. P., Jr. *Massacres in the Mountains: A History of the Indian Wars of the Far West, 1815–1875.* New York: Archer House, 1958.

Dunn, William R. *"I Stand by Sand Creek": A Defense of Colonel John M. Chivington and the Third Colorado Cavalry.* Fort Collins, CO: Old Army Press, 1985.

Edington, Thomas, and John Taylor. *The Battle of Glorieta Pass: A Gettysburg in the West, March 26–28, 1862.* Albuquerque: University of New Mexico Press, 1998.

Ellis, Richard N. *General Pope and U.S. Indian Policy.* Albuquerque: University of New Mexico Press, 1970.

Emmett, Chris. *Fort Union and the Winning of the Southwest.* Norman: University of Oklahoma Press, 1965.

Estergreen, M. Morgan. *Kit Carson: A Portrait in Courage.* Norman: University of Oklahoma Press, 1962.

Farish, Thomas Edwin. *History of Arizona.* 8 vols. San Francisco: Filmer Brothers Electrotype Co., 1915–18.

Faust, Patricia L., ed. *Historical Times Illustrated Encyclopedia of the Civil War.* New York: Harper & Row, 1986.

Fehrenbach, T. R. *Comanches: A History, 1706–1875.* New York: Alfred A. Knopf, 1974.

Fisher, Margaret M. *Utah and the Civil War.* Salt Lake City: Deseret Book Co., 1929.

Folwell, William W. *A History of Minnesota.* 2 vols. St. Paul: Minnesota Historical Society, 1924.

Franks, Kenny A. *Stand Watie and the Agony of the Cherokee Nation.* Memphis: Memphis State University Press, 1979.

Frazier, Donald S. *Blood and Treasure: Confederate Empire in the Southwest.* College Station: Texas A & M University Press, 1995.

Furniss, Norman F. *The Mormon Conflict.* New Haven, CT: Yale University Press, 1960.

Gaines, W. Craig. *The Confederate Cherokees: John Drew's Regiment of Mounted Rifles.* Baton Rouge: Louisiana State University Press, 1989.

Gilbert, Bill. *Westering Man: The Life of Joseph Walker.* New York: Atheneum, 1983.

Goetzmann, William H. *Army Exploration in the American West, 1803–1863.* New Haven, CT: Yale University Press, 1959.

Goodwin, Grenville. *Apache Raiding and Warfare.* Tucson: University of Arizona Press, 1971.

Grinnell, George B. *The Fighting Cheyennes.* New Haven, CT: Yale University Press, 1923.

Guild, Thelma S., and Harvey L. Carter. *Kit Carson: A Pattern for Heroes.* Lincoln: University of Nebraska Press, 1984.

Hafen, LeRoy R. *The Overland Mail.* Cleveland: Arthur Clark Co., 1926.

———, ed. *Colorado Gold Rush: Contemporary Letters and Reports, 1858–59.* Southwest Historical Series, vol. 10. Glendale, CA: Arthur H. Clark Company, 1941.

Haley, James L. *Apaches: A History and Culture Portrait.* Norman: University of Oklahoma Press, 1981.

Hall, Frank. *History of the State of Colorado.* Chicago: Blakely Printing Company, 1889.

Hall, Martin Hardwick. *The Confederate Army of New Mexico.* Austin, TX: Presidial Press, 1978.

———. *Sibley's New Mexico Campaign.* Austin: University of Texas Press, 1960.

Hatch, Thom. *Clashes of Cavalry: The Civil War Careers of George Armstrong Custer and Jeb Stuart.* Mechanicsburg, PA: Stackpole Books, 2001.

———. *The Custer Companion: A Comprehensive Guide to the Life of George Armstrong Custer and the Plains Indian Wars.* Mechanicsburg, PA: Stackpole Books, 2002.

Hays, Robert G. *A Race at Bay: New York Times Editorials on "The Indian Problem," 1860–1900.* Carbondale: Southern Illinois University Press, 1997.

Henson, Pauline. *Founding a Wilderness Capital: Prescott, A.T., 1864.* Flagstaff, AZ: Northland Press, 1965.

Heyman, Max L., Jr. *Prudent Soldier: A Biography of Major General E. R. S. Canby, 1817–1873*. Glendale, CA: Arthur H. Clark, 1959.

Hoig, Stan. *The Peace Chiefs of the Cheyennes*. Norman: University of Oklahoma Press, 1980.

———. *The Sand Creek Massacre*. Norman: University of Oklahoma Press, 1961.

———. *Tribal Wars on the Southern Plains*. Norman: University of Oklahoma Press, 1993.

Hollister, Ovando J. *Boldly They Rode: A History of the First Colorado Regiment of Volunteers*. Lakewood, CO: Golden Press, 1949.

Howbert, Irving. *Memories of a Lifetime in the Pikes Peak Region*. New York: G. P. Putnam's Sons, 1925.

Hughes, Thomas. *Old Traverse des Sioux*. St. Peter, MN: Herald Publishing Co., 1929.

Hunt, Aurora. *Major General James Henry Carleton, 1814–1873*. Glendale, CA: Arthur H. Clark Co., 1958.

Hutton, Paul A., ed. *Soldiers West: Biographies from the Military Frontier*. Lincoln: University of Nebraska Press, 1987.

Hyde, George E. *The Life of George Bent, Written from His Letters*. Norman: University of Oklahoma Press, 1968.

———. *Red Cloud's Folk: A History of the Oglala Sioux Indians*. Norman: University of Oklahoma Press, 1957.

———. *Spotted Tail's Folk: A History of the Brule Sioux*. Norman: University of Oklahoma Press, 1961.

Inter-Tribal Council of Nevada. *Newe: A Western Shoshone History*, Reno, 1976.

Iverson, Peter. *The Navajo Nation*. Albuquerque: University of New Mexico Press, 1981.

Jackson, Helen Hunt. *A Century of Dishonor: A Sketch of the United States Government's Dealings with Some of the Indian Tribes*. Norman: University of Oklahoma Press, 1995.

Jones, Robert H. *The Civil War in the Northwest: Nebraska, Wisconsin, Iowa, Minnesota, and the Dakotas*. Norman: University of Oklahoma Press, 1960.

Josephy, Alvin M., Jr. *The Civil War in the American West*. New York: Alfred A. Knopf, 1991.

Kappler, Charles J. *Indian Affairs, Laws and Treaties*. 2 vols. Washington, DC: Government Printing Office, 1904.

Kelly, Lawrence. *Navajo Roundup: Selected Correspondence of Kit Carson's Expedition against the Navajo, 1863–1865*. Boulder, CO: Pruett Publishing Co., 1970.

Kelsey, Harry E. *Frontier Capitalist: The Life of John Evans.* Denver: Colorado State Historical Society, 1969.

Kenner, Charles L. *A History of New Mexico-Plains Indian Relations.* Norman: University of Oklahoma Press, 1969.

Kerby, Robert L. *The Confederate Invasion of New Mexico and Arizona, 1861–62.* Los Angeles: Westernlore Press, 1958.

Kirsch, Robert, and William S. Murphy. *West of the West.* New York: E. P. Dutton, 1967.

Knight, Wilfred. *Red Fox: Stand Watie's Civil War Years in Indian Territory.* Glendale, CA: Arthur H. Clark, 1988.

Lamar, Howard R. *Dakota Territory, 1861–1889.* New Haven, CT: Yale University Press, 1956.

———. *The Far Southwest, 1846–1912.* New Haven, CT: Yale University Press, 1966.

Lavender, David. *Bent's Fort.* Lincoln: University of Nebraska Press, 1954.

Lockwood, Frank C. *Pioneer Days in Arizona: From the Spanish Occupation to Statehood.* New York: McMillan, 1932.

Long, E. B. *The Saints and the Union: Utah Territory During the Civil War.* Urbana: University of Illinois Press, 1981.

Longstreet, Stephen. *War Cries on Horseback: The Story of the Indian Wars of the Great Plains.* Garden City, NY: Doubleday & Co., 1970.

Madsen, Brigham D. *The Shoshoni Frontier and the Bear River Massacre.* Salt Lake City: University of Utah Press, 1985.

Mayhall, Mildred P. *The Kiowas.* Norman: University of Oklahoma Press, 1962.

McClintock, James H. *Arizona: Prehistoric, Aboriginal, Pioneer, Modern.* Chicago: S. J. Clarke Publishing Co., 1916.

McNitt, Frank, ed. *Navaho Expedition: Journal of a Military Reconnaissance from Santa Fe, New Mexico, to the Navaho Country Made in 1849 by Lieutenant James H. Simpson.* Norman: University of Oklahoma Press, 1964.

———. *Navajo Wars: Military Campaigns, Slave Raids, and Reprisals.* Albuquerque: University of New Mexico Press, 1972.

Meyer, Roy W. *History of the Santee Sioux: United States Indian Policy on Trial.* Lincoln: University of Nebraska Press, 1967.

Miller, Darlis A. *The California Column in New Mexico.* Albuquerque: University of New Mexico Press, 1982.

Monaghan, Jay. *Civil War on the Western Border, 1854–1865.* Boston: Little, Brown, 1955.

Moulton, Gary S., ed. *The Papers of Chief John Ross.* Norman: University of Oklahoma Press, 1985.

Nichols, David A. *Lincoln and the Indians*. Columbia: University of Missouri Press, 1978.

Nye, Wilbur S. *Carbine and Lance: The Story of Old Fort Sill*. Norman: University of Oklahoma Press, 1943.

Oates, Stephen B. *Confederate Cavalry West of the River*. Austin: University of Texas Press, 1961.

Oehler, C. M. *The Great Sioux Uprising*. New York: Oxford University Press, 1959.

Oliva, Leo E. *Soldiers on the Santa Fe Trail*. Norman: University of Oklahoma Press, 1967.

Orton, Richard H., comp. *Records of California Men in the War of the Rebellion, 1861 to 1867*. Sacramento: State Printing Office, 1890.

Osborn, William M. *The Wild Frontier: Atrocities During the American-Indian War from Jamestown Colony to Wounded Knee*. New York: Random House, 2000.

Perry, Richard J. *Western Apache Heritage: People of the Mountain Corridor*. Austin: University of Texas Press, 1991.

Pitzer, Robert Claiborne. *Three Frontiers, Memories and a Portrait of Henry Littleton Pitzer as Recorded by His Son Robert Claiborne Pitzer*. Muscatine, IA: Prairie Press, 1938.

Prucha, Francis Paul. *Documents of United States Indian Policy*. Lincoln: University of Nebraska Press, 1990.

Rampp, Lary C., and Donald L. Rampp. *The Civil War in the Indian Territory*. Austin, TX: Presidial Press, 1975.

Reichard, Gladys A. *Navajo Religion*. New York: Bollingen Foundation, 1950.

Richardson, Rupert N. *The Comanche Barrier to South Plains Settlement*. Glendale, CA: Arthur H. Clark, 1933.

Riggs, Stephen R. *Mary and I: Forty Years with the Sioux*. Boston: Congregational Sunday-School and Publishing Society, 1880.

Rister, Carl C. *Border Captives: The Traffic in Prisoners by Southern Plains Indians, 1835–75*. Norman: University of Oklahoma Press, 1940.

Robinson, Doane. *A History of the Dakota or Sioux Indians*. Minneapolis: Ross and Haines, 1956.

Roddis, Louis H. *The Indian Wars of Minnesota*. Cedar Rapids, IA: Torch Press, 1956.

Rogers, Fred B. *Soldiers of the Overland: Being Some Account of the Services of Gen. Patrick Edward Connor and His Volunteers in the Old West*. San Francisco: Grabhorn Press, 1938.

Rose, Victor M. *Ross' Texas Brigade: Being a Narrative of Events Connected with Its Service in the Late War Between the States.* Kennesaw, GA: Continental Book Co., 1960.

Sabin, Edwin L. *Kit Carson Days, 1809–1868: Adventures in the Path of Empire.* 2 vols. New York: Press of the Pioneers, 1935.

Schultz, Duane. *Month of the Freezing Moon: The Sand Creek Massacre, November, 1864.* New York: St. Martin's Press, 1990.

Scott, Bob. *Blood at Sand Creek: The Massacre Revisited.* Caldwell, ID: Caxton Printers, 1994.

Settle, Raymond W., and Mary L. Settle. *Saddles and Spurs.* Harrisburg, PA: Stackpole Books, 1955.

Slotkin, Richard. *The Fatal Environment: The Myth of the Frontier in the Age of Industrialization, 1800–1890.* New York: Atheneum, 1985.

Smith, Duane A. *The Birth of Colorado: A Civil War Perspective.* Norman: University of Oklahoma Press, 1989.

Sonnichsen, C. L. *The Mescalero Apaches.* Norman: University of Oklahoma Press, 1958.

Spicer, Edward H. *Cycles of Conquest: The Impact of Spain, Mexico, and the United States on the Indians of the Southwest, 1533–1960.* Tucson: University of Arizona Press, 1962.

Sully, Langdon. *No Tears for the General.* Palo Alto, CA: American West Publishing Co., 1974.

Sweeney, Edwin R. *Mangas Coloradas: Chief of the Chiricahua Apaches.* Norman: University of Oklahoma Press, 1998.

Taylor, Nathaniel G., et al. *Papers Relating to Talks and Councils Held with the Indians in Dakota and Montana.* Washington, DC: Government Printing Office, 1910.

Thompson, Gerald. *The Army and the Navajo: The Bosque Redondo Reservation Experiment, 1863–1868.* Tucson: University of Arizona Press, 1976.

Thompson, Jerry D. *Desert Tiger: Captain Paddy Graydon and the Civil War in the Far Southwest.* El Paso: Texas Western Press, 1992.

Thornton, Russell. *American Indian Holocaust and Survival: A Population History since 1492.* Norman: University of Oklahoma Press, 1987.

Thrapp, Dan L. *The Conquest of Apacheria.* Norman: University of Oklahoma Press, 1967.

Trafzer, Clifford E. *The Kit Carson Campaign: The Last Great Navajo War.* Norman: University of Oklahoma Press, 1982.

Trenholm, Virginia Cole. *The Arapahoes, Our People.* Norman: University of Oklahoma Press, 1973.

Trenholm, Virginia Cole, and Maurine Carley. *The Shoshonis: Sentinels of the Rockies.* Norman: University of Oklahoma Press, 1964.

Tullidge, Edward W. *History of Salt Lake City and Its Founders.* Salt Lake City: Edward W. Tullidge, Publisher and Proprietor, 1886.

Ubbelohde, Carl, Maxine Benson, and Duane A. Smith, eds. *A Colorado History.* Boulder, CO: Pruett Publishing Company, 1972, 1976, 1982.

Utley, Robert M. *Frontiersman in Blue: The United States Army and the Indians, 1848–1865.* New York: Macmillan Co., 1967.

———. *The Indian Frontier of the American West, 1846–1890.* Albuquerque: University of New Mexico Press, 1984.

Wallace, Ernest, and E. Adamson Hoebel. *The Comanches: Lords of the Plains.* Norman: University of Oklahoma Press, 1952.

Ware, Eugene F. *The Indian War of 1864.* Lincoln: University of Nebraska Press, 1960.

Weist, Tom. *A History of the Cheyenne People.* Billings: Montana Council for Indian Education, 1977.

West, Elliott. *The Contested Plains: Indians, Goldseekers, and the Rush to Colorado.* Lawrence: University Press of Kansas, 1998.

White, Helen McCann, ed. *Ho! For the Gold Fields.* St. Paul: Minnesota Historical Society, 1966.

Whitford, William Clarke. *Colorado Volunteers in the Civil War.* Denver: State Historical and Natural Society, 1906.

Whitney, Orson F. *History of Utah.* Salt Lake City: George Q. Cannon and Company, 1893.

Zolbrod, Paul G. *Dine Bahana: The Navajo Creation Story.* Albuquerque: University of New Mexico Press, 1984.

INDEX

Note: Page references in *italic* type indicate photographs or illustrations. The denotation *"pl."* followed by a number indicates a plate in the series following page 118.